Appreciative Disability Studies

Mary Ann McColl, PhD, MTS
Queen's University

Captus Press

Appreciative Disability Studies

© 2019 by the author and Captus Press Inc.

Captus Press Inc.
Units 14 & 15
1600 Steeles Avenue West
Concord, ON
L4K 4M2
Telephone: (416) 736–5537
Fax: (416) 736–5793
Email: Info@captus.com
Internet: http://www.captus.com

Library and Archives Canada Cataloguing in Publication
Title: Appreciative disability studies / Mary Ann McColl, PHD, MTS, Queen's University.
Names: McColl, Mary Ann, author.
Description: Includes bibliographical references and index.
Identifiers: Canadiana 20190064374 | ISBN 9781553223832 (softcover)
Subjects: LCSH: Disabilities-Textbooks. | LCSH: People with disabilities. | LCSH: Sociology of disability-Textbooks. | LCGFT: Textbooks.
Classification: LCC HV1568 .M33 2019 | DDC 305.9/08-dc23

Funded by the Government of Canada   Financé par le gouvernement du Canada | Canada

09876543
Printed and bound in Canada

Dedication

This book is dedicated to my late husband, W. Kirby Rowe (1948–2017), from whom I learned more than I can say about disability, but more importantly, about resilience, adaptability, and sheer bull-headed determination. He lived 41 years with a spinal cord injury. He profoundly shaped my understanding of disability and humanity, of relationships and responsibilities, of caring and support. I hope he would have been proud of what I have done in this book. I think he would have. His voice echoes in much of it.

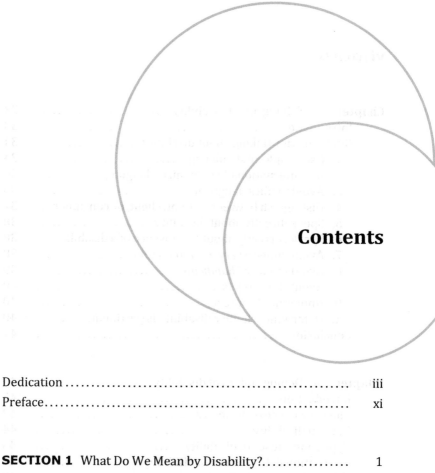

Contents

Preface

Why would someone spend a year-and-a-half writing a textbook on disability studies, when apparently the era of the textbook is finished? No one has time to read them any more ... apparently. In this era when you can sit in your pajamas and get journal articles about disability delivered to your laptop, or you can look up virtually anything you want to know on Wikipedia, or you can follow the latest activities of your favourite disability advocate or organization on their Twitter feed, why would anyone go the trouble and expense of buying and reading a book?

In a much-cited article, entitled "I have forgotten how to read", in *The Globe and Mail* (February 10, 2018), Michael Harris offers a possible response. He concludes that books transport us to a less cynical frame of mind, where

- we are not seeking instantaneous answers but rather deep understanding, and

- our problems cannot be solved with a list of strategies for becoming a better you, or a slide show of suggestions for overcoming your latest problem, or a how-to video demonstrating a step-by-step approach to solving your problems.

Instead, a book requires you to commit to a reflective process that is going to take some time.

Surely this is the best medium for learning about a topic as complex as disability. In this textbook, I have tried to imagine the situation of the novice to disability studies — perhaps the student of a health profession, a social service, or education. I imagine a reader who has elected to devote his or her career to the service of people with disabilities, and who is seeking some constructive theory as a tool for understanding the depth and breadth of disability — both as an academic discipline and as a personal experience.

I am guided by Albert Einstein's entreaty: "Everything should be made as simple as possible, but not simpler." I have tried to speak plainly and clearly from my own experience and from the scholarship about disability. I have tried to address both the real, everyday experiences of living with a disability as well as the broader social concerns of the disability movement. I hope this book will serve as a suitable introduction for those seeking to understand as best they can the challenges of living with a disability and the privilege of collaborating with people with disabilities to create a better world.

Acknowledgement: My thanks to Wayne Westfall for his creativity and his generosity in allowing me to use his artwork on the cover. Special thanks to my assistant, Shannon Jones, for her patience in assembling references and many other details.

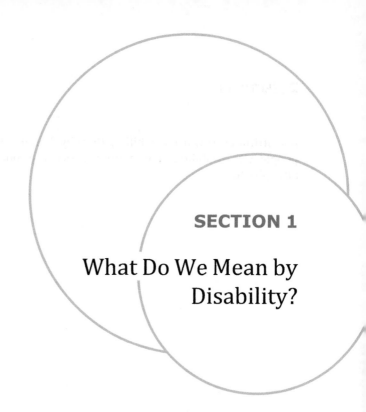

SECTION 1

What Do We Mean by Disability?

Appreciative disability studies is a new way of thinking about disability studies. Instead of focusing on disabled people as an oppressed minority, it focuses on the resilience and resourcefulness of people with disabilities in facing the many challenges encountered in interactions with their environments and with society. *Appreciative disability studies* not only examines the world as it is, but also tries to imagine the world as it might be — a world where barriers are not tolerated, where disabled people's interests are considered from the outset, and where inequities are overcome.

But first we need to understand the challenges that disabled people encounter in contemporary society in all their complexity. The first three chapters of this introductory section of the book offer a discussion of *appreciative disability studies*, as well as definitions and other models for disability, and guidance for language referring to disability. While there is no one definitive set of rules for talking about disability, different groups have different preferences for language referring to disability, and we need to be sensitive to those preferences, since they often derive from strongly held beliefs about disability and society. Chapter 4 offers a survey of statistics on disability. Who are disabled people — in Canada and in the world? Finally, Chapter 5 takes an in-depth look at attitudes toward disability, and discusses how attitudes can act as a particularly intractable barrier to opportunity and participation for people with disabilities. Further, the chapter suggests how we can all participate in improving attitudes toward disability, thereby helping to ensure that people with disabilities have better access to the good things that we all aspire to.

Chapter 1

Introducing *Appreciative Disability Studies*

Introduction

The theme of this book is *appreciative disability studies*. It is an introductory textbook on disability for students in health, education, and social sciences. I was motivated to write it after many years of teaching disability studies and being unable to find an introductory disability studies textbook — something that offered students a beginner's perspective on what it means to live with a disability in contemporary North American society, and something that would communicate effectively to young people who have chosen to devote their careers to serving people with disabilities in one way or another. I felt my task was to help them try to understand the many challenges encountered by people with disabilities in their day-to-day lives, and the various ways that one might think about providing service to them.

After reviewing about 20 contemporary, well-respected books on disability, I concluded that none fulfilled that need. I found several volumes that had a particular focus within disability studies, such as my own previous book on disability policy (McColl & Jongbloed, 2006), Prince's two books on citizenship and income security (Prince, 2009a, 2016b), and Stienstra's book on disability rights (Stienstra, 2012). These books fill an important niche in disability studies, but they are neither broad-based nor introductory.

I also found a number of highly politicized volumes that characterized people with disabilities as an oppressed minority and portrayed professionals as part of the social machinery that systematically disadvantages them. These volumes tend to be sociological or political in their discourse. They have an explicit agenda aimed at social change, and they tend to be overtly anti-professional and anti-establishment. I found them too polarized for an introductory textbook on disability.

Against this background, I hatched the notion of *appreciative disability studies* to bring together two ideas: *disability studies* and *appreciative inquiry*. Let's begin with a brief look at each.

Disability studies

Disability studies is an interdisciplinary field of scholarly inquiry aimed at understanding the experience of people with disabilities in society. Historically, disability was understood as something that happened to a person, either at or before birth or at some stage during his or her life. Disability could be caused by an illness or an injury, and it was possible to identify and understand the pathological process that led to specific deficits in the ability to do things in "the normal way". The majority of research related to disability was focused on understanding the underlying problems in the individual that caused the disability, and on what could be done to alleviate those problems. Research aimed to understand the causes of disability from the single-cell level to the level of the person as a whole. Further research focused on counting disabled people and describing their situation and the difficulties they encountered. Finally, a considerable portion of the research effort was aimed at discovering a remedy for disability in therapeutics — surgery, medication, and therapy.

Probably the majority of this research was done with the benevolent intent of making life easier and more satisfying for people with disabilities. And yet it was not experienced as such by some people with disabilities. Starting in the late 1970s, disability advocates and activists began to talk about all this attention from the medical community as a form of oppression. It was perceived as alienating, belittling, and controlling. Rather than being the subjects of disability research, disabled people wanted to be the authors of their own destiny — setting the agenda for the research effort, framing the research questions in ways that were meaningful to them, and being scientists and scholars themselves, not just "guinea pigs". (See Chapter 18 for more on disability studies versus biomedical research and rehabilitation science.)

Out of this liberating sentiment grew the field of disability studies. The Society for Disability Studies (https://disstudies.org/index.php/about-sds/what-is-disability-studies/) defines disability studies as the study of the "social, political, cultural, and economic factors that define disability". Disability studies is positioned directly in contrast to biomedical-rehabilitative studies and is characterized as

- interdisciplinary — an intersection of social sciences, basic sciences, humanities and the arts, not just the medical sciences;
- adhering to a broader causal view of disability as the result primarily of forces outside the person, that is, social forces that privilege some and disadvantage others;
- context-dependent — affected by local, national, and international factors;
- explicitly encouraging to participation by people with disabilities;
- in favour of leadership by disabled scholars;
- privileging the voices of people with disabilities; and
- inherently challenging to the biomedical approach to disability.

An offshoot of this approach to disability research is the field of critical disability studies. **Critical disability studies** represents the intersection of disability studies with critical theory. Critical theory arose in the 1930s in response to powerful ideologies, such as capitalism and fascism on the one side and communism on the other. Critical theory looks at power and dominance, and the social forces that favour the status quo. According to famous thinkers like Freud, Marx, Hegel, Kant, and Weber, critical theory focuses on how society and social structures reflect relationships of class and power that privilege some at the expense of others.

Critical disability theory claims that the medical establishment in particular, and society in general, perpetuate a view of disability that is disempowering and oppressive. This view can be seen in a number of socially constructed phenomena, such as language, images, descriptions, and portrayals of disability. It can also be seen in institutions, organization, laws, and social structures. It profoundly affects how people with disabilities are seen and treated. Critical disability studies seeks to uncover the sources of discrimination and violation that keep people with disabilities from enjoying full participation and citizenship. It exists to explicitly serve the information needs of disability activists and change agents. It upholds no allegiance to scientific objectivity or impartiality. It operates overtly from a stance of disabled persons as an oppressed minority, and powerful structures within society as oppressors. Foremost among those criticized as oppressors are health and social service professionals.

I have no argument with critical disability studies or scholars. I do not for one minute contest the appalling history of injustices that have victimized people with disabilities — eugenics, hate crimes, discrimination, and incarceration (Dolmage, 2018; Withers, 2012). However, this is not the whole story about disability, and perhaps it is not the best place to start that story for people who are seeking to learn about disability. The part that is missing in the highly politicized, monolithic perspective of critical disability studies is the day-to-day, real-life concerns that people with disabilities experience and that professionals seek to help with. The issue of disability is so complex and multi-dimensional that a hegemonic discourse on power and oppression seems inadequate to understand the depth and breadth of disability.

Appreciative inquiry

This is where appreciative inquiry comes in. **Appreciative inquiry** is an approach to knowing that asks not "What is wrong with the world?" but rather, "What does the world look like when it is at its very best, and how can we imagine moving towards that?" (Cooperrider, Whitney, & Stavros, 2008).

Appreciative inquiry is based on five principles:

1. the constructionist principle — that we co-construct reality through language and discourse;
2. the principle of simultaneity — that inquiry and change happen simultaneously, and that the mere act of inquiring about something is the seed of change;
3. the poetic principle — that language matters; the words and phrases we choose shape the discourse we engage in;
4. the anticipatory principle — that our view of the future guides what we do today; and

5. the positive principle — that change requires positive affect and energy. Positive images are at the heart of appreciative inquiry — new ideas and the will to act on them.

Appreciative inquiry follows four steps:

1. Discover — what appears to be working well?
2. Dream — what could be?
3. Design — how can we get there?
4. Deploy — where do we start?

Appreciative disability studies

So, what might the intersection of these two approaches look like? What would it look like to incorporate the best features of disability studies and appreciative inquiry as a way of studying and thinking about disability? That is what I hope to explore in this book, and what I am calling **appreciative disability studies**.

Appreciative disability studies is all of the following:

- *Collaborative:* At the very least, appreciative disability studies is undertaken and co-created in partnerships between scholars and people with disability (many of whom may be scholars themselves).

- *Interdisciplinary:* It acknowledges that the full story of disability cannot be told through the lens of one discipline, or using the language or concepts of one scholarly tradition. We must draw on the best of the sciences, the arts, and the humanities if we are to stand a chance of appreciating the complexity of disability.

- *Non-pathologized:* Having said that, appreciative disability studies resists the historical and contemporary tendency to default to a medical view of the many situations and conditions that affect human life. Medical science has grown enormously powerful in modern society, and although the scope of its ability to solve human problems is huge, the answer to how to make the world a better place for people with disabilities does not lie exclusively with health professionals.

- *Oriented toward change:* Like all earnest research inquiry, the aim of appreciative disability studies is to make the world a better place. Scholarly inquiry is not undertaken simply for its own sake, but rather for the sake of informing positive change. This is done by understanding what is and imagining what could be.

- *Balanced between objective and subjective:* In order to tell the full story, appreciative disability studies must conform to international standards of scientific rigour, but it must also reflect the authentic voices of people with disabilities. If we want disability studies to reach a broader academic and professional audience, its knowledge products must uphold the standards of the scientific community. On the other hand, if we want disability studies to address the real problems of people with disabilities, it must resonate with the real-life experience of people with disabilities. It must address important and worthwhile problems and topics.

- *Positive rather than negative in its tone:* Rather than focusing on a critique of society in its relationship to disabled people, appreciative disability studies focuses on how much we have to gain from the opportunity to work with people with disabilities. In this book, I am committed to adopting a tone that encourages people to engage with disability studies, with people with disabilities, and with careers dedicated to serving people with disabilities. I strive for a tone that is positive, constructive, and optimistic. I do not seek to deny that gross inequities exist and significantly affect the lives of people with disabilities, and we will explore these inequities in detail in the chapters that follow. I seek, however, to adopt a tone that is not alienating for readers, particularly readers who are new to disability studies.

- *Practical, rather than highly theoretical or abstract:* If we are to engage constructively with people with disabilities, we need to understand the real, everyday situations of their lives, and how best to work with them. As health, education, and social service professionals, we need to understand the issues that affect how disabled people look after themselves and find meaningful roles to shape their lives.

- *Complex:* If there were easy solutions to overcoming barriers faced by disabled people, they would have been implemented decades ago. The fact that issues persist underscores the complexity of disability issues. I will attempt to show all sides of the issues, and not oversimplify by stating the obvious — that the world should be more fair and equitable for people with disabilities. Of course it should be, but why isn't it? Usually because there are multiple perspectives to be balanced, and to deny this and simply advocate for one constituency is to ensure that no progress is made.

- *Appreciative:* Throughout this book, I will explore the theme of "appreciation" in a number of ways:
  - ¤ appreciating the challenges faced by people with disabilities in just getting through the day;
  - ¤ appreciating the resilience and resourcefulness of creative solutions developed by people with disabilities for overcoming obstacles;
  - ¤ appreciating the unique lens through which disabled people view the world, largely as a result of how the world views them;
  - ¤ appreciating how much we have to learn from people who move through the world differently than the so-called average person;
  - ¤ appreciating the complexity of creating a society that is inclusive and equitable; and
  - ¤ appreciating the gift of diversity, versus the threat of normalization.

Perspective

I have taken on the task of writing this book about disability, even though my own understanding of disability is second-hand, at best. I do not live with what most people would colloquially call a disability. I will talk more about this in a later chapter (about universality of disability and about identity politics), but for now I need to declare that I understand disability as an outsider. Readers need to understand that my perspective is not the insider perspective of someone who has first-hand experience with disability.

I have, however, had a close look at one type of disability. As I began writing this book, my husband of 27 years, to whom the book is dedicated, was marking the fortieth anniversary of acquiring his disability. I was not there when his light plane crashed, leaving him paralyzed with a spinal cord injury, nor was I on hand through the ordeal of acute care, rehabilitation, and adjustment to life with a disability. But I have been there for many of his life stages and transitions as a person with a disability, and have been a witness to joys and sorrows.

As an occupational therapist, I cannot deny that the lens through which I view the world is a problem-solving lens — a practical, rational approach to enabling people to do whatever they need or want to do. I have tried over the years to increase my awareness of the helper/service-provider orientation, and to ensure that it is not ultimately disempowering. It is at odds with the appreciative approach, and I will be challenged throughout to reconcile these two approaches.

Finally, I acknowledge the influence of having been a researcher and educator in rehabilitation and disability studies for about 35 years. Whereas the previous two lenses afford me a close-up view of disability through the experiences of clients, friends, and spouse, the academic lens requires me to step back and try to see the big picture. As a researcher, I was socialized to value objectivity, reason, and theory. As an educator, I try to deal in ideas, frames of reference, and multi-dimensionality. These ways of thinking and being can be helpful, or they can be used to objectify and diminish. I work extra hard to share the benefits of my knowledge and experience, without using them as a means to power or privilege.

Language

There is considerable sensitivity around language referring to disability. In this book, the guiding principle is inclusivity. I seek to use language that invites others into the dialogue and that welcomes a variety of perspectives. I refer to federal guidelines for non-discriminatory language. I seek neutrality, precision, and clarity of communication in language. (For more about language referring to disability, see Chapter 3.)

How this book unfolds

This is an introductory textbook on disability for students from a variety of fields. The primary audience members are

- university students in the health, education, and social service professions (such as occupational therapy, physical therapy, rehabilitation psychology, kinesiology, nursing, special education, and medicine);

- college students in health and social disciplines (such as rehabilitation assistance, orthotics and prosthetics, attendant care, nursing assistance, educational assistance, child care, and social services); and

- graduate students in disability studies, social anthropology, human geography, and medical sociology.

A secondary audience includes working professionals in all areas of life dealing with people with disabilities, from health professionals (physical and occupational therapists, nurses, social workers, psychologists, physicians), to educators, legal professionals, and workers in community agencies and social services.

The book contributes new information on the situation of people with a disability in North American society 37 years after the International Year of Disabled Persons (1981). It offers a practical and hopefully even-handed discussion of disability in contemporary society, including the most up-to-date information available from research and scholarship, as well as government and consumer sources, on issues affecting people with disabilities in the course of their everyday lives.

The book is divided into five sections — What Do We Mean by Disability? Disability and Self-care; Disability, Productivity, and Leisure; Disability in Society; and Themes in Appreciative Disability Studies. The three concepts of self-care, productivity, and leisure derive from my background as an occupational therapist, but they have proved to be a most effective means of categorizing the challenges encountered and strategies employed by individuals and groups affected by disability. These are the issues that people with disabilities encounter as they seek to be healthy, happy, self-sufficient, productive, and contributing members of society.

Chapter 2

Thinking about disability: Models and definitions

Introduction

Defining *disability* seems like a relatively straightforward thing to do. Surely it simply refers to things that people can't do. What else could it be? And yet, disability means much more than that. In this chapter, we will consider

- the historical ways of thinking about disability and the conditions that gave rise to them;
- the contemporary models of disability and some of the advantages and disadvantages of them;
- the implications of defining disability; and
- the qualities of a good definition.

Historical models and definitions

Disability is defined etymologically as a compound word made up of the prefix *dis*, meaning "away from", and *ability*, meaning "capacity or competence" — from Latin to Middle French to Middle English and ultimately modern English.

According to *Merriam-Webster's* online dictionary (https//www.merriam-webster.com/dictionary/disability), the word *disability* has been with us since the 1500s, and can refer to a functional inability, a lack of financial means, or a legal impediment. But the concept of disability has of course been with us much longer than that — thousands of years, in fact. One of the oldest documents we have — the Hebrew Bible — refers to disability, using words like *blind, lame, leper, possessed of demons, defect, impurity*, and others that fall hard on our ears today (Stiker, 1999). The Bible gives us a striking picture of the appalling social and material conditions that people with disabilities endured in the ancient world. Because of beliefs about the relationship of disability to sin, disabled people were shunned, ostracized, and forced to derive a livelihood by begging.

Over the intervening centuries and up to recent times, four other definitions of disability have evolved (McColl & Bickenbach, 1998). In each instance, disability was defined by various authorities in society that in one way or another controlled the destiny of people with disabilities.

1. Until the middle of the 20th century, the most common way of thinking about disability was using the **charitable model**. Disability was defined by religious authorities, who identified a sense of mission toward people they saw as the victims of misfortune and objects of pity. They determined that the appropriate response to disabled people was one of charity and benevolence. While this definition on the surface sounds benign, it reduces disabled people to passive recipients of philanthropy, without agency to care for themselves or to control their own circumstances. They were literally at the mercy of well-meaning others.

2. By the middle of the 20th century, the development of the field of rehabilitation led to a situation where people with disabilities could realistically contemplate a life beyond disability. It was a different life than the one they had expected, but it was a life nonetheless. The rehabilitation system had socialized them to strive for independence and to master their own personal care and daily activities. They were encouraged to take their place in society, even to the extent of contributing their labour in limited ways. This environment gave rise to the **economic model** of disability. The labour market, specifically employers and businesses, defined people with disabilities according to their ability or inability to work, to be economically self-sufficient, and to represent an economic force in

society. The worth of people with disabilities was defined by their productivity. In the absence of the ability to generate a reasonable income, the responsibility of society toward people with disabilities was to acknowledge their limitations and their need for financial supports, and to develop programs and systems to provide them with a subsistence living. This era gave rise to vocational rehabilitation, sheltered workshops and disability pensions, to name a few examples of expressions of the economic definition. While this view of disability acknowledges the need of all people to have a productive outlet and to contribute to something beyond themselves, it stops short of truly honouring the contributions disabled people are capable of making to society. Instead it relegates them to the role of recipients of welfare, rather than contributors to society. It also tends to entirely disregard their needs and preferences as potential customers.

3. By the 1950s and 1960s, post-war prosperity had led to a zeal for social reform and an affinity for the good life. Scientific developments seemed to promise unbridled progress and improvements to social status for many. The middle class was growing as all aspired to the social ideal of full employment, home ownership, higher education, and perhaps even a few luxuries. The **sociological model** grew out of this milieu. The justice system and powerful institutions within society were charged with upholding these social norms and the expectations of citizens. People with disabilities, particularly those with mental or emotional impairments, were seen as being outside the mainstream of society, at the margins — a minority group (Imrie, 1997). This specification provided justification for these people to be segregated from society — hospitalized, institutionalized, or even incarcerated.

4. By far the most prevalent definition of disability to have evolved in the 20th century was the **biomedical model**. As people became increasingly enamoured of developments in medical science, health professionals became powerful sources of authority in modern society. The biomedical definition of disability hinges on the idea that there is an impairment, a fault, a flaw in some tiny part of the person, and if only we could find it and correct it, then the person could be restored to health, happiness, and function. This

reductionistic approach situates disability in objective, organic findings, and it assumes that if the biological problem can be overcome, then all will be well. The appropriate response from society toward disabled people is to ensure that timely and compassionate diagnosis and treatment are available. Consistent with the previous definitions, the bio-medical model situates disability inside the person, and defers to an external authority to decide what is needed to remediate the situation.

The preceding definitions prevailed at different times over the past 100 years. All reflect what was important in society at the time. Until the 1980s, and arguably even up to today, these models were all evident in images and portrayals of disability around us. How disability is portrayed signals to us the underlying definition of disability that is being invoked.

Here's an example:

For years, a major national fundraising campaign for childhood disability took place over the Labour Day weekend and featured images of children with obvious disabilities and elfin smiles. The rhetoric accompanying these images was heavily weighted with stories evoking pity, pathos, and sympathy. These emotional portrayals were meant to tug at our heartstrings and loosen our purse strings. And they did — they brought donations flooding in, raising millions of dollars to provide goods and services for children with disabilities.

This is, of course, an example of the charitable definition. It seems horrifying to our modern sensibilities to think of exploiting disabled children in this way as a means of raising money. But if that money is to be used to promote their welfare, is it really so terrible? It was not undertaken with malevolent intent, but rather with benevolent intent — to provide necessary goods and services to children with disabilities, to alleviate the burden of cost on families with a disabled child, and to raise awareness in the general population of the struggles and challenges faced by some. It was an expression of society at that time. Like most definitions, it tells us at least as much about those doing the defining as it does about those being defined!

Challenge for readers #1

Google *disability* and look at some of the images and articles it brings up, particularly those in the popular media (rather than the academic press). See if you can identify the underlying definition of disability that shapes the language and ideas expressed.

- For the charitable model, look for words like *victim*, *suffered*, and *brave*, the intentional elicitation of an emotional response, and ideas about the benevolent impulse to help.
- For the economic model, look for references to the financial and economic situation of people with disabilities, inferences that competitive work is not an option, and passive images of receiving without reciprocally giving back or contributing to society.
- For the sociological model, look for words like *normal* and *abnormal*, references to people with disabilities as a risk to the safety of others, and images of disabled people intended to evoke fear.
- For the biomedical model, look for images of disabled people as patients. Look for medical professionals with them. Watch for them to be shown in bed, in hospital gowns, and undergoing medical or technical procedures.

What proportion of the images you see fall into each of these categories? What does this brief exercise suggest are the most prevalent definitions of disability in our society today? Are you surprised?

On the downside, of course, is the disempowering effect such portrayals have on the people portrayed, and the perpetuation of an image of disability as helpless and pitiable.

Modern definitions

In the early 1980s, people with disabilities responded to the many social movements that were afoot in the previous two decades — the civil rights movement, the peace movement, the women's movement. The disability movement became the "last civil rights movement" (Driedger, 1989). In response to the rallying cry "Nothing about us without us", people with disabilities insisted that they, and only they, were qualified to define the condition of disability.

The year 1981 was identified as the United Nations International Year of Disabled Persons, and the decade from 1982–1993 was the UN Decade of Disabled Persons. We still celebrate December 3 each year as the International Day of Persons with Disabilities, as a reminder of the lofty goals that were set as part of the World Program of Action concerning Disabled Persons (United Nations, 1982, Resolution 37/52).

The following definitions of disability have arisen in the past 35 years, in keeping with the post-modern paradigm — experiential, context-dependent, relativistic, subjective:

1. The first alternative definition of disability to challenge the medical model was the **independent living model** of disability. The independent living movement arose in the United States to assert the right of self-determination for people with disabilities. The independent living movement thus defined people with disabilities as consumers (rather than patients or clients) — meaning rational decision-makers in control of the resources that shape their lives. Choice is at the heart of independent living — specifically, the same range of choices enjoyed by non-disabled people within a society. Key themes in independent living are housing, living situation, employment, personal support services, social opportunities, and advocacy. Independent Living Centres arose in cities across North America, providing services "of, by and for people with disabilities".

2. Disability activists in England offered another alternative definition of disability — the **social model** of disability (Oliver, 1990). They viewed disability as entirely socially constructed by a society designed without their needs in mind. Disability did not exist in any objective reality of impairment or diagnosis, but rather in the barriers that society erected to inhibit the full participation of disabled people. This model proposed that the remedy to disability, or the appropriate social response to disability, would be the removal of all barriers that create inequities for people with disabilities. Hosking (2008) describes the social model as the "mighty shove" needed to shift the dominant discourse away from the biomedical model to something more structural

rather than individualized — away from individuals to society at large — as the origin of disability.

The social model became so dominant in disability advocacy and activism around the turn of the 21st century that it was virtually hegemonic. To subscribe to any other definition of disability was heresy. But that sort of dominance cannot be sustained — it is a set-up for criticism, and sure enough, criticisms of the social model began to emerge:

- The social model was utopian and unrealistic. The ideal of a barrier-free society was unattainable.
- The social model didn't deal with the practical realities that people with disabilities face today, and in the future.
- The social model simply replaced the oppressive language of medicine with the equally alienating and esoteric language of sociology and political science.
- The social model failed to deal with the heterogeneity of disability. Structural solutions were simply too remote to deal with intimate and personal issues.
- Disability research based on the social model categorically rejected the scientific paradigm, in favour of participatory and emancipatory research approaches. While these methods responded to the need for an alternative to traditional research methods, they situated disability studies entirely outside of mainstream science.

Finally, the most damning critique of the social model was that it failed to acknowledge the lived experience of disability and the individuality of disability. For example, for people who experience pain and its implications for daily life, no amount of social engineering is going to make that go away.

3. A subset of the social model is the **human rights model**. It focuses on the potential for an insensitive society to discriminate against people with disabilities by virtue of society's failure to account for the needs of disabled people when establishing structures and programs within society. Discrimination can arise from deliberately excluding people with disabilities, but more often, it arises unintentionally — by failing to give a thought to how people with disabilities will interact with the physical, social, and legal environment. The remedy, according to the human rights model, is to challenge prevailing structures where they lead to discrimination, and

to systematically alter laws and policies to ensure equity for people with disabilities. Discrimination against people with disabilities must be eliminated case by case, whether intentional or unintentional.

4. Another corollary of the social model of disability is the **critical disability approach**, which was discussed in Chapter 1. This approach characterizes disability as an issue of power and a source of historical oppression. Disability arises when dominant forces in society exercise their privilege regardless of its implications for others. The critical disability approach rejects all attempts at objectivity or rational inquiry into disability, since these are expressions of the dominant normative discourse that privileges the status quo and silences the voices of disabled people.

5. The **biopsychosocial model** arose in an attempt to reconcile the critique of the social model as being inadequately attentive to the lived experience of disability. Over time, as the social model failed to produce the changes it sought in social structures, critics pointed to its often alienating rhetoric, its utopian view of the world, and its denial of real personal challenges accompanying disability. The biopsychosocial model attempts to reconcile these issues by situating disability at the interface of a person with an impairment and a society that fails to adequately adapt for that impairment. It represents a swing of the pendulum away from an entirely structural perspective on disability toward a perspective that also recognizes the individual experience. However, unlike the medical model, the biopsychosocial model offers no objective indicator of who does and does not have a disability.

6. Another approach to conceptualizing disability is found in the **capabilities approach**. The capabilities approach was first proposed by Sen (1980) as a means of understanding the inequality and disadvantage experienced by some individuals and groups in society. Capabilities are defined as opportunities to partake in certain activities or goals in life by virtue of having the ability, resources, means, knowledge, and external circumstances to do so. Nussbaum (2000) built on the capabilities approach by specifying 10 "functionings" that are considered essential to human flourishing: life/survival; bodily

health; bodily integrity; use of the senses, thought, and imagination; emotions; practical reasoning; affiliation; relating to
other species; play; and control over one's environment.
Rather than a normative concept of ability, the capabilities
approach emphasizes freedom to live a life of one's choosing,
including autonomy and human rights (Baylies, 2002;
Burchardt, 2004; Riddle, 2010).

7. The last model in this list was proposed by Swain and French
   (2000) and is called the **affirmation model** of disability. This
   model attempted to turn the tables on disability definitions.
   The authors maintained that all of the above models are still
   "tragedy" models, in that they focus on disability as a problem
   — as a source of oppression, discrimination, ignorance, and
   disregard. The affirmation model of disability focuses on the
   advantages experienced by people with disabilities. Some of
   the advantages they enumerate include the ability to eschew
   class distinctions, freedom from society's expectations and
   requirements, and empathy for other oppressed minorities.
   They point to expressions of disability pride in the arts scene
   — in dance, visual arts, poetry, comedy, and music.

Together with the four historical definitions of disability, there
are no less that 11 definitions of disability that you may encounter
currently in circulation. It is essential when talking about disability
that we make it clear what we mean and that we understand the
implications of our definition.

Why do we need a definition of disability?

According to Stiker (1999), we define things when we want to differentiate them from other things. We define childhood (vs. adulthood)
so that we can differentiate the age below which people can't be
expected to be self-sufficient, to take responsibility for their actions,
and to function as citizens. We define cultural and ethnic back-
grounds so that we can understand different ways of thinking and
acting, according to different historical reference points, belief systems, and social norms.

But why do we define disability? Why is it important to point
out where someone moves through the world differently?

First and foremost, it is important to be able to speak precisely about disability in order to honour the experience of some of those in our midst — people who see, hear, look, feel, or move differently. To minimize the experience of disability by refusing to give it a name is the ultimate denial of that experience. To deny that disability exists does the ultimate injustice to people for whom daily life is more of a struggle than it is for many of their non-disabled counterparts. Consistent with the theme of this book, we seek to talk candidly about disability, so that we can appreciate what it means to people — if we are to have real, meaningful conversations with disabled people. To shy away from it, or to treat disability as a political football, is to disrespect one of the most influential aspects of a person's life.

Another reason for being able to define disability is to create a shared identity among people with disabilities. Ability and disability exist on a continuum. Somewhere on that continuum of ability-disability there is a threshold beyond which people say they have a disability. They self-identity as having a disability, or being disabled. They claim the label of disability.

Why would someone do this? Surely there are things that each of us can't do; but if asked if they were disabled, about 85% of the population would say no. For those people who say yes, the disability is a part of how they interact with the world and how the world treats them. It has become a part of who they are; it has been internalized as an identity.

Disability is recognized as a non-normative experience. It sets people apart in their experience of the world from their non-disabled contemporaries. It is what Solomon (2012) refers to as a horizontal identity. Unlike a vertical identity, which is derived from one's family, either by birth or by socialization, a horizontal identity differentiates one from his or her family. It requires him or her to find a peer group with whom to affiliate and consolidate identity. Thus, the horizontal identity of disability unites disabled people with others who experience disability. It affords them "membership" in a peer group with shared values, experiences, language, and assumptions. We all have multiple identities — student, athlete, wife, boyfriend, sister, pianist, and so on. Disabled people participate in all of these identities, but they also carry an identity as a person with a disability. The ability to label this aspect of their lives provides coherence to their overall identity.

In some instances, groups of disabled people express that identity in the form of a social movement. They extend their personal identity through affiliation and solidarity with other people who share similar experiences in the world. They express their reality through the power of numbers, seeking to be heard as a social and political force. They derive purpose and meaning from knowing there is a contingent of people who subscribe to a similar cause.

Another reason to define and label disability is to communicate realistic expectations of performance both to the self and to others. In the absence of knowledge about the presence of a disability, we all make assumptions about what is appropriate to expect of people, both in our private circles and in society at large. We expect that people will conduct themselves in certain ways in public and that they will uphold certain social standards. We expect that people will communicate in certain ways, that they will strive for independence and economic self-sufficiency, and that they will observe the privacy of others. These are but a few of the many expectations we assert in everyday life without even thinking about them. But for disabled people, some of these expectations may be beyond their abilities. Knowing about the presence of a disability allows us to adjust expectations so as to be fair and considerate.

But what if the disability is not immediately evident? What if the disability is invisible, like many sensory, psychological, or intellectual disabilities, or like disabilities arising from pain or fatigue? Or what if the circumstances in which we encounter someone don't highlight his or her disability? Then we rely on the person to self-identify as having a disability — to trust us enough to reveal that part of their life to us. It has been called "the dilemma of difference". When do we proclaim the presence of a disability and when do we hide it?

I am reminded of a friend who immigrated to Canada from his home country, which had become oppressive and which afforded limited opportunities for him and his family. When he returned to visit his native country, even years later, he said he would stand in the customs line to enter the country with a knot in his stomach, trying to figure out whether to show his Canadian passport and say as little as possible in his accented English, or show his original passport and use his unaccented first language to address the customs officer. Which identity would get him past the necessary authorities with the least delay and difficulty?

A similar dilemma faces people whose disability is not immediately evident, even though that dilemma faces them every day. Do you assert your privacy to not reveal the presence of a disability, or do you claim the disability right from the start? Of course, the implications of either course of action are obvious. By withholding information about disability, you avoid the risk that people will make assumptions about what you can and cannot do — assumptions that in many instances may be grossly unfair and the product of stereotyping and stigma about disability. At the same time, you forfeit the possibility of any special considerations or services. On the other hand, revealing the disability means that you can expect some adjustment to expectations in keeping with real limitations on ability and performance, but you risk the abuse of that information to disadvantage and limit your chances.

A final reason that we need to know what we mean by disability is that, as a society, we strive to create equity and inclusion of people with disabilities by affording certain benefits, services, and supports. In order to distribute those goods and services fairly, we need to know who is eligible to receive them and who is not. Perhaps the most obvious example is disability pensions. In Canada, when someone incurs a disability, the federal government compensates him or her for productive years lost by paying out a pension. Public servants responsible for this program need to have some basis upon which to make judgments about who can receive the pension. Another example is the Disability Tax Credit. In recognition of extraordinary costs associated with living with a disability, the federal government gives a tax credit to people who qualify by virtue of having a disability. But what constitutes a disability? Some of these policy dilemmas have at their core the need for a definition of disability.

How does it feel to have an important condition of your life defined by others? In an attempt to understand the importance of how disability is defined, I invite readers to take the Challenge for readers #2.

Qualities of a good definition of disability

A number of scholars have attempted to enumerate the qualities of a good definition of disability.

1. There appears to be consensus on the necessity for an underlying health condition as the basis for defining a disability (WHO, 2001; Leonardi, Bickenbach, Ustun, Kostanjsek, & Chatterji, 2006). We would not say that someone had a dis-

Challenge for readers #2

I am assuming that most of the readers of this book will be students of one description or another. (Even if not enrolled in a formal academic program, the fact that you are seeking to learn about disability entitles you to claim the role of a student.) Go out into your community and your circle of acquaintances and ask them how they would define what a STUDENT is. When you feel that you have heard from enough people to have got a range of different responses and ideas, stop and look over the definitions you have been given.

1. What appear to be the common themes in people's definitions of a student?
2. What elements of the definitions do you agree/ disagree with?
3. As an "insider" to the student role, how does it feel to have "outsiders" defining the conditions of an impor- tant aspect of your life?
4. Imagine how it would feel if this definition was used to determine whether or not you got benefits or ser- vices that you consider essential.

Now remember that your status as a student is temporary and, in fact, quite privileged. Imagine what it feels like to have a disability — which may be prolonged or even life- long — defined by others, often by others who have no idea of the day-to-day reality of living with a disability.

ability who couldn't function in a particular community because he or she didn't speak the language of its members. But we would say someone had a disability if he or she couldn't speak because of dysarthria or some other health condition that rendered him or her unable to speak and be understood. Although no clear link can be established between any particular health condition and its manifestation as disability (Paetzold, 2005), it is clear that a health condition must be present. The presence of a health condition "legiti- mizes" disability, according to Depoy and Gilson (2011). For example, an ataxic gait may be considered "legitimate" if it is associated with cerebral palsy, whereas the same gait pattern associated with inebriation may not.

2. There is also broad agreement that a disability is inherently an inability to perform some important function or role. While not a perfectly objective state, disability must be more than a subjective experience or a negative evaluation of quality of life (Leonardi et al., 2006). Pain is not a disability, nor is depression or hemiplegia; rather, these are conditions that inhibit the ability to *do* certain things. It is that inability to *do* that constitutes a disability. A disability is a specific limitation or restriction that has important consequences for a person's life.

3. Most authors agree that disability is a universal phenomenon — that we all experience some degree of disability with regard to some activities. And yet, for some people, disability is one of the most important factors that affects how their life unfolds, while for others it is a mere inconvenience. Where is the threshold beyond which a person crosses over to having a disability or being considered disabled? This is one of the thorniest questions we face when trying to configure a definition of disability. The simple response is to say that disability is a self-identified phenomenon; however, this approach is inadequate for some of the situations described above, such as when governments afford benefits or supports to people who qualify as disabled.

4. There is no agreement in the literature about who is qualified to assess or measure disability. Medical or health professionals are often the default assumption about who can authenticate a disability status. And yet, medical professionals are qualified only to testify to the underlying medical condition, and not to the disability itself (Corson-Rikert & Christmas, 2009).

5. A good definition of disability must align with current knowledge, practice, and ideology about disability. Thus, in the current climate, the only acceptable definition of disability is one that places at least equal emphasis on the role of society (vs. the role of the individual) in creating a disability situation.

6. The best definition of disability must be context-free under some circumstances, and context-dependent under others (Scanlon, 2013; Letizia, 2002; Paetzold, 2005). When considering policy aimed at *equity* or *access*, the definition of disabil-

ity should be context-free; that is, the policy should address all types of disabilities, regardless of the particular manifestations in different situations. On the other hand, when considering policy aimed at providing *supports*, the definition of disability must be context-dependent. It must reflect the specific needs of those individuals who are tactically disadvantaged in participating in a particular life area by virtue of their disability. (More on disability policy in Chapter 17.)

7. Some situations that call for a definition of disability require a severity indicator, often as a means of establishing eligibility for goods or services (Scanlon, 2013). Severity of disability is usually related to the ability to be independent. The International Classification of Functioning Disability & Health (WHO, 2001) rates the severity of disabilities as follows:
    *   the *capacity* to perform an activity;
    *   actual *performance* in a particular environment;
    *   the *frequency* with which the limitation has occurred in the last 30 days — rarely, occasionally, frequently, every day;
    *   the *intensity* of the effect of limitations — 25% of the time, less than 50%, more than 50%, more than 95%; and
    *   the extent of *interference* of the limitation — tolerable, interferes with day-to-day life, partially disrupting of daily life, totally disrupting of daily life.

    Severity is also sometimes rated according to the number of areas of life affected. A disability is seldom classified as severe if it affects only one particular sector of life (vs. affecting multiple areas of daily living).

8. A good definition also allows for the fact that disability doesn't look or act the same way in every person. Disability interacts with personal and environmental factors, and may be temporal or situational:
    *   Relapsing/remitting conditions, where the underlying health condition has a natural course of exacerbation and remission: These conditions result in a disability that is more acute at some times than at others, and these episodes are seldom very predictable. In such circumstances, the person may be virtually disability-free during some periods, and experience greater or lesser degrees of impairment depending on the state of the illness. This cate-

gory might include disabilities associated with conditions like multiple sclerosis, mental illness, or chronic pain/fatigue syndromes. It might also include conditions where treatments render the person temporarily disabled, such as chemotherapy or serial surgeries.

- Conditions for which the prognosis is unknown: Even though there is a verifiable disability at the time of assessment, there may be recovery to a state where no disability remains. An example would be complex musculoskeletal injuries and back, neck, or head injuries (including concussion). Another example in this category might be cancer or HIV/AIDS, where the ultimate outcome cannot be anticipated.

- Conditions that arise in response to particular activities or conditions: When they occur, they can be legitimately disabling, but at other times they may not be in evidence at all. Examples of these conditions might include migraine, back pain, and neck pain.

Try Challenge for readers #3, and compare your definition with other contemporary definitions.

Challenge for readers #3

1. Name five people you know who have a disability, and beside each of their names, write down what you consider to be that person's disability.
2. Now look across the five disabilities you have described, and try to identify the qualities or characteristics that are common to all.
3. On the basis of your observations, try to write your own definition of disability.

My definition of disability:

_____

_____

_____

Contemporary definition of disability

The international standard for defining disability currently is the World Health Organization's definition (Escorpizo, Stucki, Cieza, Strumbo, & Riddle, 2010), expressed in the *International Classification of Functioning, Disability and Health* (ICF; WHO, 2001). The ICF defines disability as

> ... an outcome of interactions between health conditions (diseases, disorders and injuries) and contextual factors:
> * external environmental factors — for example, social attitudes, architectural characteristics, legal and social structures, as well as climate, terrain and so forth; and,
> * internal personal factors, such as gender, age, coping styles, social background, education, profession, past and current experience, overall behaviour pattern, character.

Another international standard for the definition of disability is contained in the *United Nations Convention on the Rights of Persons with Disabilities* (UN, 2006) to which Canada became a signatory in 2012:

> Persons with disabilities include those who have long-term physical, mental, intellectual, or sensory impairments, which in interaction with various barriers, may hinder their full and effective participation in society on an equal basis with others.

Some important features common to these two definitions are as follows:

* Both situate disability not exclusively in the person and not exclusively in the environment, but rather as a product of an interaction of a person with an environment.

* Both acknowledge that a health condition must be present in order for a disability to be present. The simple fact of not being able to do something can result from many situations, but the only one that we label *disability* is the one that arises in the presence of a health condition.

* Both identify the concept of barriers — environmental factors that inhibit ability.

- The UNCRPD definition refers to participation in society and equality as the outcomes that all people, in particular people with disabilities, seek.

- The ICF definition also enumerates personal characteristics that affect the experience of disability.

Conclusion

This chapter shows us the incredible complexity of disability and the necessity to be precise and deliberate in our use of the term. We have explored no less than 10 ways of thinking about disability — some historical and some contemporary. And yet, I suspect that all can be found in discussions about disability today.

Appreciative inquiry asks us to imagine what the world would look like at its very best. It follows four steps — *discover, dream, design,* and *deploy.* For each chapter of this book, I will apply this framework to summarize what we have learned from the current chapter.

We have discovered that there is no universal consensus on how we should think about disability. Some models are very practical and specific, while others are abstract and esoteric. There are certainly models that are less acceptable than others, such as the charitable model or the medical model, but we are left with no clear instruction as to which model is best. That depends to some extent on our philosophical approach and the purpose for which the definition is being used.

We have also *discovered,* and this theme will be revisited throughout this book, that there is a discernable historical trajectory in how we think about disability. The development of historical consciousness about disability has been layered over broader social movements and ideologies. We can see a relationship between perspectives on disability and those on other social factors, such as race, gender, and sexual orientation.

On a personal level, I hope we have *discovered* something about the feeling of being labelled or categorized. It can be disenfranchising indeed to have the sum total of your life experience reduced to a single word or pigeonhole. Often that label has important practical consequences as well as social or emotional ones.

While we may *dream* of a world where we can all agree about what it means to have a disability, it is probably unrealistic to think that a single definition will satisfy all applications. It is more important that we understand and consider the implications of different definitions and models of disability than it is to drive toward consensus on a single definition.

These definitions are part of the *design* of our society, and of many of the structures and processes that we see around us. As we analyze the institutions, policies, programs, and services that make up our society, our analysis will be strengthened if we can recognize how the designers were thinking about disability when they made up the rules or when they built the institutions.

As we prepare for a career in the health, educational, or social sciences, we may be called upon to *deploy* programs that will be used by people with disabilities. A key step in this process is to circumscribe who is and is not eligible to participate in the program or to receive the goods and services offered by the program. When designing eligibility criteria, it is essential to think about who we include and who we exclude when applying different definitions or conceptualizations of disability.

Chapter 3

Talking about disability

Introduction

As we have alluded to in previous chapters, the language we choose for talking about disability is important. It describes a central feature of the lives of many people, and the words we use can communicate — whether intentionally or unintentionally — our underlying beliefs about disability.

Talking about disability is something that makes people nervous if they are not accustomed to it, and if they have no guidelines for how to proceed. There are a number of possible reasons for this. Most people seek, first and foremost, not to offend. They do not want to contribute to the unease of another by using language or terminology that the other person would find demeaning or inappropriate. They don't want to appear insensitive or ignorant. They don't want to reveal their lack of understanding or sophistication by the use of language that is out of date, out of fashion, or out of step. For professionals in particular, they want to convey their competence by using correct terms for issues or topics within their purview.

Yet, we are not born knowing how to use language to communicate effectively about disability. Furthermore, there is little consensus about what language is best or most acceptable. It may seem at times like it is impossible to select language that is correct in every situation — and to some extent, this is true.

Guidelines for talking about disability

This chapter offers a few guidelines to ensure that the language we use is inclusive and respectful, rather than alienating, distancing, or even insulting.

1.   People-first language?

There is a broadly held view that the correct way to talk about people with disabilities collectively is to put the people first and the disability second. Many authorities, including the Government of Canada, insist on this language; however, there is a significant contingent of disability scholars and advocates who say no to people-first language. They claim that people-first language situates the disability entirely within the person (i.e., the person has the disability), and that is at odds with the contemporary definitions discussed above. Instead, they prefer the term *disabled people*, because it affirms that we are talking about people who have been disabled by their circumstances. Some of the factors that disable may be within the person, but some are entirely external to the person. Disability is at least partially the result of physical barriers, such as stairs; informational barriers, such as lack of knowledge about disability; attitudinal barriers, such as stereotypes and misplaced assumptions; and systemic barriers, such as inadequate policy consideration. Many of these are barriers over which the individual has little or no control.

In this book, we will use both terms interchangeably, in deference to both schools of thought. But, more importantly, we will strive to always use language that invites others into the dialogue, and that welcomes a variety of perspectives. We refer to federal guidelines for non-discriminatory language (HRSDC, 2006). When talking about particular organizations or groups, we will use the language that they prefer, if we can find a statement of preference. Overall, we seek language that communicates clearly and precisely.

2.   Use internationally recognized language

So, what might language that is clear and precise look like? As discussed above, the international standard for classifying disability is the World Health Organization's *International Classifica-*

tion of Functioning, Disability and Health (ICF; WHO, 2001). The ICF is the result of an international collaborative process that has been underway since the 1980s, when it initially became evident that existing classifications of diseases (i.e., the WHO's ICD — *International Classification of Diseases*) were inadequate to capture the experience of disability. For example, the ICD offers a classification of 164 for the condition of a stroke, one of the most common sources of disability. And yet a stroke can manifest dramatically differently in different people. For some, a mild stroke may result in no real functional change. Recovery is complete, and the individual returns to his or her former activity level. For others, the results of a stroke can be devastating, including the loss of physical function on one side of the body; speech, visual, and sensory perceptions; and even cognitive functions. Furthermore, depending on personal characteristics, such as age, marital status, or language abilities, the lived experience of a stroke may also be dramatically different. Layer upon that the accessibility and supports available in the environment, and the impact of a stroke changes again, either for better or worse.

The ICF attempts to capture this complexity in its classification system for functioning and disability. It is beyond the scope of this book to provide a complete discussion of the ICF. For that, I refer the reader to the ICF website (http://www.who.int/classifications/icf/en/). As a brief summary of what the ICF offers, here are the main elements of the classification system:

- The primary contribution of the ICF is the classification of activities and participation. Activities are defined as tasks or actions; participation is a broader concept defined as involvement in life situations. Disabilities are specifically classified as **activity limitations** (difficulties an individual may have in executing activities) or **participation restrictions** (problems an individual may experience in involvement in life situations). Activity limitations and participation restrictions pertain to nine areas:
  - learning and applying knowledge;
  - general tasks and demands;
  - communication;
  - mobility;
  - self-care;
  - domestic life;
  - interpersonal interactions and relationships;

¤ major life areas; and

¤ community, social, and civic life.

- The ICF also offers a classification of **environmental factors**, including

  ¤ products and technology;

  ¤ natural environment and human-made changes to environment;

  ¤ support and relationships;

  ¤ attitudes; and

  ¤ services, systems, and policies.

- Finally, the ICF offers a way of classifying the impairments to body structure and function that may be associated with disability:

  ¤ **Impairments of body structure** include structure of the nervous system; eye, ear, and related structures; structures involved in voice and speech; structure of the cardiovascular, immunological, and respiratory systems; structures related to the digestive, metabolic and endocrine systems; structures related to genitourinary and reproductive systems; structures related to movement; and skin and related structures.

  ¤ **Impairments to body function** include mental functions; sensory functions and pain; voice and speech functions; func-tions of the cardiovascular, hematological, immunological, and respiratory systems; functions of the digestive, metabolic, and endocrine systems; genitourinary and reproductive functions; neuro-musculoskeletal and movement-related functions; and functions of the skin and related structures.

For more information on definitions and terms, see the primer on the ICF published by the WHO (2001): *Towards a Common Language for Functioning, Disability and Health*, available as a PDF file on the WHO website (http://www.who.int/classifications/icf/icfbeginnersguide.pdf?ua=1).

3. Avoid medical language

The technical terms above describing impairments may have led readers to believe that the best way to talk about disability is to use technical language or perhaps even medical language. But remember that impairments are not disabilities. Impairments are underlying medical conditions, whereas disabilities are related to everyday activities and aspects of life. *A disability is not a diagnosis.* As we have discussed in the first chapter, diagnoses are inadequate to capture the complexity and multi-dimensionality, as well as the variety, of disabilities. It is far more descriptive to use ordinary, everyday language to describe disabilities — language that resonates with the real difficulties that people experience in trying to get through their day.

4.   Distinguish between patient, client, or consumer

Related to the fact that a disability is not a diagnosis, neither is a person with a disability a patient. There are at least three words that describe people who are the recipients of health and social services. We want to be clear about how we use these words in relation to people with disabilities:

- A **patient** typically refers to someone who is ill and who has placed his or her care in the hands of a medical professional. When we become a patient, we forfeit some of our autonomy in order to receive the best guidance and judgment of a professional. We often don't have much choice in our situation as a patient — we depend on others to make good decisions on our behalf.

- As a **client**, we retain more authority in the relationship with a professional, in that we choose to enter into a relationship with a professional. We still count on his or her expertise and good judgment, but we expect to make choices about how the process will or won't unfold.

- As a **consumer**, we are ultimately in charge of what goods and services we will accept, in that we are either paying for them or authorizing payment from a third party.

You can see that these three types of relationships exist on a continuum from less power in the hands of the recipient and more in the hands of the professional, to the opposite. People with disabilities typically consider themselves either clients or consumers of service, depending on the extent to which they can exert the fullest degree of power in the relationship and maintain control of the conditions of their life.

5.   Speak directly about disability

Particularly when talking about disability in the popular media, we often hear what I refer to as euphemistic language about disability — "differently able", "diverse-ability", "visually challenged", and various other configurations that seem to go to great lengths to avoid talking about what is right in front of us. To me, these euphemistic terms suggest or imply that it is somehow inappropriate to speak directly about disability, that it is something we need to conceal behind more socially acceptable language. I caution against the use of these alternative formulations for disability and advocate instead for clear, direct language. We strive to speak about disability as a condition of life, a reality that has profound implications for someone's life. We don't need to make it socially acceptable by using alternative language.

6.   Speak correctly about the absence of a disability

Another aspect of talking about disability is how we talk about those who don't have an obvious disability — the non-disabled. We sometimes hear the term *able-bodied*, but of course that only refers to people who don't have a physical disability. And as some disability advocates are quick to point out, we are all only temporarily able-bodied (or TAB), in that we will all probably acquire disabilities as we age. The assumption that we want to avoid making at all costs is that the absence of a disability renders us "normal". That word has considerable historical freight, associated with the sociological definition discussed earlier in this chapter. At best, it is a highly ambiguous term; at worst, it sets the stage for significant discrimination and various types of abuses.

7.   Avoid unnecessary emotional tone

Another guideline for speaking as a professional about disability is to avoid an unnecessary emotional tone — either positive or negative. While having a disability can be an emotional experience in many ways, it is not appropriate to impose an emotional overtone on our dialogue about it. We certainly want to avoid negative assertions that a disability is a tragedy or a burden, or that the person experiencing it is a victim or is unlucky. On the other hand, we also want to avoid casting him or her as a hero or superhuman. This sort of hyperbole makes it difficult to have real, authentic relationships with people. Instead, we simply want to acknowledge that different people live out their humanity in different ways; that the conditions of life are different for each of us. To the extent that we can talk about disability in an even-handed and matter-of-fact way, we permit people to encounter each other on their own terms, and to discover details about each other's lives in the context of real relationships.

8.   Avoid the word *handicap*

A word we usually avoid when speaking about disability is *handicap*. Handicap was a feature of the previous version of the ICF (WHO, 2001), known as the *International Classification of Impairment, Disability and Handicap* (ICIDH; WHO, 1991). You will notice in comparing the two that the words *impairment* and *disability* persist, but the word *handicap* has disappeared. **Handicap** referred to a situation where a person experienced a significant social disadvantage because of a disability. There were six types of handicap (WHO, 1991):

1. Orientation — the ability to orient oneself to the surroundings;
2. Physical independence — the ability to sustain a customarily effective independent existence;
3. Mobility — the ability to move about effectively in one's surroundings;
4. Occupation — the ability to occupy time in a manner customary to age, sex, and culture;
5. Social integration — the ability to participate in and maintain customary social relationships; and
6. Economic self-sufficiency — the ability to sustain customary socioeconomic activity and independence.

The use of this language has receded in our way of thinking about and talking about disability. It was perceived by some as derogatory and has therefore been replaced by the notion of participation restriction in the new taxonomy. As often happens, something is lost when something else is gained. The idea of social disadvantage associated with disability is indisputable, as future chapters will illustrate, and it is somewhat of a shame to have lost the ability to talk succinctly about this social disadvantage by invoking the concept of handicap. However, we must also acknowledge that in general parlance, few people made the distinction between the more neutral concept of disability and the more negatively charged concept of handicap, and used the two interchangeably. Perhaps the only way to overcome the negative attribution that disability is always handicapping was to do away with the word *handicapped* altogether. In any case, it has become a word we do not use in referring to people with disabilities.

9. Avoid stereotypes

Obviously, we want to avoid stereotypes about disability. We will talk more about stereotypes in Chapter 5, but basically a stereotype is a whole constellation of characteristics that we attribute to a person, simply because he or she possesses one of those characteristics. It usually results from overgeneralizing a fixed set of qualities to a group of people, rather than recognizing that each person is unique. Stereotypes prevent us from understanding the truth about a given individual because we are misguided by our assumptions. A good rule of thumb is generally not to make assumptions, and to understand that what we see is not always all there is to understand. People may appear to have a disability and yet be perfectly functional in their roles and contexts. Alternatively, people may appear to have no disability and yet be constrained on many fronts by their lives and their functioning.

10. Understand context

Like many minority groups, disabled people sometimes use words to describe disability that would be considered an insult or a slur if they were expressed by someone without the disability. These words are often self-deprecatory or an expression of black humour. They are words that "outsiders" simply may not use, because they are considered offensive. They are often an expression of how society has historically spoken about people with disabilities. By appropriating these words, disabled people mitigate their power to wound and oppress.

11. Determine whether disability is pertinent

A final rule of thumb is to ask yourself if it is necessary to talk about disability at all. Is it necessary to describe a person as someone with a spinal cord injury, or a mental illness, or a learning disability? Or is it more pertinent to talk about them in the context of their social roles, their community connections, their achievements and talents? Disability is only one of many characteristics that define who a person is and how he or she moves through the world. In many instances, it is not the most important thing we need to know about someone.

Conclusion

It may seem as though there is no clear answer to the question of how best to talk about disability, and to some extent that is true. Disability is such a complex and multi-dimensional concept that to think we can find a simple solution to talking about it is unrealistic. Instead, these few guidelines offer some hints upon which to develop your own judgment about what is the most respectful way to talk to people about the aspects of their daily life

- that are impeded by obstacles,
- that take an inordinately long time to complete,
- that require the assistance or supervision of someone else, or
- that they simply cannot do.

The best advice is to listen to how people talk about their own disability and how they refer to themselves. There is nothing wrong with asking people what language they prefer for talking about their disability, and being guided by those preferences.

Using the Appreciative Inquiry framework, I hope this chapter has helped you to *discover* the many ways that people refer to disability. Further, I hope it has helped you to listen with a new ear to the language used by others to refer to disability. The more acutely you listen, the more you will learn about the ideas that people are trying to communicate when they talk about disability.

I suppose we can *dream* about a time when there is consistency in the way we talk about disability, and yet, I suspect that dream may be elusive, simply because of the complexity of disability. Instead, maybe it makes more sense to dream of a time when we can hear beyond the words to the meaning conveyed. Further, we can dream about language that is so commonplace in our lexicon — language that is sufficiently inclusive and respectful — that it does not risk offending.

With regard to *design*, I hope the chapter has given you some options and ideas for language that you can use and be comfortable with. You may be already familiar with talking about one type of disability, but not sure if this is suitable for other disabilities. Hopefully, the chapter has helped to expand your lexicon and permit you to speak with confidence, but also with sensitivity and openness, about various aspects of disability.

In terms of *deployment*, as a health, education, or social service professional, you have a unique opportunity to help the people you work with to communicate effectively about their own disability and the disabilities of others. Although the trend currently is that people with disabilities should not have to divulge the nature or extent of their disability, it can be enormously helpful for people with disabilities to learn to speak candidly with others about their disability and their needs. Professionals, if armed with a few ideas about language, might assist in this valuable process of finding ways to communicate with others about this important aspect of life.

You will also have an opportunity to speak out about language used to discuss disability in public. People seldom choose to be offensive or ignorant in their use of language; however, they often do offend by applying terms that are outdated, insensitive, or inaccurate. As you hone your language skills and choices, you may feel empowered to share those with others who have not had the benefit of your experience with people with disabilities. They can learn to be more inclusive in their language and, in most instances, they will thank you for a constructively delivered suggestion.

Chapter 4

Demographics of disability

Introduction

While numbers never tell the whole story, they are useful for offering an overall picture of how many, how much, and how often. This chapter represents an attempt to provide some numbers about disability, and to situate disabled people in the context of entire populations, both internationally and in Canada. Although this chapter treats disability as a single entity, it is in fact a very diverse and heterogeneous category, as we will repeatedly learn throughout this book. While it can be somewhat deceptive to enumerate the disability community as if it were a unified whole, it at least gives us a starting point to recognize how many among us are affected by disability.

The prevalence of disability

According to *Disability World* (a disability news and information website: www.disabled-world.com), disabled people are the world's largest minority group. About 1 billion people in the world are estimated to live with a disability — that's approximately 15% of the world's population, or one in seven people. About 20% of those, or 200 million, have a moderate to severe disability, or one that significantly impacts the conditions of life (Handicap International, 2012).

The number of people with disabilities around the world is up from about 10% in the 1970s (World Health Organization, 2011). Disability is increasing worldwide, and there are a number of possible explanations for that:

- Disability is significantly more prevalent in older age groups, primarily due to the increased incidence of chronic diseases with age. As the population ages and the profile of the world population tips toward an older average age, higher rates of disability accompany this demographic shift.

- As medical expertise and technology continually improve, people survive conditions and circumstances that would have been fatal in days gone by. Often that survivorship is accompanied by a residual disability.

- Exposure to disabling situations and environments is increasing. Occupational exposures, vehicular and pedestrian accidents, natural disasters, and conflict situations all have the collateral problem of creating disability.

- As disability becomes more common and more mainstream, the willingness to report disability also changes. People are less reluctant to claim that they have a disability when they believe there are fewer negative consequences for them — less stigma, less stereotyping, less social and economic fallout.

- There have been significant differences in the way disability has been defined and measured over the approximately 50 years that statistics have been kept on disability. Definitions have generally become increasingly broad and inclusive.

Data on disability

Disability statistics are typically collected either by a population-based census or by a sample survey. Censuses have the benefit of covering the entire population (thereby picking up regional differences), and of being repeated at intervals, albeit typically infrequently. However, they are costly and resource-intensive, and may be impossible in countries where the population is not stable or accessible (Bickenbach, Cieza, & Sabariego, 2016). Surveys, on the other hand, tend to be more focused and detailed, but require inference to generalize to the population. Sampling becomes an issue particularly if there are exclusions, such as children or people in institutions. Also, the completeness of surveys will vary depending on the data collection method — phone, mail, door-to-door, online, or web-based. Needless to say, different countries will have different capacities in terms of producing reliable and complete data on disability using either of these methods.

As an example of how survey methods can affect results, we looked at five national surveys in Canada conducted between 1991 and 2001, to compare the different portraits of disability that were created using different definitions of disability (McColl, James, Boyce, & Shortt, 2003; McColl & Jongbloed, 2006). The surveys showed dramatically different levels of prevalence of disability, ranging from 6.3% to 14.5% of the population, depending mostly on the use of the biomedical vs. economic definition of disability. They also showed vastly different levels of educational attainment (ranging from 12% to 35% achieving post-secondary education) and employment (42% to 55% employed). Some of these differences could be explained as a function of the date of the survey, but mostly they were a reflection of how disability was conceptualized and operationalized.

Types and causes of disability

The most common form of disability is a walking disability, experienced by an estimated 30.6 million people around the world; 3.6 million of those use wheelchairs. Twelve million have a disability relating to their everyday tasks, such as self-care. Eight million have difficulty seeing, and 7.6 million experience difficulty hearing.

Disability has different health conditions associated with it in different regions throughout the world. For example, in Africa, South Asia, and South America, infectious diseases represent a significant source of disability. Diseases we seldom see in North America but that are almost endemic in the developing world are major contributors to disability worldwide — for example, tuberculosis, meningitis, malaria, and leprosy. Also, diseases that have been either virtually eradicated or at least controlled in the developed world still have devastating effects on populations and individuals in the developing world — diseases such as HIV/AIDS, measles, mumps, and polio. Eighty percent (80%) of the world's population live in developing countries, and so disability disproportionately affects vulnerable populations in those countries (UN Development Programme, 2016).

Non-communicable or chronic diseases are more prevalent than communicable diseases in the developed world, and they are significant contributors to the prevalence of disability — cardiovascular disease, respiratory disease, cancer, arthritis, mental illness, and sensory conditions. Together, chronic diseases are estimated to account for two-thirds of all of the years lived with disability worldwide (World Bank & WHO, 2011).

The third most common cause of disability is injuries and accidents — auto or other road accidents, occupational injuries, violence, and humanitarian crises. It is estimated that 20 to 50 million people worldwide per year sustain injuries that result in disability (World Bank & WHO, 2011).

International differences in disability

As one might expect, disability prevalence differs between countries. The *World Report on Disability* (World Bank & WHO, 2011) provides data on disability from 59 countries, representing 64% of the world's population. The report is restricted to adults 18 years of age and older. For countries included in the report, the average disability prevalence is 15.3%, with a range between 14.0% and 16.4%, as shown in Table 4.1.

Many of the same factors that affect differences across time also affect differences between countries:

- differential health risks in the population;
- the prevalence of specific conditions in different regions of the world;
- economic factors in general, and poverty in particular, with attendant differences in the conditions of life, such as nutrition, safety, and opportunity;
- industrial and geo-political environmental exposures, such as vehicles, natural disasters, conflict, crime, and accidents;
- cultural factors, such as views about disability and willingness to report;
- accessibility of medical and rehabilitation services;
- data-collection procedures; and,
- population demographics.

Table 4.1: Prevalence of moderate and severe disabilities by region and national wealth

	Moderate & severe disabilities	Severe disabilities only
World	15.30%	2.90%
Europe	16.40	3.00
Southeast Asia	16.00	2.90
High-income countries*	15.40	3.20
Africa	15.30	3.10
Western Pacific	15.00	2.70
South & Central America	14.10	2.60
Eastern Mediterranean	14.00	2.80

* Countries with gross national incomes (GNI) of more than $10,600 US per capita (2004); all other regions represent countries with low to middle income.

Source: World Bank & WHO, 2011.

Table 4.2: Median age (in years) of disabled population, changes from 1950–2050 (projected)

	1950	1975	2005	2050
World	23.9	22.4	28	38.1
Low-income countries*	19.5	17.6	19	27.9
Middle-income countries**	21.8	19.6	26.6	39.4
High-income countries	29.0	31.1	38.6	45.7

* GNI of less than $3,250 US (2004).
** GNI of more than $10,600.

Source: World Bank & WHO, 2011.

Age distributions differ significantly from region to region, and disability disproportionately affects older people. Table 4.2 shows how the disability population is aging, and how those trends differ from high- to low-income regions. In high- and moderate-income countries, the average age of the disabled population is expected to increase about 17 years over the century from 1950 to 2050. In low-income countries, the average age of disabled people has stayed about the same since 1950, but is expected to increase about 8 years in the next 50 years. These numbers are significantly affected by the fact that the fastest growing age cohort in the world is 80- to 90-year-olds, most of whom have at least one form of disability.

According to European statistics on disability including 27 European countries (Eurostat, 2015), 42.2% of all disabled people in Europe were over 65 years of age, 35.5% were between 45 and 64, and 22% were between 15 and 44. The prevalence of disability in Europe goes from 8.5% of the population 15 to 44 years of age, to 18.8% of the population between 45 and 64, and 35.6% of those over 65. According to the *Canadian Survey on Disability* 2012 (Statistics Canada, 2012), that proportion goes up to 42.5% for those over 75.

Across the age spectrum and in most regions of the world, women experience higher rates of disability than men. Table 4.3 shows the sex ratio (women to men) for those 60 and older in seven regions of the world. In five of the seven regions, women experience between 1% and 14% higher rates of disability than men. Some of this is due to the fact that women survive longer than men, and thus there are more of them in the older age group who have disabilities. Women also have higher rates of some disabling conditions, such as arthritis, where their rate is double that for men. Particularly in poorer countries, women are less likely to receive needed health care, less likely to be educated or literate, more likely to live in poverty, and more likely to experience poor work conditions. All of these factors are associated with disability, as we will explore further in subsequent chapters.

Where does Canada fit in?

The prevalence of disability in Canada is estimated at 13.7% (Statistics Canada, 2012) — an estimate that falls between the World Health Organization's global estimate of 10% and the *World Report on Disability* estimate of 15.6% (Mitra & Sambamoorthi, 2014). Among high-income countries, Canada is in the middle of the pack. The Organisation for Economic Co-operation and Development (OECD, 2003) offers statistics on disability prevalence among adults (20–64) in 19 countries. In the adult age group, Canadian disability

Table 4.3: Sex ratio (F/M) for moderate and severe disabilities by region (age > 60)

	Moderate & severe disabilities	Severe disabilities only
World	46.3 / 45.9 = 1.0087	10.5 / 9.8 = 1.0714
South & Central America	43.6 / 45.1 = .9667	9.2 / 9.2 = 1.0000
Europe	41.1 / 41.9 = .9809	7.2 / 7.3 = .9863
Western Pacific	47.0 / 46.4 = 1.0129	10.3 / 9.8 = 1.0510
Eastern Mediterranean	54.4 / 53.1 = 1.0245	13.0 / 11.8 = 1.1017
High-income countries*	37.4 / 36.1 = 1.0360	9.0 / 7.9 = 1.1392
Southeast Asia	60.1 / 57.5 = 1.0452	13.2 / 11.9 = 1.1092
Africa	54.3 / 52.1 = 1.0422	17.9 / 15.7 = 1.1401

* GNI of more than $10,600.

Source: World Bank & WHO, 2011.

prevalence is 16.1%, compared to 10.7% in the United States, 12.8% in Australia, 18.2% in the United Kingdom, and 20.6% in Sweden.

The most common types of disability among adults in Canada are those associated with (Statistics Canada, 2012) the following:

- pain   (9.7%)
- flexibility   (7.6%)
- mobility   (7.2%)
- mental illness (3.9%)
- dexterity   (3.5%)
- hearing   (3.2%)

- seeing   (2.8%)
- memory   (2.3%)
- learning   (2.3%)
- development   (0.6%)

These issues total to 56.4%; thus, there are obviously many people reporting more than one type of disability. The average number of different types of disability reported by the 13.7% of the population with disabilities is 4.12.

With regard to severity, about half of adult disability in Canada is considered mild or moderate (51.5%), and about half is severe or very severe (48.5%), as shown in Table 4.4.

The average age of onset of adult disability in Canada is 43 years (Arim, 2015). Adult disability in Canada is more prevalent

- among those over 65 (33.2%) compared to those 15 to 64 (10.1%) and
- among women (14.9%) compared to men (12.5%), for a sex ratio of 1.19.

Among children, the rate of disability is low — 1.7% for children below 4 years of age, and 4.6% for children 5 to 14. Among adults with disabilities, 13% report that they acquired their disability in childhood (Statistics Canada, 2012).

Table 4.4: Severity of disability among adults in Canada (15–64 years)

	Proportion of disabled adults (%)	Proportion of total population of adults (%)
Very severe	26.0	3.6
Severe	22.5	3.1
Moderate	19.8	2.7
Mild	31.7	4.3

Source: Statistics Canada, 2012.

Conclusion

This chapter helps us to appreciate just what a significant population the disability community represents around the world. It has led us to *discover* the size of the disabled population — about 1 billion people worldwide. Many authors consider this an underestimate, because of the difficulty of collecting information about disability in some countries.

About 14% of Canadians have a disability. Furthermore, if you assume that at least one other person — a parent, spouse, sibling, or adult child — is directly involved in helping to manage the requirements of the disability, then the number affected is closer to one-third of the population. That is an enormous number — one in three Canadians directly affected by disability — and apparently it is on the rise!

When you look around your classroom or other group, can you tell who the 30% are who are affected by disability? Don't forget to count not just the obvious disabilities, like someone using a mobility device or expressing some other overt sign. How many have invisible disabilities or disabilities that they cope seamlessly with? How many are caregivers or primary supporters of people with disabilities?

My *dream* in response to the information in this chapter is for people to become more aware of the presence of disability, and to begin to wrap their heads around our responsibilities as individuals and groups toward people with disabilities.

The challenge of course is that disability looks so different from person to person, making it difficult to *design* programs, communities or organizations that will meet the diverse needs of all. We will talk further about policy and design to address this challenge in Chapter 17.

In the meantime, we all have the opportunity to *deploy* our voices to raise awareness of disability whenever we have the opportunity. Ask the question out loud, "How would someone with a mobility disability manage this entrance?" "How would someone with a hearing disability participate in this seminar?" "How would someone with difficulty speaking make his or her situation understood?"

Chapter 5

Attitudes toward disability

Introduction

In this chapter we will try to appreciate how Canadians think and feel about disability, why they might hold the views they do, and what can be done to improve attitudes about disability.

Before going further, I invite readers to take a moment to think about the importance of context in discussing attitudes (Challenge for readers #4).

Since attitudes are culturally mediated, it makes sense to talk about Canadian attitudes, recognizing that there may also be regional and local attitudes, and there are also probably universal

---

Challenge for readers #4

Think about three different situations where you might encounter someone with a disability — in the grocery store, as a family member, or as a client or patient in your practice/classroom. Imagine how you might view, greet, and interact with each of these three individuals. Think about people with different types of disabilities and how that might affect your impressions, greetings, and approach. Write yourself a few notes on each of these three different scenarios.

---

attitudes about the pervasive human condition of disability. We will use research from Canada, but also from other developed Western democracies, such as the United States, the United Kingdom, and Australia, to explore Canadian attitudes toward disability.

What do we mean by attitudes?

An **attitude** is a learned idea that grows out of socialization and experience. It represents a response toward a person, place, or thing. Attitudes have both a cognitive and an emotional component. They include an evaluation of their object, and that evaluation is usually expressed as either negative or positive. A positive attitude characterizes something or someone as good, useful, worthy, likeable; a negative attitude characterizes its object as inadequate, unattractive, having limited utility, unworthy.

Attitudes typically serve four purposes:

1. *Utilitarian:* They streamline our decision-making in particular situations by providing us with a summary judgment of key elements of a situation;
2. *Knowledge:* They help us to interpret new information and assimilate it into our existing filing structure;
3. *Ego-defensive:* They uphold our sense of self and consolidate our identity; and
4. *Value-expressive:* They express to others who we are and what our core values or beliefs are.

Attitudes may be both implicit and explicit (Aaberg, 2012). Explicit attitudes are often expressed as opinions; they are thoughts that can be shared with others about how we feel about a certain person, group of people, or real or abstract thing. Implicit attitudes, on the other hand, usually exist just beneath the level of consciousness. They are typically emotional responses, rather than intellectual responses, and they are expressed through behaviour and must be imputed or interpreted from behaviour. In order to be aware of our own implicit attitudes, we need to scrutinize our thoughts and behaviours, and reflect on how we are thinking and feeling toward something or someone. As service professionals, we need to apply meta-cognitive processes to enhance our awareness of attitudes.

Why are attitudes important? Attitudes are important because, whether conscious or unconscious, they guide our behaviour. They govern how we react to people and situations. They communicate our evaluation of those persons or objects. They restrict our choices by asserting social norms — what is and isn't acceptable in our society (Reeve, 2014)

Attitudes are important also because they can be sensed and perceived by those to whom they apply. Indeed, disabled people are profoundly affected by the attitudes held by all those they encounter or interact with (Reeve, 2014). They are affected both in objective and subjective ways. Objectively, their material well-being is influenced by the attitudes of employers, co-workers, law-makers, service workers, health professionals — in other words, all those who play some part in the way our society operates. Subjectively, their emotional well-being and sense of self is affected by the reactions they see in the faces of others — strangers, family members, friends and neighbours, service professionals, intimate partners. The reflected evaluation that is communicated in an attitude can't help but be internalized and incorporated into one's own evaluation of self-worth. Ultimately, disabled people even begin to restrict their own choices and options because they adopt the prevailing attitudes and social norms about what they can and can't do (Reeve, 2014).

Attitudes are important in disability studies because we all have deeply held beliefs about disability based on our experiences and our learning. Attitudes are especially challenging for health and social service professionals, since disability does not fit the prevailing medical model that professionals are typically socialized into. We can't always treat or mitigate disability; we can't promise a positive outcome; we can't control the choices disabled people make (Byron & Dieppe, 2000). If we are to work effectively with people with disabilities, we need to ensure that our attitudes are constructive. We need to plumb our own psyches to ascertain what attitudes we hold, where they came from, and whether or not they are compatible with our goal of being a health, education, or social service professional.

What do Canadian attitudes toward disability look like?

Perhaps the best word to describe Canadian attitudes toward disability is *ambivalent*. Prince (2009b) characterizes them as "pride and prejudice" — pride that we have made significant progress in recent years, and that we are relatively enlightened in our views toward people with disabilities; prejudice in that significant inequalities and negative attitudes persist. Research shows that although 92% of Canadians say that accessibility for people with disabilities is a human right, only 50% say that it should be a priority for policymakers, and only 40% say that environmental modifications are useful and worthwhile (Angus Reid Institute, 2015b).

Similarly, Daruwalla and Darcy (2005) find that the public verbalizes positive attitudes toward disability, but actually holds deeper negative attitudes. When asked their opinion, people are aware that there are socially desirable attitudes toward disability — attitudes that favour equity, access, and opportunity. Social desirability arises when people seek to be consistent with peers, to conform with the prevailing culture, and to avoid social sanctions. Research shows that when covert, subconscious measures are employed to get at deeper emotional attitudes, a more disturbing story emerges. (For a fuller discussion of measures of implicit and explicit attitudes toward disability, see Palad et al., 2016.)

In 2015 and 2016, the Rick Hansen Institute commissioned the Angus Reid Institute to explore Canadian attitudes toward disability. They encountered four identifiable mindsets toward disability, based on how responses clustered on a number of issues (Angus Reid Institute, 2015a; Korzinski, 2016).

1. *On-side:* About 34% of respondents cared deeply about people with disabilities and empathized strongly with their issues. They tended to be older and were more likely to be female; they often had first-hand experience with disability.

2. *Young Bystander:* The next largest group (28%) were young and idealistic. They believed in human rights and access, but they were not particularly involved with people with disabilities on a day-to-day basis, nor were they very aware of their issues.

3. *Older Detached:* The third group (22%) were older and more aware of the issues, but did not feel that they were their issues, despite the fact that they were closer to acquiring age-related disabilities.

4. *Indifferent:* The last group, and thankfully the smallest (15%), expressed indifference toward disability issues. Equity and access were characterized as nice ideas, but not rights, and particularly not if there was a cost associated, or if the result could negatively affect non-disabled people.

The area where attitudes toward disability are perhaps most ambivalent is employment. Although 88% say we are missing out by not employing the talents and skills of people with disabilities in the workforce, 50% say it is understandable that employers would not want to hire someone with a disability. Prince (2009b) observed that while survey respondents acknowledge that workplace discrimination is unacceptable, they also believe that opportunities for disabled workers should not financially or practically disadvantage employers or other workers.

Dualistic and paradoxical attitudes

Attitudes toward disability are characterized by numerous authors as being both dualistic and paradoxical. Let's explore some of the ways in which attitudes toward disability are both of those things.

Attitudes toward disability are dualistic or binary in that they typically contrast disabled people with non-disabled people (Hammell, 2016; Hughes, 2007). Disability exists only in opposition to a non-disabled norm. We have alluded briefly in the previous chapter to the idea that there is a threshold beyond which everyday limitations in performance become disabilities. We acknowledge that some people have more difficulty with some things than others, and there is a range of performance that we consider non-disabled or normal. Beyond a certain point, however, individual deviations from the norm are considered disabilities. Where exactly is that point, and who decides?

When we think of "normal", we often think of the normal curve. This bell-shaped curve represents the distribution of many naturally occurring phenomena in the world. According to this symmetrical curve, about 64% of virtually any characteristic (such as a particular ability) falls within ± 1 standard deviation from the mean, and 95% within ± 2 standard deviations. If we take the example of agility, about 64% of people are of average agility — they can probably stand on one foot for a brief period of time. About 15% are slightly better than average — maybe they are amateur athletes or recreational dancers. About 15% are also slightly worse than average — maybe they are at risk of falling or are otherwise accident-prone. Then there are 2.5% at either extreme of the distribution — at the top end are Olympic gymnasts; at the bottom end are those who have difficulty coordinating any type of movement.

Phelan (2011) suggests that this highly precise and objective notion of "normal" is not the construction we use when judging disability. Instead, he maintains that the notion of "normal" we apply when talking about disability is entirely socially constructed. It is the product of social ideals and beliefs about beauty, self-sufficiency, and conformity. *Normal-ness* is a label that is wielded like a weapon, to include some and marginalize others. To the extent that a particular definition of *normal* becomes hegemonic or predominant, it represents a force or a power that can be used against groups within society.

The media of course is one of the most powerful communicators and purveyors of attitudes toward disabilities. The media also indulges in dualism when referring to disability. The tendency in the media is to either "lionize or demonize" people with disabilities (Daruwalla & Darcy, 2005). The rhetoric tends to portray people with disabilities as being super-human in some instances, and pitiful, hopeless, or even frightening in others. In the first instance, the "hero" narrative imposes an expectation on people with disabilities that is almost impossible to live up to. In the second instance, the characterization reinforces social distance and alienation of people with disabilities.

Another dualistic tendency in media portrayals of disability is to focus almost exclusively on the disability. The disability is typically featured in the foreground, and all other characteristics recede into the background. The only thing we notice is the person's disability, and not the many other qualities that make people who they are. By focusing on the disability, disabled people are reduced to two-dimensional characters, which ignores the depth and breadth of their humanity.

A paradoxical tendency in portraying disability is over-attribution or under-attribution (Byron & Dieppe, 2000).

- **Over-attribution** refers to situations where every detail of the person's story or behaviour is seen through the lens of his or her disability. We are led to believe that the disability is the most important quality the person possesses, and that it affects everything else in his or her life.

- **Under-attribution** is when inadequate consideration is given to the fact of a disability. The person is described or characterized as though the disability did not exist. Any discussion of the disability is strategically avoided.

Somewhere in the middle is a balance, where the disability is given due consideration for its role in the person's experience of the world, but where it does not overshadow the many other qualities that go into making up the whole person. Simply to be aware of this tendency is the first step toward checking ourselves to ensure that we are not seeing the disability and nothing else. After all, disabled people are just as likely or unlikely as anyone else to be careless or thoughtful, happy or disagreeable, patient or aggressive.

Another pervasive and paradoxical way to think about disability is to characterize it as a series of losses — loss of a body part, loss of a functional ability, loss of the old self, loss of the anticipated future. Watermeyer (2009) rejects this approach as sentimental and exploitative. While he acknowledges that loss exists, it is only one aspect of the complex experience of disability. The story in Figure 5.1, *Welcome to Holland* by Emily Perl Kingsley (1987), beautifully illustrates an alternative to the loss discourse about disability. In addition to being a writer for *Sesame Street* for many years, Ms. Kingsley is also a parent of a child with a disability.

Stereotypes

The most dangerous aspect of all of these attitudes is the extent to which they contribute to cultural scripts about who disabled people are and how we should relate to them. These cultural scripts often take the form of stereotypes. **Stereotypes** are preconceived notions about individuals or groups of people. They are typically over-simplified and fixed in people's minds. They usually exist at a subconscious level, and they result in the attribution of a whole constellation of characteristics to a person simply because he or she possesses one particular characteristic. For example, cultural stereotypes exist about university professors. When we hear that someone is a university professor, many people conjure an image of someone who wears glasses, is socially awkward, detached from the real world, physically uncoordinated, and absent-minded. One need only watch television for evidence of the parameters of this stereotype. A similar process happens with stereotypes about disability. Whether they are aware of it or not, most people hold fixed views about disability. Here's an exercise to help with insight about your own deeply held views of disability.

Figure 5.1: Welcome to Holland (by Emily Perl Kingsley)

I am often asked to describe the experience of raising a child with a disability — to try to help people who have not shared that unique experience to understand it, to imagine how it would feel. It's like this ...

When you're going to have a baby, it's like planning a fabulous vacation trip to Italy. You buy a bunch of guidebooks and make your wonderful plans — the Coliseum, the Sistine Chapel, Michelangelo's David, the gondolas in Venice. You may learn some handy phrases in Italian. It's all very exciting. After months of eager anticipation, the day finally arrives. You pack your bags and off you go. Several hours later, the plane lands. The flight attendant comes in and says, "Welcome to Holland." "Holland?! What do you mean, Holland? I signed up for Italy! I'm supposed to be in Italy. All my life I've dreamed of going to Italy."

But there's been a change in the flight plan. They've landed in Holland and there you must stay. The important thing is that they haven't taken you to some horrible, disgusting, filthy place, full of pestilence, famine and disease. It's just a different place. So you must go out and buy a new guidebook. And you must learn a whole new language. You will meet a whole new group of people you would never have met. It's just a different place. It's slower paced than Italy, less flashy than Italy. But after you've been there for a while and you catch your breath, you look around, and you begin to notice that Holland has windmills, Holland has tulips, Holland even has Rembrandts.

But everyone you know is busy coming and going from Italy, and they're all bragging about what a wonderful time they had there. And for the rest of your life you will say, "Yes, that's where I was supposed to go. That's what I had planned." The pain of that will never ever go away, because the loss of that dream is a very significant loss. But ... if you spend your life mourning the fact that you didn't get to Italy, you may never be free to enjoy the very special, very lovely things about Holland.

Source: © 1987 by Emily Perl Kingsley. All rights reserved. Reproduced by permission of the author.

The exercise in Challenge for readers #5 is attributed to Beatrice Wright (1960), a pioneer in the field of rehabilitation psychology.

Dr. Wright has done this exercise repeatedly with groups of health professionals and with groups of disabled people, and the result is always the same, no matter how much actual disability is present in the audience. The majority of people end up with a negative score. In other words, they evaluate other people's disabilities as more troublesome than their own.

Wright offers a number of explanations for this finding, but the main theme in her discussion is that no matter how disabled they are, people typically see the disabilities of others as more demanding, more difficult, or more limiting than their own. What they fail to account for, of course, is the fact that people have experience and coping mechanisms for overcoming their own disability, whereas they can't imagine how they would cope with the limitations imposed by a different disability.

Although it may appear sympathetic, a negative rating is really also saying, "I would hate to have to live with that limitation. I evaluate that type of a life as negative on balance, and certainly worse than my own life." This pervasive negative evaluation is at the root of many of our underlying attitudes about disability, and is perhaps the most destructive feeling we can harbour.

Another way to think about stereotypes of disability was proposed by Fiske, Cuddy, Glick, & Xu (2002). Fiske and colleagues offer the Stereotype Content Model, which proposes that there are two relevant dimensions along which we situate everyone we encounter when we make social evaluations: warmth and competence. These two dimensions are called different names in different models, but numerous models have characterized the two dimensions of social judgments similarly (Abele, Cuddy, Judd, & Yzerbyt, 2008).

- *Warmth* refers to social and moral qualities — the extent to which a person is judged to be likeable, approachable, and friendly.
- *Competence* refers to intellectual and motivational qualities — the extent to which a person is judged to be capable and respected.

These qualities form a two-dimensional space that can be used to explore the judgments we impose when we encounter individuals

Challenge for readers #5

1. In the table below, under column A, write down the names (or initials) of five people you know who have a disability.
2. Under column B, write a word or two to capture the nature of what you consider to be each of their most significant disabilities.
3. In column C, rate each person's disability on a scale of 1–10, in terms of the extent to which you estimate it affects his or her everyday life. A rating of 1 means it hardly affects the person at all; a rating of 10 means that his or her disability affects virtually every aspect of the person's life.
4. In column D, write your own name five times, and in column E, write down your own most significant disability five times. Now rate your own disability in column F in terms of how significantly it affects *your* life. (Write down the same number five times.)
5. In column G, for each row, or each person you know, subtract the value in column C from the value in column F, i.e., (F – C). Now total up the values in column G for a grand total. The value in the white square will be positive, negative, or neutral.

	A	B	C	D	E	F	G
	Name	Disability	Rating	Name	Disability	Rating	(F – C)
1.							
2.							
3.							
4.							
5.							
Total							

What does the total in Column G mean?

- If the value is positive, it means that, on average, you tend to rate your own disability as more severe than that of others you know with a disability.
- If the value is neutral, it means that you rate your own disability as equally affecting compared to other people you know.
- If the value is negative, it means that you consider the disabilities of others as more difficult to deal with, more demanding, and more interfering than your own disability.

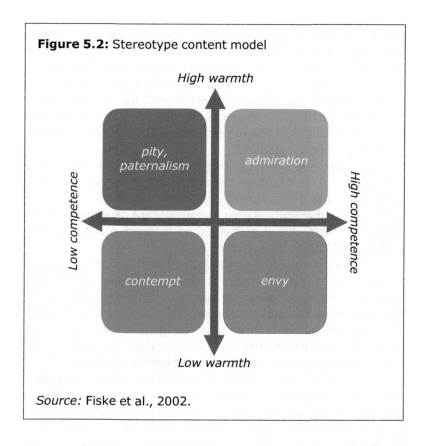

Figure 5.2: Stereotype content model

High warmth

Low competence

High competence

pity,
paternalism

admiration

contempt

envy

Low warmth

Source: Fiske et al., 2002.

(see Figure 5.2). Each quadrant typically evokes an emotional response or an attitude. The combination of high warmth and high competence (upper-right quadrant) leads to admiration, whereas low warmth and high competence leads to envy. Low warmth and low competence elicits contempt, while high warmth with low competence elicits pity and paternalism. Research across cultures, settings, and age groups shows that people with disabilities are usually situated in the latter quadrant — high warmth and low competence (Cuddy et al., 2009; Fiske et al., 2002). The disability stereotype is thus one where people with disabilities are judged to be kind, warm, and friendly, but vulnerable, dependent, and low status.

This mixed stereotype model (one high and one low evaluation) is thought to be a response to social awareness against prejudice. According to Rohmer and Louvert (2012), people with disabilities are "strongly normatively protected", meaning that there are strong social mores against discrimination toward people with disabilities. The social norm declares that people with disabilities are not to be held responsible for their situation, but rather are meant to be afforded all due considerations. Thus, one interpretation of the high warmth rating is as compensation for a low competence rating, and to permit the respondents to uphold an image of themselves as non-prejudiced.

However, when social editing can be overcome using implicit ratings scales — that is, those that are designed to get at underlying attitudes — negative evaluations of warmth have also been seen, confirming that prejudices exist that people are reluctant to report explicitly or are skilled at concealing in overt social discourse (Aaberg, 2012; Rohmer & Louvert, 2012).

The ultimate paradox about disability exists for disabled people themselves — whether or not to claim the label of disability, whether to assume disability as a part of one's identity, whether to speak out about disability, or whether to distance oneself from it. By claiming the label, one is absolved of considerable responsibility (or blame) for certain inabilities; however, one risks the negative attributions that may go along with being identified as disabled.

Alternatively, one can forgo the label of disability and any negative stereotype associated with it, but in doing so one may also forfeit whatever legitimate considerations that might go along with the label. Is it better to be ignored or misunderstood — perhaps even reviled (Watermeyer, 2009)? Is it better to be denied consideration, or to be thought too demanding? What would you be prepared to give up just to be considered "normal"? People with disabilities report that in addition to confronting stereotypes in their own lives, they also feel the additional pressure of constantly needing to disprove them — to show that not all people with disabilities are the same.

To apply a stereotype is to forfeit the opportunity to know a whole person, and yet the insidious nature of stereotypes is that we think we do know them! The cluster of beliefs that constitutes a stereotype is so ingrained in our view of the world that is ceases to even raise questions. It becomes a truth that we apply without critical thought. This is the basis of **ableism** — the systematic discrimination or disadvantaging of people with disabilities, simply because of the fact of their disability, and because of a constellation of beliefs that accompany the idea of disability.

How can we account for attitudes toward disability?

What is at the root of attitudes toward disabilities? As shown in the stereotype content model (Figure 5.2), emotions have a great deal to do with our responses toward people with disabilities. Feelings are evoked by our perceptions of who disabled people are to us, and how they affect our lives and our prospects, including what our duty to them is.

By far the most prevalent emotion evoked by disability according to the literature is fear (Hughes, 2007). But what is there to fear from people with disabilities? To understand fear, we need to understand a bit about our "old brain" and how it is designed to promote our survival and reproduction. The old brain, made up primarily of the cerebellum and brain stem, is where our primitive instincts reside. The old brain operates at an unconscious level, and at about 20 times the speed of the new brain, or cerebrum. The old brain is the automatic, involuntary, survival-oriented part, while the new brain is the conscious, effortful, cognitive part (Kahneman, 2011). While it takes about two seconds for the new brain to form a coherent thought, it takes only a split second for the old brain to react to stimuli and initiate biological processes, such as the secretion of hormones or neurotransmitters, in response to its instinctual reaction.

The old brain governs immediate, reflex, or routine reactions that are "hard-wired" for survival and reproduction. The old brain scans every piece of incoming information from the senses and instantaneously assesses it for the potential for risk or opportunity. For example, it recognizes danger in an unknown dog lunging toward us with teeth bared, and initiates a series of manoeuvres to prepare us to either fight or flee — that is, to confront the impending threat or to high-tail it away from the scene! At the same time, the new brain initiates a process of analytically evaluating the threat. Is it a chihuahua that we can block from attacking us and that is unlikely to do us much harm anyway? Or is it a big dog that could go straight for our throat? Is there a fence between us and the dog? Is the owner in the yard? Is the dog on a leash? All of these mitigating factors, and many more subsequent observations, are used by the new brain to realistically assess the level of threat and mediate the reaction that our old brain initiated.

The old brain evolved millions of years ago, and has changed very little in the interim. While it is perfectly designed to react quickly to threatening situations, it is not always fine-tuned to respond to the many complex situations that arise in the way humans live today. For example, the old brain recognizes the difference between people who look like us and people who don't — people who are of our tribe and people who are not. In the ancient world, people who were different from us might have been a threat to our individual or collective survival. They could have been after our food, our homes, or our territory. The old brain raises the level of alertness when we encounter someone who is different from us.

Of course, in modern diverse society we encounter people all the time who look different from us, and our big new brain (our cerebral cortex) immediately rejects that warning as unnecessary, even to the point of eventually teaching the old brain that that particular reaction is obsolete. The more we encounter diversity, the more our brains learn that there is nothing to fear. Given a second or two for the new brain to kick in, we muster a response that is much more appropriate to our contemporary context, and suppress the primitive fight or flight response of fear (Galli & Pazzaglia, 2016).

The same process happens with regard to people with disabilities (Pryor, Reeder, Yeadon, & Hesson-McInnis, 2004). Our old brain responds to difference with fear — fear of our own vulnerability, fear of dependency, fear of difference. This is clearly a reaction that is not adaptive and that has no survival value in our current context. In fact, rather than enhancing our social and survival advantage, the old brain's fearful reaction to people with disabilities is counterproductive. It prevents us from engaging effectively with 15% of the population!

There are two other unconscious reactions emanating from the old brain that may result in poor attitudes toward disability if they are unchallenged by the more rational and higher-functioning cortex. The first is what Hughes (2007) refers to as disgust. It seems a harsh word, but what he is referring to is our reaction to "messiness" — to things that are supposed to be on the inside of the body appearing on the outside of the body — blood, mucus, saliva, urine, feces. Certainly not every disability is associated with the excretion of bodily fluids, but some health conditions associated with disability include impairments to systems or structures that regulate the expression of bodily fluids. To assume that all people with disabilities are "messy" is an extreme example of the kind of stereotype we discussed above — taking one characteristic of a person and assuming that a whole constellation of other characteristics also applies. Disability is such a complex and multi-dimensional phenomenon that we can make no assumptions about how it affects individuals.

The third emotion that can perpetuate negative attitudes toward disability is pity (Hughes, 2007). Although not malicious, it can still be very damaging toward people with disabilities. Pity situates the other person in a subordinate position, by objectifying and diminishing that person. Even though pity comes from a tender and sympathetic reaction, it has the same limiting effect as other single, simple emotional responses. It denies the fullness and complexity of our humanity, and situates the entire response to a person on only one of his or her many characteristics. It is another form of stereotyping in that it makes a whole series of assertions about what a life with a disability is all about, on the basis of an isolated piece of information.

At the heart of stereotypes regarding disability is ignorance — just as ignorance is at the root of virtually all stereotyping. Along with this ignorance goes discomfort — a more benign but equally alienating reaction — that we will somehow feel awkward, that we won't know what to do or say, that we will make a social blunder, that we will upset the person and cause a scene, that our ignorance will be on display for all to see. If people don't understand how many different manifestations of disability there are, if they don't recognize the different systems that can be affected (or unaffected) by disability, if they don't appreciate how profoundly disability is lodged in a person's sense of himself or herself, or if they don't have any experience with disabled people as individuals, it is easy to imagine how a one-dimensional image of disability can take hold. What is required for positive attitudes toward disability is an understanding of disability that allows for the complexity, subtlety, depth, and breadth of the issue.

What can be done about attitudes toward disability?

The way we approach changing attitudes toward disability is informed by our understanding of how attitudes are formed (Daruwalla & Darcy, 2005). Based on the evidence, there are five approaches that can be taken, with some degree of evidence for their success.

But first, let's talk about the two common approaches that *don't* work. The most common approach to changing attitudes, and the one that probably springs immediately to mind, is the public awareness or media campaign. Based on the sound assumption that poor attitudes stem from ignorance, the obvious approach is to overcome that ignorance with accurate and timely information. Efficiencies are achieved by reaching the broadest cross-section of people through mass media. You can probably think of television spots or roadside billboards you've seen, carrying messages of hope and possibility for disabled people.

Evidence is lacking about what kind of saturation would be needed to significantly change attitudes, but the common wisdom is that this approach is not targeted or concentrated enough to make a difference. The audience sees or hears the message, but does not internalize it. This broad, impersonal approach allows people to accept the information without challenging their own implicit attitudes. In fact, it sometimes even validates people who hold problematic implicit attitudes, by permitting them to distance themselves from the issue. Attitudes tend to be so deeply held that even though behaviour might change for the better, underlying negative attitudes may persist. Attitudes can be entirely independent of behaviour, and can be relatively impervious to external motivators.

The other strategy that has been shown *not* to work to change attitudes is simulations. For example, non-disabled people spend a day in a wheelchair (to simulate paralysis), or with earplugs in (to simulate hearing impairment), or with Vaseline smeared on their glasses (to simulate visual impairment), or with a headset constantly transmitting negative messages (to simulate auditory hallucinations). The basis for this type of program is the "walking a mile in your neighbour's shoes" approach — developing empathy by undergoing the experience. Simulation programs continue to be used in a number of different sectors, despite evidence that they are ineffective at best, and damaging at worst (Flower, Burns, & Bottsford-Miller, 2007; Leo & Goodwin, 2016). As Silverman, Gwinn, and Van Boven (2014) point out, they usually backfire, leaving participants with even more negative impressions of life with a disability.

Wright (1960) contends that the main problem with simulations is that they fail to take account of the skills and aptitudes that disabled people develop as a means of coping with daily requirements. Instead, the non-disabled person is encountering every challenge for the first time, with all its frustrating, alienating, overwhelming impact. Using the same logic as her exercise offered above — that other people's challenges usually look more daunting than our own — Wright cautions that simulations can have the unexpected negative consequence of making non-disabled people feel horrified by the idea of living with a disability. While this feeling may promote empathy, it does not contribute to positive attitudes toward disability or toward disabled people.

Just as attitudes are made up of both cognitive and emotional components, the most successful strategies for attitude modification target both informational and emotional components. It is easy enough to teach people what they ought to think, and then show that they can parrot that back. But does that mean that their attitude has changed, or does it simply mean that they have become more aware of social desirability bias and how to circumvent it? Implicit measures of attitudes are much more reliable indicators of underlying attitudes (Rudman, Ashmore, & Gary, 2001). They show us that approaches that focus on both the cognitive and emotional components are superior when it comes to changing underlying attitudes. Several authors refer to the importance of this "dual process" model for attitude change, including both theory and real-life experiences (Campbell, Gilmore, & Cuskelly, 2003; Monteith & Mark, 2005; Rudman, Ashmore, & Gary, 2001).

Here are five strategies for which there is evidence of effectiveness in changing attitudes.

1. Contact

The best evidence available shows that the programs that are most successful in promoting positive attitudes toward disabled people are those that bring people into contact with people with disabilities in the context of usual daily roles. It doesn't appear to matter what they do together — only that they spend the time together and get to know how the other person operates (Shields & Taylor, 2014). Galli and Pazzaglia (2016) invoke the inter-group contact hypotheses (Allport, 1954) and transformational learning theory (Mezirow, 2000) to explain the importance of direct, real-world contact as a means of promoting positive attitudes. An interesting example was a program where students accompanied disabled individuals on an accessibility audit of their university campus (Byron & Dieppe, 2000).

However, it appears that contact alone is not enough. Contact was shown to positively impact the warmth aspect of disability stereotypes, but not necessarily the competence aspect (Kittson, Gainforth, Edwards, Bolkowy, & Latimer-Cheung, 2013). Contact made students feel more tender and sympathetic toward disabled people, but it did not necessarily make them evaluate them higher in terms of their ability to be independent and effective. Unless contact is paired with some theoretical or cognitive learning, it tends to fall short of mitigating both elements of warmth and competence in stereotypes (Campbell, Gilmore, & Cuskelly, 2003).

Particularly effective are those programs that also include an element of co-participation, or active engagement alongside people with disabilities in leisure-time activities (Barg, Armstrong, Hetz, & Latimer, 2010). Imagine the effect of a program that trains elite skiers to assist sit-skiers — young people who typically use a wheelchair for daily mobility. The "instructor" sees his or her sport in a whole new light — appreciating the good fortune of having skiing as part of his or her life. Seeing disabled individuals in an active lifestyle, coping with challenges, implementing adaptive strategies and functioning in healthy ways was significant in eliciting positive attitudes (Gainforth, O'Malley, Mountenay, & Latimer-Cheung, 2013; Kittson et al., 2013). In particular, integrated sporting events, where disabled and non-disabled events occur side by side are effective in increasing awareness and positive attitudes (such as the integrated Commonwealth Games, see Paradis, Misener, McGillivray, & Legg, 2017).

2. A focus on children

Attitudes are formed early in life, when implicit preferences are encoded during the basic socialization process (Daruwalla & Darcy, 2005; Galli & Pazzaglia, 2016). Therefore, there is good evidence that attitudes are influenced most easily and effectively among children. Preventing young people from developing fearful or otherwise negative attitudes toward disability is a more effective and efficient approach than waiting until poor attitudes emerge and then trying to override them. Armstrong, Morris, Abraham, Ukoumunne, and Tarrant (2016) studied British children 7 to 16 years of age and found that the more naturally occurring contact they reported with disabled people (whether they were friends, family members, schoolmates, or even more remote contacts), the more likely they were to have positive attitudes toward disability. This relationship between contact and attitudes was not altered by social class or gender, but it was stronger the earlier the contact was experienced.

3. A focus on health professionals

Health professionals are powerful sources of authority in our society, and they are important gatekeepers to many of the goods and services that society has to offer to people with disabilities. Furthermore, they are central to the struggle to maintain health, prevent complications, and delay further functional limitation. A considerable amount of the research conducted on attitudes toward disability has involved students in the health professions, particularly medical students. During the years of their training, there is an opportunity to address this "captive audience" with positive messages and information about disability. University training programs for health professionals are notoriously demanding, leading to very full timetables for students. Typically, only a few hours are devoted to learning about how to interact with people with disabilities in the context of a busy medical curriculum. And yet, studies have shown that these programs can be remarkably effective, even when the contact is brief and indirect, such as through films, vignettes, and videos (Barg, Armstrong, Hetz, & Latimer, 2010; Bu, Veloski, & Ankam, 2016; Byron & Dieppe, 2000; Galli & Pazzaglia, 2016; Schwartz et al., 2010).

4. Rewards and incentives

You often hear people say that the real test of improved attitudes is improved behaviours — but that is only partly true. Behaviour responds to incentives, and if you can line up the right sort of incentives, people will do whatever is required to obtain the carrot or avoid the stick. While you can't directly change attitudes by changing behaviour (i.e., with external rewards), you can use incentives to create a situation where contact occurs, and where some of the co-participation processes described above take place. For example, you can offer wage subsidies to incentivize employers to consider disabled job applicants. By offering to supplement the wage of the disabled employee for a period of three months, you offer the employer the opportunity to gain experience with a disabled worker — to discover the many known benefits of hiring disabled workers, to overcome his or her prejudices about how a disabled worker would perform and what he or she might require, and to confront his or her own fears and sensitivities about disability (Dana, Lalwani, & Duval, 1997). An experience like this can shake loose many of the attitudinal barriers to employment, in return for a relatively modest investment.

5. Discrepancy awareness

The final strategy that has been shown to be effective in changing attitudes toward disability is an educational approach called discrepancy awareness or meta-awareness (Dana et al., 1997). This approach usually takes the form of an interactive educational forum where individuals are brought into contact with their implicit attitudes. Using situational learning, scenarios are acted out that create an opportunity for learning about implicit attitudes. Using another workplace example, the following situation is "workshopped":

> A hiring committee is provided with resumés from prospective job applicants. When candidates appear for their interviews, they have disabilities that were not evident from the application — one uses a wheelchair, one has a developmental disability, one has expressive speech difficulties. As each candidate enters the room and at intervals throughout the process, the hiring committee is invited to stop the action and share their thoughts and concerns. A skilled facilitator unpacks the implicit attitudes being revealed and invites participants to examine them.

The truest test of improved attitudes is increased empathy and decreased social anxiety in dealing with disabled people (Armstrong et al., 2016); feeling more comfortable and confident, and more aware of the other's feelings (Bu, Veloski, & Ankram, 2016); and being able to take the perspective of someone with a disability (Galli & Pazzaglia, 2016). If we accept the argument put forth earlier that the main basis for poor attitudes toward disability is fear, then surely overcoming that fear and indifference is our main objective (Byron & Dieppe, 2000).

Conclusion

This chapter set out to help us appreciate the pervasive nature of attitudes toward disability and the potentially damaging effect of negative attitudes. I hope it has helped readers to *discover* some technical aspects of attitudes that they may not previously have been aware of, such as the fact that attitudes are made up of both cognitive and emotional aspects, that attitudes can exist at both conscious (explicit) and unconscious (implicit) levels, and that attitudes have a number of purposes that may not continue to be relevant at our current stage of evolution.

I hope we have also *discovered* the challenge of changing attitudes toward disability in a country like Canada, which is already fairly progressive, at least in its overt or explicit attitudes. When people think they are already doing all that needs to be done, it is difficult to get their attention on the need for change. And yet, as long as people with disabilities are significantly socially and economically disadvantaged, as they are in Canada (as we will see in subsequent chapters), the need for change persists.

Our *dream*, of course, is for true equity and inclusion of people with disabilities. In order to achieve this, we need greater transparency around attitudes toward disability, and alignment of what people say and do with what they actually think. It's not enough to be able to give the correct responses on a survey. The dream is for a time when the words, beliefs, and actions all line up to create opportunities for people with disabilities.

In order to optimize attitudes, we may have the chance to participate in the *design* of intervention strategies.

- We know that these strategies must focus both on the cognitive and emotional aspects of attitudes.
- We know that we need to go beyond explicit attitudes and increase awareness of implicit attitudes — those that people may not even know they hold.

Two subsets of the population have been featured in the research — children and health professionals. Both of these groups have been shown to be highly amenable to interventions to improve attitudes toward disability, and both have the potential to be influential in creating a more inclusive world.

Furthermore, according to Angus Reid, half of the population ("young bystanders" and "older detached") are potentially sympathetic to disability issues, and could be shifted to be "onside". This would leave only 15% who are "indifferent", and who would thus be effectively marginalized.

As we contemplate *deploying* strategies for changing attitudes, the evidence is clear that there are strategies that do and don't work. The two most popular strategies — awareness campaigns and simulations — have been shown to not only be ineffective, but perhaps even damaging. There are however five approaches that have shown promising results — contact and co-participation, a focus on youth, a focus on health professionals, rewards and incentives, and discrepancy awareness. All of these seek to increase empathy, decrease social anxiety, and promote a positive view of disability.

SECTION 2

Disability and Self-Care

Now that we have explored the definition and scope of disability, the next two sections of this book examine how disability affects people in the three major domains of life (McColl, Law, & Stewart, 2015):

- self-care, meaning the ability to manage one's basic needs and to prepare for participation in other activities;
- productivity, referring to those activities that fill the main portion of a person's day, and that afford one a livelihood, entail an obligation, represent a contribution, or include achievement; and
- leisure, meaning those activities that one engages in when one is freed of the obligation to be productive.

In this section on self-care, we will explore definitions of *self* and *self-care*, types of self-care disabilities, and the prevalence of self-care disabilities. In addition, we will explore the idea of independence, which lies at the root of our concern for self-care. Several subsets of self-care warrant particular attention, including spirituality, sexuality, and health care.

We will strive to appreciate the many challenges that people with disabilities encounter before they even leave the house in the morning, and the resourcefulness and ingenuity that permits them to overcome these challenges — challenges to what most people would consider mundane tasks, taken for granted, completed quickly and efficiently in order to get on with the real business of living. However, they are essential for survival, and the inability to complete these tasks — like bathing, dressing, eating, and toileting — casts them in a whole different light. They become massive barriers to the things we want to do, like to do, or need to do.

Chapter 6

The depth and breadth of self-care

Introduction

Our interest in self-care arises with our concern for the "**self**" — a constructed entity that represents the individuality and identity of each person. The self is an abstract notion or consciousness about one's own nature. It is our understanding of where "I" ends and the rest of the world begins. The self constitutes an individual's uniqueness, and his or her distinctness from other "selves". It is made up of our essential qualities, our knowledge, memories, beliefs, desires, and needs. It is the agent responsible for our thoughts, feelings, and actions. The self is known through cognitive, affective, and sensory experiences.

Self-care thus is defined as all of those activities that one undertakes that provide maintenance and support to this entity called the self. The International Classification of Functioning, Disability and Health (WHO, 2001) defines *self-care* to include the array of personal tasks and duties outlined in Figure 6.1.

Impediments to the ability to engage in self-care may come from a variety of sources, both internal and external to the individual. Within the individual, physical factors like decreased strength, mobility, coordination, or sensation may require individuals to carry out personal care with assistance or using adaptive aids. Pain and fatigue are physical factors with a profound impact on the ability to complete self-care. Cognitive factors, like the ability to plan and exe-

77

Figure 6.1: ICF definition of self-care

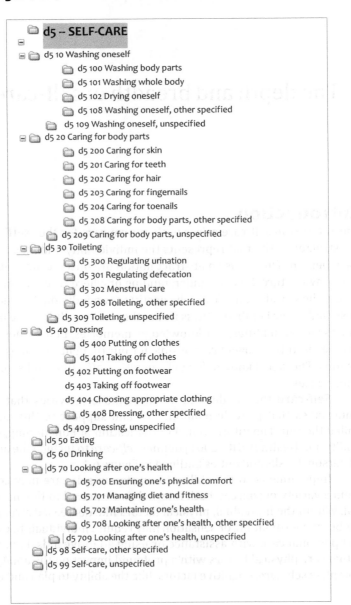

Source: WHO, 2001.

cute a task, or the ability to remember the components of a task, may affect the ability to be independent in self-care. Psychological factors, like one's self-awareness or self-esteem, may affect performance of self-care activities. And finally, the environment may make the completion of personal care tasks either more difficult or more manageable. The presence of appropriate physical space, economic resources, tools, equipment, and supportive others can have profound effects on an individual's ability to complete personal care. Each of these factors alone, or several in combination, may be enough to result in a disability in self-care.

To begin this section, I offer an updated version of a chapter written for a previous book that is no longer in print (McColl & Bickenbach, 1998), which I feel offers a number of interesting perspectives on the breadth of self-care. It draws on the voices of seven people with disabilities. I use the text of their extraordinary biographies and other writings to offer examples of self-care disabilities and to illuminate the subtle and yet pervasive ways that self-care disability affects one's life.

- In *My Left Foot* (1954), Christy Brown recounts the story of his life with cerebral palsy.
- In *A Leg to Stand On* (1984), Oliver Sacks describes his experience of a severe peripheral nerve injury to his leg.
- In *The Body Silent* (1987), anthropologist Robert Murphy describes his evolving understanding of disability, due to the progressive onset of quadriplegia caused by a spinal tumour.
- In *In the Jaws of the Black Dogs* (1995), John Bentley Mays invokes the metaphor coined by Winston Churchill to discuss his experience with depression.
- In *Slow Dance* (1997), Bonnie Sherr Klein describes her recovery and rehabilitation from two brainstem strokes.
- In a series of articles and presentations, Patricia Deegan (1988) and Esso Leete (1989) describe their experiences with schizophrenia.

Although some of these accounts are now quite old, they deal with timeless concepts. While some of the language used might seem dated, these extracts illustrate the nature and effects of self-care disabilities.

When we think of caring for the self, we often think primarily of the physical self; however, in this chapter, I propose a broader definition of caring for the self, including not only the physical self but also the emotional, intellectual, and spiritual self.

Physical self-care

Caring for the physical self is a broad category that refers to those abilities that help us to maintain our health, our bodies, and our physical presentation to the world in a condition that allows us to undertake whatever other activities our daily life holds in store. **Physical self-care** consists mainly of the basic personal functions that we do every day or otherwise routinely and regularly. Murphy (1987) describes them as follows:

> ... how to get on and off the toilet, how to dress, how to shave, how to brush his teeth how to get in and out of bed, how to carry out all the minor chores of life with minimal dependence on others. These are the activities that most of us — or I should say most of you — carry out unthinking automatically, but each presents a great challenge to a paraplegic and almost an impossibility to a quadriplegic. (p. 55)

Murphy (1987) and Klein (1998) both describe many technological and methodological adaptations they have made to daily activities, like showering, dressing, and emptying one's bowel and bladder. They also discuss the need for assistance from another person from time to time. For some people with more severe disabilities, much of their self-care is performed by hired attendants or family members. Murphy poignantly illustrates some of the difficulties inherent in this.

> I haven't been able to scratch my back or shoulders for the past ten years.... For this I depend on Yolanda, and when she isn't around, I grit my teeth and wait for the itch to pass. (p. 199)

Murphy (1987) talks further about the idea of independence, and the extent to which it dominates the self-identity of people with disabilities. Independence, self-reliance, and personal autonomy are central values in North American culture.

> Lack of autonomy and unreciprocated dependence on others bring debasement of status in American culture and in many other cultures.... Overdependence and non-reciprocity are con-

sidered childish traits, and adults who have them — even if it's not their fault — suffer a reduction in status. (p. 201)

Mays (1995) also talks about the independence ethic, and its effect on people with mental illnesses. He takes a different perspective, commenting on how the independence ethic may drive people with mental illness into even greater withdrawal and social isolation.

Thus does depression hide its true lair — the proposition that staunch individualism and self-reliance are the root virtues from which we've allowed ourselves to drift.... The torment of depression springs, at least in part, from the fact that we are independent, even if we don't want to be.... The experience of intense isolation as a strategy for coping with the confusion of the world makes the depressive a true believer in [independence]. (p. 109)

Murphy (1987) also talks about the necessity of planning in every aspect of daily life, including his most basic self-care:

Whereas once I could act on whim and fancy, I now had to exercise planning and foresight. This was true of even the simplest actions.... The house had become a battlefield, my movements well-thought out strategies against a constant foe.... Gone were the days when I could wander into the kitchen for a snack or outside for a breath of fresh air. This loss of spontaneity invaded my entire assessment of time. It introduced a calculating quality into an existence that formerly had been pleasantly disordered. (p. 76)

Klein (1998) too talks about the need for planning in personal care to save unnecessary steps, and the toll it takes.

I used to run out the door grabbing my bag, knowing my keys, wallet, notebook, pens, phone lists were all there. Now when I go even downstairs, I have lists that I check and re-check — and still I forget things. Planning is hard work. Pressure work. But I'm learning to be patient and recognize what I really need and what I can do without. (p. 256)

Murphy (1987) refers to the fatigue associated with having to plan every aspect of his life in minute detail.

Beyond the physical symptoms, I have been overtaken by a profound and deepening sense of tiredness — a total, draining weakness that I must resist every waking minute. It starts in the morning when I struggle to awaken.... Facing the world every day is an ordeal for everybody.... It is much worse to confront the day with a serious deficit. The wish to turn my back on the world continues through my daily ablutions, which grow longer and more tedious every year. (p. 89)

Deegan (1988) tells us of the force of sheer will that is needed to overcome this fatigue.

Something more ... is needed [for] the person to get out of bed, shake off the mind-numbing exhaustion, get dressed, overcome the fear of the overcrowded and unfriendly bus, and face the fear of failure in the rehabilitation program. In essence, disabled persons must be active and courageous participants in their own rehabilitation, or it will fail. (p. 12)

Also included in physical self-care are issues of safety, health, and lifestyle. All of these involve choices, conscious or unconscious, that individuals make about caring for the physical self. Murphy (1987) talks about the importance of guarding against falls and further injury, and of maintaining the care and integrity of one's skin when sensation is impaired. Klein (1998) too mentions impaired sensation, and the need to be vigilant against injuring oneself. Mays (1995) refers to the necessity of seeking care in a timely fashion when ill, and the difficulty of separating real symptoms of physical illness from somatic experiences of mental illness.

Emotional self-care

The ability to care for the emotional self, or **emotional self-care**, refers to the skills and aptitudes that individuals possess for understanding their feelings, coping with them, and seeking resolution of stressful or troublesome feelings. The experience of living with a disability carries with it a number of its own emotional experiences, in addition to those shared with the non-disabled population. Murphy (1987) deals with these in detail, but summarizes them as follows:

The four most far-reaching changes in the consciousness of the disabled are: a radical loss of self-esteem; the invasion and occupation of thought by the disability; a strong undercurrent of anger; and the acquisition of a new and undesirable identity.... Our lives are built upon a constant struggle between the need to

reach out to others and a contrary urge to fall back into ourselves. Among the disabled, the inward pull becomes compelling, often irresistible. (p. 108)

Emotional self-care consists of methods for coping with these
and other emotional experiences that might otherwise stand in the
way of living in the world. Coping in this context refers to strategies
or manoeuvres undertaken to deal with an emotionally stressful situation. Some of the coping strategies invoked by the seven authors
are detailed here. Leete (1989) refers explicitly to her coping
approach as follows:

> All of my coping strategies largely consist of four steps: recogniz-
> ing when I am feeling stressed (which is harder than it may
> sound); identifying the stressor; remembering from past experi-
> ence what helped in the same or similar situations; and, taking
> action as quickly as possible. (p. 199)

Some of the actions she refers to include keeping busy, structuring her time, using trusted others for reality checks, and trying
not to be judgmental of herself and others, but rather being more
accepting of actions and attitudes.

Deegan (1988) talks about the need for action as a coping strategy to find one's way out of the "darkness" of disability. She likens
her own experience with mental illness to that of a man with whom
she was acquainted who had quadriplegia.

> The paralyzed man and I began in little ways, with small tri-
> umphs and simple acts of courage. He shaved, attempted to read
> a book, and talked with a counsellor; I rode in the car, shopped
> on Wednesdays, and talked to a friend for a few minutes. He
> applied for benefits, got a van and learned to drive; I took
> responsibility for my medications, took a part-time job, and had
> my own money. ... One day at a time, with multiple setbacks, we
> rebuilt our lives on the three cornerstones of recovery — hope,
> willingness and responsible action. (p. 14)

Mays (1995) describes how strong emotions, such as anger and
love, helped him to cope with the emotional withdrawal of depression.

> The gift of real emotion, even anger, is the working of a wonder,
> the creation of a setting in which a patient can allow genuine
> feeling into a human interchange. If I was angry, ... I was at least

making the first honest contact in a lifetime of concealed angers, suffocated emotions. (p. 71)

Both Mays (1995) and Deegan (1988) refer to the importance of love as a strong emotion that may be used in coping or caring for the emotional self. Mays states that "Love is depression's most potent enemy."

Klein (1998) talks about humour and laughter as a means of coping with the emotional aspects of disability.

> I laughed at anything, and my family laughed with me. We laughed when I dropped or spilled things. We laughed that I sounded like a drunk with marbles in my mouth.... We laughed in part for our own protection. Did we sometimes laugh too loud to mask the tragedy of my illness? I don't think so.... All of a sudden, the future was gone, too fragile to imagine, and there was just the moment. It was hilarious. (p. 201)

Brown (1954) discovered that both painting and writing were ways of caring for himself emotionally, and affording himself some relief from the feelings of isolation and exclusion that dominated his adolescent experience.

> I had a feeling of pure joy when I painted, a feeling I had never experienced before and which seemed almost to lift me above myself.... I'll sit for hours painting in the bedroom upstairs, unconscious of everything — including myself. (p. 57)

Brown (1954) also discussed an important idea that is raised by other authors as well. On a trip to Lourdes, he encountered others with disabilities for the first time, and reflected on the importance of recognizing that there are others both better off and worse off than oneself. We refer to this phenomenon as **social comparison**, and it is an important informal process that happens for many disabled people in rehabilitation, or in participation in disability-specific organizations, activities, or events.

> As I saw all those people, each with his or her own suffering, a new light began to dawn on me. I was rather bewildered.... I had been rather like a snail shut away in his own narrow little shell.... I felt as if I had been blind all along and that only now was I seeing with my eyes and feeling with my heart the plight of others whose burdens were so great as to make mine seem nothing in comparison. (p. 95)

Several of the autobiographies dealt with a conscious process of coping aimed at finding a more positive way of perceiving one's experience of disability. Klein (1998) used books to meet other people with disabilities, and learn from their experiences (much as we are doing in this chapter). Through these accounts, she experimented with alternative conceptualizations of the disability and the self, and ultimately developed a more constructive perception of her situation. Murphy (1987) offers a similar insight:

> It then occurred to me that this is the universal human condition. We all have to muddle through life within our limitations, and while I had certain physical handicaps, I retained many strengths.... Some people are unable to do what I do because they lack the mental equipment, and in this sense, they are disabled and I am not. Everybody is disabled in one way or another. (p. 212)

Finally, Christy Brown (1954) says,

> It was a bitter realization, but a true one and a necessary one.... It made me sad and bitter for a time, but in the end it made me stronger within myself. If I could never really be like other people, then at least I would be like myself, and make the best of it. (p. 137)

Intellectual self-care

Caring for the intellectual self, or **intellectual self-care**, refers to engaging in activities that maintain one's interest, that offer stimulation or intellectual challenge, and that provide reassurance of a competent level of cognitive functioning. Some people do crossword puzzles, others participate in discussion groups, and others read. All of these are examples of activities or abilities that we engage in to keep ourselves mentally alert, and to reassure ourselves that our cognitive skills will not let us down.

Intellectual self-care refers to those activities one undertakes in an effort to stimulate one's brain, to advance one's learning, or to test one's intellectual capacities. Leete (1989) talks about the necessity of creating space in her life for intellectual activity by attempting to decrease some of the stimuli reaching her brain.

> One of the main differences between the brain of a normal person and one who has schizophrenia is a major difficulty filtering

or screening out background noise. I am hyper-alert, acutely aware of every sound or movement in my environment. I am often confused by repetitive noises or multiple stimuli and become nervous, impatient and irritable. To deal with this, I make a deliberate effort to reduce distractions as much as possible. (p. 197)

Klein (1998) talks about using a journal to bring order to a jumble of thoughts and ideas:

I asked [a friend] for a journal of my own.... I had always insisted that I had no time for that sort of thing, but now I began keeping one in earnest.... It was a tool for my survival. I was processing the strange and troubling events occurring in my body; recording thoughts I couldn't trust my damaged mind to remember; trying to make coherence out of chaos. Writing in my journal became as necessary a part of my daily routine as brushing my teeth. (p. 197)

Mays (1995) also talks about keeping diaries, both as a way of processing thoughts and as a means of expressing thoughts that could not be shared with others.

And there are of course, the diaries — pages where my leaking, fugitive mind hid itself in blasphemies. (p. 38) ... It does not require the intimacy or good fellowship required by many other activities.... Hard questions must be asked and answered — a process that one can carry on creditably even when deeply depressed. (p. 139)

A compelling portrayal of the importance of expression for intellectual well-being is found in the account by Brown (1954), from his initial discovery of his ability to communicate with a piece of chalk held in his left foot, through his painting and drawing, and ultimately through his writing.

I had lots of ideas that I couldn't express through my paints and brushes. The sudden inspiration to try and pin them down on paper through the use of words came.... Immediately I got a sixpenny jotter and began to write. I hardly knew what I was doing. I just sat there, writing down whatever came into my head. It was a crazy jumble of words, sentences and paragraphs.... Later I began to connect them and tried to weave them into a pattern.... Finally I started to put thoughts behind what I wrote. (p. 84)

Brown (1954) talks about the intellectual stimulation of learning and reading — geometry, Latin, and literature. Of Shaw he says,

> If meeting Shakespeare was like a breeze from Heaven, meeting Shaw was like a fresh wind from the sea in March.... Reading his plays was as brisk and stimulating an exercise for me as a morning run along the sea strand is for most people. (p. 173)

Spiritual self-care

Spiritual self-care refers to an abstract set of abilities that allows individuals to preserve faith, connection, belief, and trust, and to achieve some measure of peace with the shape their lives have taken and with their place in the world. Spiritual self-care may involve the development of an alternative view of causation or attribution that allows an individual to experience justice and fairness in his or her lot in life, and satisfaction from his or her ability to contribute to the world.

The accounts of disability reviewed for this chapter are full of references to the spiritual self, and to insights gained through a spiritual view of disability. Despite being entirely secular in their presentation, these accounts all offer evidence of the spiritual self and efforts to care for the spiritual self. Murphy (1987) ends his highly analytical and insightful volume with a chapter entitled "There's no cure for life", in which he states,

> For if all other meanings and values are arbitrary and culturally relative, then the only transcendent value is life itself.... Life has a liturgy that must be continuously celebrated and renewed; it is a feast whose sacrament is consummated in the paralytic's breaking out from his prison of flesh and bone, and in his quest for autonomy. (p. 230)

Further on the topic of meaning, Murphy (1987) notes that many people with disabilities strive to find meaning in their condition.

> The disabled, for understandable reasons, are more interested than most people in the conundrums posed by their affliction. Some resign themselves to God's inscrutable design, or believe they are being tested by Divinity for some special purpose. This attitude has the virtue of answering the query, "Why me?" ... There may be no final meanings, but we do live in a meaningful

universe; otherwise we could not abide intelligent existence. Our meanings, however, are humanly contrived.... Disability does indeed have a meaning, albeit one that is bestowed humanly. (pp. 222–223)

Klein (1998) also raises the "Why me?" question, but much like Murphy (1987), she dismisses it as a dead end in the search for meaning in life lived with a disability.

I felt strangely peaceful. Whatever was going on in my body was clearly out of my control. I didn't believe in any Divine Plan, but neither did I believe this was a random accident. I didn't ask "Why me?", but felt rather that it was my turn — I who had always been so privileged and lucky. (p. 26)

Sacks (1984) too refers to recognizing a greater force, and the experience of a peaceful passivity that accompanies this recognition.

Now, for the first time in my life perhaps, I had tasted, been forced to taste, something quite different — to experience in patienthood the profoundest passivity; and to realize this was the only proper attitude at the time. Socially, I had to try to be active and adult, and avoid more than the minimum necessary dependence on others; but spiritually — inwardly — I had to relinquish all my powers and pretensions, all my adult masculine enterprise and activity, this being the only proper posture of the soul at this time. (p. 88)

Several authors also refer to the spiritual theme of hope, and the various ways that hope serves to care for the spiritual self. Sacks (1984), Murphy (1987), and Brown (1954) all refer to a secretly held hope for "a miracle", despite their intellectual knowledge that it is impossible. Deegan (1988) takes the importance of hope a step further, and suggests to caregivers and service providers that they engage in a "conspiracy of hope ... build a community of hope which surrounds the one who may have lost all hope".

Finally, three of the authors reviewed referred to religious ritual and the comfort it brought them, much to their own surprise in some cases. In each of these accounts, the connection with religion is experienced as a connection with a childhood memory. Klein (1998) tells of the comfort experienced through visits from her rabbi.

Rabbi Ron was more important to me than either of us would have expected.... [He] connected me to a piece of my life ... a piece of my childhood, my upbringing in a traditional Jewish family. (p. 29)

Murphy (1987) recounts the experience of overhearing someone repeating the Apostle's Creed one night in the hospital.

> Silently I followed the prayer; a prayer I had not said since childhood, remembered not by the words or meaning, but rather by the cadence of its recital.... The prayer cast a momentary spell in its brief and atavistic resort to old forms, a spurious kind of solace that faded with the sounds. (p. 2)

Spirituality has been defined as a sense of connection with the self, the world, and a higher power (McColl, Bichenbach, Johnston, Nishihama, Schumaker, Smith, & Yelland, 2000). To the extent that thoughts and activities reinforce this connection to others, the world, and a greater power, they may be considered spiritual self-care activities.

Conclusion

I hope the chapter has helped us to *appreciate* that self-care is much more than dressing, bathing, and eating. The autobiographical accounts offered in this chapter provide insight into the range of self-care required by people with different types of disabilities. Self-care represents the background, behind-the-scenes activities that the outside world seldom sees. It is an essential aspect of a full and satisfying life, but it is not an end in itself. It is simply a means to other valued activities, such as productivity and leisure.

We have *discovered* that the self is a complex, multi-dimensional concept, made up of physical, social, psychological, mental, and spiritual identities. Thus, caring for the self is more than hygiene and social presentation. It is a collection of carefully balanced tactics and strategies that allow people with disabilities to be participants in their daily lives. The business of caring for the self is as complex as the notion of the self. To treat self-care in the uni-dimensional way too often done in rehabilitation is to undermine the efforts of the individual to create and sustain a full and functioning self. We share with our clients the *dream* of being understood as a unique and valued self, in all one's fullness and vitality.

We have also *discovered* how different disabilities can affect self-care. We have considered examples in this chapter that range from relatively practical constraints, such as those experienced by Robert Murphy resulting from his quadriplegia, to very abstract limitations, such as those described by Patricia Deegan associated with her mental illness. Regardless of their cause, self-care disabilities interfere with peoples' abilities to get on with their lives. Self-care is a necessary but not sufficient condition for participation and personal autonomy.

In our work as health, education, and social service workers, we have the opportunity to *design* self-care programs that don't simply uphold social standards and norms of hygiene, dress, and comportment, but rather that validate the total selves of our clients. This means adopting a broader definition of the self, and by extension of self-care. It means resisting the temptation to assume that if a person can dress, bathe, and toilet himself or herself, that your job is done. There is so much more to the self that needs to be appreciated, cultivated, and supported in order to flourish.

Finally, as we *deploy* these programs, it is worthwhile to consider the courage that it takes every day to continue to care for a self that is more demanding and difficult than others you see around you. As we will see in the next chapter, people with disabilities spend considerably more time in self-care than their non-disabled counterparts. Because of the disability itself, because of the potential for complications, because of the need for special equipment or supplies, because of coordination with assistants where necessary, and because of constraints on time, self-care becomes an act of courage, resistance, and commitment, as much as it is an act of personal maintenance.

In closing, I commend to the reader the original sources for all of these first-person accounts. They offer a fuller understanding of how personal, emotional, intellectual, and spiritual self-care interact with the many other demands in the lives of people with disabilities.

Chapter 7

Demographics of self-care disability

Introduction

In the preceding chapter, we talked about what it means to be a "self" and to care for the self. We noted that self-care is a precondition for many other types of participation, in that it gets us ready for other activities. We emphasized different manifestations of the self — the physical, emotional, intellectual, and spiritual selves — and the importance of caring for all of these. Furthermore, we drew on the voices of people with disabilities to explore the many different issues that arise in self-care. Finally, we strove to appreciate the challenge of self-care when a disability is present — the courage, commitment, and discipline required to do what others take for granted, even when it is inordinately difficult, takes an undue amount of time, or requires coordination or cooperation with other people.

In this chapter, we will seek to understand the scope and breadth of self-care disabilities in Canada. As always, we will benefit from research and experiences in other countries, but we will focus on the situation in Canada, and the extent to which self-care disabilities affect people in Canada. In order to do that, we will focus on a somewhat more restricted definition of self-care. Statistics Canada refers to what we typically call **activities of daily living (ADLs)** and **instrumental activities of daily living (IADLs)**.

- ADLs include personal care — bathing, dressing, eating, toileting, grooming, and functional mobility in the home.

- IADLs refer to a broader span of self-care activities, including interactions with the community, light and heavy housework, meal preparation, errands/appointments, finances/bill payments, care for children or others, and minor health care procedures, such as taking medications and administering injections.

Who experiences self-care disability?

The 2011 Canadian Survey on Disability (Statistics Canada, 2012) estimates that 8% of the population 15 or older receives help with IADLs, and about 2% receive help with personal care (ADLs). Similarly, in the United States, 2.7% of the non-institutional population has a personal-care disability (Disability Statistics, 2015). Among all Canadians with disabilities (14% of the population), approximately 1.5 million adults and 1.2 million seniors need assistance with daily activities (Fournier-Savard, Mongeon, & Crompton, 2010; Statistics Canada, 2007).

The most common self-care disabilities involve instrumental activities of daily living. Among those reporting a self-care disability, 83% report needing help with transportation, 67% with housework, 53% with home maintenance, 40% with finances, and 34% with medications and treatments. Only 25% report needing assistance with ADLs or personal care (Statistics Canada, 2012).

A number of factors affect the need for assistance with self-care: age, gender, severity of disability, and type of disability, to name a few. Older age is associated with higher degrees of self-care disability: 40% of those with self-care disabilities are over 65 years of age, 31% are between 45 and 64, and 29% are between 14 and 44 years of age (Sinha & Bleakney, 2014). The *Disability Status Report: United States* (Disability Statistics, 2015) tells a similar story. Whereas only 2.7% of all disabled people reported needing self-care assistance, 13.7% of disabled people over the age of 75 needed self-care assistance.

Women constitute 56% of the population with self-care disabilities, in part because of their longer survival, and thus the joint effects of age and disability. Severity and type of disability also obviously affect the nature and extent of self-care disability. Self-care disabilities are highest among those with severe and very severe disabilities (87% and 95%, respectively). Sixty-seven percent (67%) of

Table 7.1: Average minutes per day spent in self-care activities

	Canadians with disabilities		Canadians without disabilities		Americans with disabilities
	1992	2010	1992	2010	2010
Light housework	108.2	109.0	83.2	84.1	109.8
Personal care	85.6	97.5	59.6	71.3	98.7
Home maintenance	34.2	32.5	32.0	27.1	25.3
Errands/services	33.2	31.6	28.6	30.9	28.1
Child care	13.2	14.5	24.8	27.4	9.6
Adult care	1.3	4.4	1.0	2.5	1.0

moderately disabled and 40% of mildly disabled report that they need assistance with self-care.

With regard to the time spent on self-care activities, Table 7.1 compares Canadians with disabilities (Statistics Canada, 1992; Statistics Canada, 2010) with all Canadians and with Americans with disabilities (Wilson, McColl, & Parsons, 2015; Wilson & McColl, 2017).

The most notable observation is the additional time required by people with disabilities over people without disabilities. It takes them almost an extra hour per day to complete their most basic self-care — personal care took 26 more minutes (in 2010) and light housework took 25 more minutes. This difference probably reflects many of the issues discussed in the previous chapter — the fact that things take longer and that there are often additional self-care duties involved in living with a disability. It is interesting to note that Americans with disabilities look very similar to Canadians with disabilities in these areas.

Home maintenance and errands are not all that different between disabled and non-disabled Canadians. This is probably accounted for by the fact that those who can do these things for themselves probably do them in ways not dissimilar from those without disabilities. Child care takes up considerably less time among people with disabilities, perhaps reflecting differences in marital status and childbearing between disabled and non-disabled people.

Unmet needs for assistance with self-care

Among those who report a self-care disability, only some receive the assistance they feel they need. Thirty-four percent (34%) report needing no assistance to manage their self-care disability, and 66% report that they need assistance. Of those who needed assistance, 37% get the help they need, 24% don't get enough help, and 5% don't get any care at all. These percentages vary with the severity of disability, as shown in Figure 7.1.

Among those who are very severely disabled — 95% of whom require assistance with self-care — 37% get the care they need, 53% get some care but less than required, and 7% receive no care despite needing it. Only 5% of those who are severely disabled report needing no assistance with personal care. A similar story is

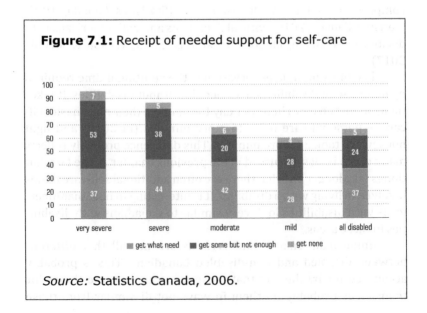

Figure 7.1: Receipt of needed support for self-care

Source: Statistics Canada, 2006.

told by those with less severe disabilities. Among the 87% of people with severe disabilities who need help with self-care, only 44% actually get what they need, while 43% do not. Forty-two percent (42%) of people with moderate disabilities get the care they need, while 26% do not. Even among people with mild disabilities, 28% get the care they need, while 32% do not.

Below are the main reasons stated for unmet needs for self-care (Statistics Canada, 2006):

- It is too expensive to hire someone to provide help (29.4%).
- People don't know how to obtain help (12.7%).
- Help from family or other informal sources is not available (12.4%).
- Help is not available in the geographic area (5.9%).
- The type of help needed is not covered by the person's insurance (5.1%).

Who provides assistance with self-care?

More than 80% of assistance to people with disabilities is currently provided by families, including spouses, parents, siblings, and children (Fournier-Savard et al., 2010). Eighty-four percent (84%) of Canadians live in families (Statistics Canada, 2007). The family is an essential unit of economic and instrumental support in Canadian society. It is a resource that serves both individuals and the national interest by providing inestimable services and supports to Canadians at no cost.

Both American and Australian data show that 75% of disabled adults live with family, and 23% are dependent on their families for practical and financial support (Dow & Meyer, 2010; Fujiura, 2010). Among disabled people, 4.3% are adult children living with (and financially dependent on) their parents. In the United States, just under 1% (0.8%) of the total population are disabled adult children living with their families of origin. In more than half of those cases (55%), the primary wage earner in the home is 60 years of age or older (Fujiura, 2010).

Living situation obviously significantly affects who provides care. For those living with family in Canada, 80% of care comes from a family member. Other sources of help are extended family, friends, or individuals associated with agencies designated to provide help — 24% of the care needed comes from extended family or friends, and 17% comes from paid helpers. These percentages add up to more than 100% because many people have more than one caregiver: 28% have two, and 29% have three or more people who share caregiving duties (Fournier-Savard, Mongeon, & Crompton, 2010).

Women with disabilities are twice as likely as men to live alone (24.6% vs. 12.3%), less likely to be married or partnered (50% vs. 58.4%), and more likely to be single parents (11.0% vs. 7.8%). They are therefore more likely to receive any needed help from agencies or volunteers. For those living alone, 56% of care comes from family and 57% from friends or other volunteers. A further 35% comes from paid helpers — twice as much as for those living with family (Burlock, 2017).

On average, care recipients received 7 hours a week of care; however, that estimate varied widely depending on the reason for needed care and the source of the care. The highest volumes of care were provided to people with dementia, averaging 37 hours per week, and the lowest were provided to people with mental illness, averaging 3 hours per week.

Over their lifetimes, almost half of Canadians (46%) will provide care to an aging or disabled loved one. In the preceding year, just over one-quarter of Canadians (28%) have provided such care. Almost as many men (26%) are caregivers as women (30%) (Sinha, 2013).

Thirty-eight percent (38%) of all care is provided to parents (27% to mothers, and 11% to fathers; 24% to parents living with the adult child providing care). Eight percent (8%) of care is provided to spouses and 5% to adult children. The remaining 49% is provided to extended family and friends. Eighty-nine percent (89%) of primary caregivers had been fulfilling the role for more than a year, 50% for more than 4 years, and 29% for more than 10 years (Sinha, 2013; Sinha & Bleakney, 2014).

In total, it is estimated that 233 million hours of care are provided per week to people with self-care disabilities in Canada (Turcotte, 2013). Spouses provide the highest amount of care — on average 14 hours per week. Parents provide an average of 10 hours to their adult children, and adult children provide an average of 4 hours per week to their parents. Other family members or friends generally provide about 3 hours per week.

Caregiving typically does not happen in isolation, but rather against a background of other responsibilities. Twenty-eight percent (28%) of caregivers were also caring for children at the same time as providing care to another adult. Sixty percent (60%) were working outside the home in addition to providing care (Sinha, 2013). Caregiving has been shown to have psychological, economic, and health-related consequences for caregivers. In addition, it fundamentally changes the relationship between care recipient and caregiver, and often exacerbates whatever dynamics already existed between the two people.

Several studies attempted to estimate the costs of informal caregiving on a nationwide basis, including social spending, medical costs, and lost productivity:

- Dow and Meyer (2010) estimated that 6 million Americans, 6 million Britons, and 2.6 million Australians provide informal care to family members. They estimate that 74% of all care provided in Australia is provided informally, accounting for $30.5 billion US per year in savings to society. They similarly estimate the value of care provided by family members at $87 billion per year in the United Kingdom (approximately equivalent in value to the National Health Service), and $257 billion in the United States.

- An Australian study estimated the overall cost of caregiving at $968 AU per household per week, or $49,818 per year (Access Economics, 2010).

- The market value of family caregiving in the United States was estimated at $304 billion US in 2004 (Fujiura, 2010).

Children with disabilities

The discussion to this point has focused on adults who receive help with self-care. It is somewhat more difficult to assert what a self-care disability is in childhood. A certain amount of parental caregiving in self-care is normative with children, and so it is unclear exactly where that expectation for parental assistance should end and where continued need for assistance represents a disability.

The most recent survey of disability in Canada, the *Canadian Survey on Disability 2012* (Statistics Canada, 2012) included only adults aged 15 and older, so we have to rely on the previous survey, the Participation and Activity Limitation Survey (Statistics Canada, 2001; 2007), or the one before that, the Health and Activity Limitation Survey (Statistics Canada, 1991), for information about disabled children. Those surveys found that 3.7% of children aged 14 and under lived with a disability — compared to 14.3% in the total population. Among disabled children, 42.5% had a severe or very severe disability, 24% had a moderate disability, and 33.5% had a mild disability (Statistics Canada, 2007).

In more than half of households where there was a disabled child (54%), the family reported that their situation was significantly affected by the need to provide care to that child. In 70% of households, mothers reported being affected by caregiving for a disabled child, 11% for fathers, and 14% for both parents. These effects could include working fewer hours (47%), altering work hours (44%), refusing a job because of childcare responsibilities (42%), having to quit work to provide care (30%), or turning down a promotion because the demands of the job would conflict with caregiving (26%) (Behnia & Duclos, 2003). Only 5% of households caring for a disabled child reported no effect on the economic and practical aspects of life.

Most households, however, reported being self-sufficient in caring for their disabled child — 64% of parents reported needing no additional help. Among the remainder, 11.5% of parents reported getting all the help they needed, 8% reported getting some help but needing more, and 13.5% reported getting no help despite needing some (Behnia & Duclos, 2003).

Attendant care

In several instances throughout this chapter, we have discussed care provided by paid others or agencies outside of the informal support system. These assistants are usually called personal support workers, although they can also be called attendants, home support workers, health-care aides, orderlies, or nurse's aides, depending on the agency and the setting. They typically work under the supervision of a nurse or other health professional, even though that person may supervise remotely. They are usually qualified with a college certificate in a related field, or with on-the-job training. **Attendant care** may range from light housekeeping and meal preparation to the most personal and intimate care, such as assistance with bathing, toileting, and dressing.

In most jurisdictions in Canada, personal supportive care is available in the home for people with severe disabilities, through a home-care program or a comparable publicly funded organization.

Care is usually provided by an agency and authorized for a certain amount of time per week. The agency is responsible for bonding and supervising care providers, as well as for scheduling and monitoring.

As you can imagine, there are certain challenges associated with receiving personal assistance from a stranger with whom you have no formal relationship or accountability. Here are just a few examples.

- Attendants often come with their own ideas about how a certain function should be performed, such as transferring an individual from his or her bed to a wheelchair. Attendants may have learned a particular way of doing this, whereas the person receiving service prefers a different way. Some attendants will be skilled in negotiating these discussions and compromises, while others may not, leading to tension. For people with disabilities who have already had to surrender a certain amount of independence and control over intimate aspects of life, this additional violation of their autonomy may be unacceptable.

- Scheduling of attendants is challenging both for agencies and for individuals receiving service. Most people receive one to two hours of assistance per day, and they need that assistance at particular times — usually around getting up in the morning and preparing to retire to bed at night. It is obviously difficult for an agency to meet all of these requests in a timely manner, and so clients are asked to adapt their schedules to meet those of the agency. This is a particular challenge for people who have other obligations, such as going to work or caring for a family.

- Imagine having someone help you take a shower or bath, evacuate your bowels, or feed yourself. If you think about all the people you know, there are some you would be more comfortable with providing that type of assistance than others. Now imagine that a stranger is being sent to your home to assist with those same functions. You may have to give this person a key to get into the home this person may be male or female, young or old, gentle or gruff, share your interests or not. A very particular type of trusting relationship is required between attendant and client. Over time, many clients and attendants develop that type of relationship — one of deep caring and unspoken understanding; however, it is also sometimes the case that clients are required to accept help from someone who is not at all compatible.

Finally, we need to remember that personal support workers too have a life — a life that their work requires them to schedule around the particular needs of someone outside of their own family and friends. They are paid a modest wage (currently averaging about $18 per hour in Canada), and they are asked to do a job that many people simply would not be capable of doing. They must find a way with every client to truly care for and about that person — his or her most basic needs and personal dignity.

An alternative to agency-provided attendant care is available in some jurisdictions — self-managed or direct-funded personal care (Yoshida, Willi, Parker, & Locker, 2004). Under this model, funds are allocated to individuals to hire, train, supervise, and sometimes fire their own attendants. They become employers, with a business registered with the Canada Revenue Agency, and a direct line of accountability between them and their attendants. They are responsible for providing statutory benefits (such as Canada Pension, Employment Insurance, and Workers' Compensation) and holidays to their employees, and for carrying liability insurance to protect them in the event of injury.

This model of attendant care arises out of the independent living approach to disability supports (see Chapter 2), placing the resources needed for independence directly in the hands of disabled people. It has obvious benefits in terms of compatibility and scheduling of workers, but it also has significant responsibilities associated with being an employer and managing public funds.

Non-human assistance with self-care

To this point, we have talked about human assistance with self-care, but there is also the possibility of assistance from non-human sources, particularly service animals and assistive devices.

Service animals include any animal trained to perform specific tasks to assist a disabled person. They are usually dogs, but can also be horses, monkeys, or even birds. They can go where regular pets or companion animals are not permitted, while in the course of practising their function.

The prevailing definition used to specify which animals qualify as service animals comes from the *Americans with Disabilities Act* (U.S. Department of Justice, Civil Rights Division, 1990):

A service animal is "any guide dog, signal dog, or other animal individually trained to do work or perform tasks for the benefit of an individual with a disability, including, but not limited to, guiding individuals with impaired vision, alerting individuals with impaired hearing to intruders or sounds, providing minimal protection or rescue work, pulling a wheelchair, or fetching dropped items ... generally, a public accommodation shall modify policies, practices, or procedures to permit the use of a service animal by an individual with a disability."

As inferred in the definition, there are a number of tasks that service animals can be specifically trained to do, and a number of different categories of service animals:

- *Guide animals* provide guidance and direction to blind individuals. The first service animals recognized in North America were guide dogs, trained at the Seeing Eye Institute in Morristown, New Jersey, since 1929.

- *Hearing animals* guide people with hearing impairments to the location of a sound, such as a doorbell, alarm clock, or emergency signal.

- *Medical emergency animals* are trained to recognize the onset of an emergency such as a seizure, fall, or heart attack, and to respond in particular ways, such as going for help, fetching medication, or even dialling 911 on a specially designed interface.

- *Mental health companion animals* provide support and comfort to people with mental illness.

- *Service animals* include all other animals specifically trained to fulfil the needs of particular disabled individuals, such as retrieving items, pulling a wheelchair, opening doors, and many other functions.

According to the Canadian Foundation for Animal-assisted Support Services (CFAS), there is currently no standard for identification and certification of service animals in Canada. Nor is there any registry or database for locating service dogs. The cost can vary from $3,000 to $50,000, depending on the training and specialization needed, and dogs are usually obtained from a registered charity or not-for-profit organization. Although the Standards Council of Canada is currently in the process of developing standards for service dogs, the message is still "Buyer beware" when contracting for a service dog. As with any relationship where there is a power differential, the relationship between service animals and the agency, breeder, trainer, client, and/or disabled person is not free from ethical issues (Wenthold & Savage, 2007). Managing expectations, ensuring the health and well-being of the animal, and planning for the termination of the relationship are all issues worthy of consideration.

Assistive devices, or **adaptive equipments**, are the final category of assistance with self-care that we will consider in this chapter. Assistive devices include any external tool, machine, or electronic aid that is designed specifically to enable someone with a disability to perform a specific function. Assistive devices can include everything from wheelchairs to adapted door openers and light switches, dressing aids, computer programs, and interfaces. Eighty percent (80%) of disabled people in Canada report that they use at least one assistive device, and many use more than one. Those with learning disabilities and mobility disabilities use the most — an average of 3.8% and 2.5% assistive devices per person, respectively.

The use of assistive devices is related to age and severity of disability, with 90% of those over 75 and 95% of those with severe disabilities using at least one assistive device (Statistics Canada, 2012). Assistive devices differ, of course, depending on the nature of the disability and the task performed. Table 7.2 shows the three most common devices used for each category of disability as captured in the 2006 Participation and Activity Limitation Survey (Statistics Canada, 2007). Mobility disabilities are the most common type of disability, and thus wheelchairs, scooters, canes, crutches, and walkers are the most commonly used assistive devices.

Not everyone who needs assistive devices has them, so there are unmet needs here too. The extent to which needs are met differs by category of disability and by severity of disability. On average 61% of disabled people who need assistive devices report that they have them; however, 10% have none of the devices they need, and 29% have only some of the devices they need. While people with mild disabilities are the most likely to have their need for assistive devices met (75.9% vs. 41.3% of people with very severe disabilities), people with very severe disabilities are the least likely to report that they have none of their needs met (6.9% vs. 11.2% for people with mild disabilities).

Table 7.2: Most commonly used assistive devices by type of disability

Type of disability	% of total disabled population	Assistive device	% in category using
Mobility disability	28.7	Cane	71.6
		Walker	33.3
		Manual wheelchair	16.0
Hearing disability	14.2	Hearing aid	79.7
		Volume-control telephone	35.5
		Computer	13.1
Agility disability	8.5	Reacher	54.6
		Grab bars	43.5
		Upper-limb orthotic	31.1
Seeing disability	6.3	Magnifier	91.3
		Large print	42.5
		Talking book	16.7

Source: Statistics Canada, 2007.

Below are the most common reasons for unmet needs for technology:

- the cost to purchase or maintain the device,
- lack of availability in the area,
- not knowing where or how to obtain the device, and
- not qualifying for funding for the device.

In some jurisdictions in Canada, there is financial assistance from the province for the purchase of adaptive equipment; however, the availability, amount, and eligibility for funding differ significantly from one jurisdiction to another (Smith, Roberts, McColl, Martin Ginis, & Miller, 2017). Family is still the main source of payment for assistive devices (70.3%), while public sector funding covers only 12.1% of the reported devices in the survey.

Conclusion

In this chapter, we have attempted to describe some of the characteristics associated with self-care disabilities, as well as the implications they can have for overall functioning. We *appreciate* that additional time taken for self-care cuts into the other activities that the individual wishes to achieve in a given day, and that time affords relatively little in terms of intrinsic satisfaction.

We have *discovered* that a relatively small proportion of people with disabilities experience self-care disabilities in the area of personal care. While dressing, bathing, and toileting may be the activities that come most readily to mind, they are not the ones that present the greatest problems in the area of self-care. Instead, the most troublesome activities are household and community activities — making meals, changing beds, vacuuming, shopping, preparing meals, banking, budgeting, and cutting grass and shovelling snow, to name a few.

We have also *discovered* that assistance is not necessarily readily available to help with these functions. A significant proportion of self-care needs remain unmet, and many are delegated to family members in the absence of disability support services in the community. This may be considered normative in the case of disabled children, but adults do not typically continue to receive assistance with self-care beyond the usual transition at adolescence. For disabled adults, community support services are essential to preserving independence in self-care.

We have explored the concept of personal support workers or attendant care, and we *dream* of a system where the many obstacles and logistical challenges to appropriate and timely attendant care can be overcome. One *design* that offers promise is self-managed attendant care, particularly for those individuals who have the desire and the ability to function as an employer and supervisor in their own care. We have also looked at two non-human options that can be *deployed* to enable or facilitate self-care — adaptive equipment and service animals.

Chapter 8

Independence, autonomy, and capacity

Introduction

Armed with an understanding of the depth and breadth of self-care, and of the scope and magnitude of self-care disability, this chapter explores a concept that is central to the discussion of self-care disability — independence.

Independence literally means freedom from outside control or authority; not supported by or dependent on another; capable of thinking and acting by oneself. Tamaru, McColl, and Yamasaki (2007) refer to five types of independence that are relevant to discussions in the context of disability:

- *Personal or self-care independence:* The ability to perform one's own personal care, such as dressing, bathing, toileting, and mobility without assistance from others.

- *Vocational independence:* The ability to procure and sustain work, and to function without assistance (including close supervision) in the workplace.

- *Economic independence:* The ability to generate sufficient revenue to meet one's needs, and to manage financial resources without assistance or oversight.

- *Social independence:* The ability to function in society without assistance, including relationships with individuals, organizations, and groups. This includes the ability to encounter people, interact with them, and set appropriate limits on interactions.

- *Psychological independence:* The ability to see oneself as a unique self who is valuable, functional, and self-determining.

Independence is usually measured as the extent to which one does or does not require assistance. The International Classification of Functioning Disability and Health (WHO, 2001) rates independence in self-care, as in all activities, in the following categories:

- *No problem* (negligible, none, ...): meaning needing assistance 0% to 4% of the time
- *Mild* (slight, low, ...): 5% to 24% of the time
- *Moderate* (medium, fair, ...): 25% to 49% of the time
- *Severe* (high, extreme, ...): 50% to 95%
- *Extreme* or *Complete* problem (total, ...): 96% to 100% of the time

Gignac and Cott (1998) make a further distinction in the conceptualization of independence, also based on the need for help. Independence occurs when one neither needs nor receives help, and dependence occurs when one both needs and receives help. The state of needing but not receiving help is referred to as being "not independent", and the state of not needing but receiving help is called "imposed dependence" (see Table 8.1).

Table 8.1: Spectrum of independence–dependence

		Receives assistance	
		Yes	No
Needs assistance	Yes	Dependent	Not independent
	No	Imposed dependence	Independent

History of independence

The history of the concept of independence is closely tied to the development of the field of rehabilitation (Stiker, 1999; Reaume, 2012). The field of rehabilitation as we know it today is barely a century old. It arose in response to a number of forces in civil society in the early 20th century — not least of which was the First World War. Rehabilitation developed as a way of repaying the debt of honour owed to injured veterans. Injuries obtained as a consequence of military service needed to be reversed, if possible, or at least mitigated so as to return the injured soldier to his former life. This social imperative shaped a number of institutions in society — not just health care.

War veterans were not the only disabled people who were suddenly attracting the attention of social reformers. Industrialization and automation of production resulted in previously unknown levels of workplace accidents and injuries. Agricultural mechanization similarly produced disabilities. As automobiles became more prevalent, these too led to disabilities. Finally, tuberculosis created a cadre of patients who had lost the ability to be productive and were rendered remote and idle for long periods of time. Consequently, disability came to be understood as a departure from a prior state, and also as a departure from the prevailing norm. The responsibility of rehabilitation was to restore the person to that former or normative state.

Alongside the restoration of the physical condition of the injured veteran was an imperative for social restoration as well — a return to productivity and community. Independence was seen as the precondition to dignity, respect, and meaningful participation, both by others and by people with disabilities themselves. Rehabilitation was tasked with restoring independence so that disabled persons could be fully assimilated in society. The ultimate success of rehabilitation would mean that disabled persons were indistinguishable from the emerging middle class, enjoying the rewards of productivity and prosperity.

Throughout the middle decades of the 20th century, the emerging field of rehabilitation developed a preoccupation with asserting its legitimacy and establishing its rightful place as a medical specialty (Tamaru et al., 2007). The surest way to do this was to demonstrate the effectiveness of rehabilitation using outcome measures. What better outcome to show the value of rehabilitation than independence? If participating in rehabilitation could lead to independence, then the foundations of the field would be validated and its worth affirmed.

A number of outcome measures were developed that are still in wide use today to quantify the extent to which an individual was capable of being independent. A prominent example is the Functional Independence Measure (FIM) — part of the Uniform Data Set for Medical Rehabilitation (UDSMR, 2012). The FIM consists of 18 items each scored from one to seven, with lower values representing greater need for assistance and less independence. Using normative data, FIM scores can actually be calibrated to suggest the number of hours per day of physical assistance needed with basic daily activities (mostly self-care). The proliferation of such measures throughout the 1960s and 1970s led to a commodification of the concept of independence and establishment of its primacy as a driving force in rehabilitation.

By the late 1970s and early 1980s, the civil rights movement that had so definitively shaped the previous decade reached the consciousness of other disenfranchised minorities, such as women, visible minorities, the poor, gay and lesbian groups, and eventually people with disabilities (Driedger, 1989). Labelled the fifth civil rights movement, people with disabilities began to resist the notion that others defined and controlled the conditions of their lives, particularly health professionals and institutions. Instead of being identified by a medical diagnosis, people with disabilities claimed political and social power by insisting that society treat them as consumers, not patients. Their slogan, "Nothing about us without us", encapsulates the impetus to take control of the resources and processes that influenced their lives — a social movement called the independent living movement (DeJong, 1979; Prince, 2009a).

The independent living movement resulted in the development of Independent Living Centres across Canadian and American cities, providing services "by, for and of" people with disabilities (Boyce et al., 2001). The movement was characterized by self-help, advocacy, and peer support, and its main concerns were integration and the removal of barriers. One of the most dramatic examples of programs developed under the independent living flag was supported housing options for severely disabled people, including those with ventilator needs. (For an example, see the Nucleus Housing program in Toronto, Ontario; Reaume, 2007.)

The independent living philosophy was a first step on the road to the social model of disability. Oliver and Barnes (2012) acknowledged the empowering ideal underlying the independent living movement, but they felt that it still focused too heavily on the individual and what he or she was able to achieve. They critiqued it for inflicting the burden of independence on disabled people themselves, and for exposing people with disabilities to the vagaries of market forces. With independence comes the expectation that disabled people will be able to operate in a competitive world, despite not being afforded equal terms. (A fuller discussion of the social model is found in Chapter 2, but its essence lies in the location of disability outside the person — in the social and political realm, and not just in the personal realm.)

Finally, by the early 21st century, there is evidence for a new understanding of independence that is compatible with our relativistic, post-modern view of the world. MacPherson (2006) offers a definition of independence that is not norm-referenced. In other words, he suggests a situational or context-dependent definition of independence that is entirely subjective. He asserts that no one is better positioned to evaluate independence than the individual himself or herself. That evaluation need not be tied to any objective or shared definition of what independent functioning looks like; nor is it tied to the way a person used to do an activity or seeks to do that activity in the future. Rather, it involves the extent to which an individual's way of carrying out an activity is compatible with human dignity and equality of opportunity.

Independence versus autonomy

The idea of independence is deeply rooted in our North American psyches. It is a value that is central to our way of life. We prize our ability to look after ourselves and our own, without depending on others. Leipoldt (2006) characterizes Western society (as we experience it here in North America) as being governed by a number of powerful ideas — all of them related to the over-arching ideal of independence:

- *Individualism:* The valuing of the goals and aspirations of the individual above those of the collective or of the state. Individualism upholds the freedom of individuals to act in their own best interests, and usually involves an explicit opposition to the participation or interference of the state in matters of personal preference.

- *Materialism:* The idea that what is important is the physical world, and not so much ideas or consciousness. Materialism places ultimate value on things and posits that material things, rather than ideas, underlie the social structure.

- *Consumerism:* A social movement aimed at the acquisition and consumption of goods and services. Consumerism is an economic idea that suggests that the will of people is expressed in what they consume.

- *Utilitarianism:* A theory of morality that says that the correct thing to do is that which achieves the most good for the most people. It is a form of moral relativism, in that morality is considered relative to a particular set of circumstances. Utilitarianism stands in opposition to a morality based on principles of absolute right and wrong.

- *Bureaucratization:* The idea that bureaucracies or institutions control much of our lives and that this is necessary for the efficient, orderly operation of society. Bureaucracies tend to be hierarchical, impersonal, and role- or policy-bound.

- *Commercialism:* The idea that free enterprise, capitalism, and an open market are the best ways to ensure prosperity and productivity. Commercialism literally means that value is based on the ability to generate revenue.

- *Competitiveness:* Valuing competitiveness begins by acknowledging that people living together in a society must sometimes act in opposition to one another in order to secure scarce resources. In a competitive society, the strongest thrive, and it is tacitly accepted that the weak will perish.

- *Self-sufficiency:* This term can refer to individuals or systems, and it means that the circumscribed person or group is capable of survival without any input from outside itself. It can supply all its own needs without having to depend on external resources. Although this is mostly an ideal rather than a reality, in North America it is a highly prized ambition — to be self-sufficient.

One can readily see from this list that North American society can be a difficult place to be a person with a disability. Donchin (2000) asserts that it can also be a difficult place to be a woman or a member of virtually any disadvantaged group. As Leipoldt (2006) describes it, North American society favours the strong, the quick, the wealthy, and the sophisticated.

Donchin (2000) recommends that instead of focusing on independence, we think about autonomy. Autonomy, she posits, is relational and collaborative. It is relational in that it acknowledges the social nature of human beings and the fact that human societies are organized on principles of reciprocity and connection. It is collaborative in that it acknowledges the power of each person to contribute to the extent that he or she is able.

Autonomy is defined as the capacity to be self-governing; to make informed decisions without the involvement of another person or organization. It focuses on decision-making rather than actual doing, and allows for situations where the desired function can be achieved by directing another to act in one's place. An example in the disability area is where an attendant or personal support worker performs self-care functions under the supervision of someone with a significant impairment. To the extent that the attendant adheres to the direction of the individual with a disability, and performs the task as he or she is asked to do, the individual can still experience autonomy, even though strictly speaking he or she is incapable of being independent.

Tamaru, McColl, and Yamasaki (2007) performed a qualitative exploration of the concepts of independence and autonomy among people in rehabilitation. They discovered that independence was a relatively concrete concept, made up of particular competencies and skills — the ability to live alone, to return home and resume one's prior life, to be safe, to require relatively minor amounts of help, and to use equipment to augment independence.

Autonomy, on the other hand, was a much more complex construct, made up of the more subtle qualities of self-governance and self-realization.

- Self-governance included the freedom to act on the basis of one's own free will, to assert oneself, to claim needs and act positively to obtain necessities, and also to decline activities and participation.

- Self-realization included shaping one's own life, expressing individuality, acting authentically in concert with one's values, accepting one's disability and overcoming feelings of shame or inferiority, accepting one's own reality with a degree of maturity, and having affirming feelings about one's own life.

Tamaru et al. (2007) identified a psychological profile compatible with autonomy that included

- taking initiative, doing as much as possible given one's limitations, making an effort, and being fully engaged, even enthusiastic and committed to life;
- being deliberate, decisive, and responsible in one's actions; and
- having a sense of control over one's destiny, the perception that one was able to accomplish what was necessary in life.

Other important ideas

In addition to independence and autonomy, there are several other ideas that have been introduced by various authors to help us to approach this dominant idea of independence, and as Oliver and Barnes put it (2012), to free disabled people from the tyranny of independence.

Free will

In the discussion of autonomy, the idea of exercising free will has been mentioned by several authors. Free will is one of the qualities that makes us human. **Free will** refers to the ability to choose one's own destiny, and to act in ways that are compatible with our beliefs, requirements, and values. To limit the free will of another is to compromise his or her autonomy, and ultimately to dominate or oppress the other.

Autonomy and the exercise of free will is the foremost governing principle in most systems of morality. Upholding the other person's autonomy is an acknowledgement of his or her humanity, and it is the basis for moral or ethical behaviour toward others. Behaving ethically toward others consists of four qualities:

1. *Autonomy:* Honouring the rights of others to make their own decisions;
2. *Beneficence:* Acting in the best interests of the other;
3. *Non-maleficence:* Doing no harm; and
4. *Justice:* Treating others fairly, according to a consistent code.

Choice

For people with disabilities, Rabiee and Glendenning (2010) identify seven areas of life where choice is important:

- *Health care:* What treatments to accept, by whom, and when;
- *Equipment: What adaptive aids are compatible with one's lifestyle, finances, and self-image;*
- *Housing:* Where to live, with whom, and with what level of support;
- *Education:* What level of education is needed for one's life aspirations, and whether integrated or specialized education is more suitable;
- *Personal care:* What functions require help, by whom, where, and when;
- *Employment:* What level of employment one aspires to, and what accommodations are needed; and
- *Leisure:* What interests one wishes to pursue.

Choice involves a process of identifying options and selecting among them. According to Rabiee and Glendenning (2010), choice depends on having alternatives, having information about those alternatives, anticipating the consequences of different options, balancing short- and long-term consequences, being able to process information analytically, and having the level of support/resources needed to make specific options possible.

In health care and social services, we are often called upon to offer choices to clients and to participate in decisions. Our utmost ethical duty in so doing is to ensure that we do nothing to violate the autonomy of our clients. By upholding their right to make decisions for themselves, we acknowledge their humanity and their dignity, even if we don't always agree with their choices.

Risk

For service providers, the principle of autonomy is tested when clients make choices that we disagree with, or that we think are not in their best interests — perhaps something dangerous or risky. Imagine a client with a cognitive impairment due to a brain injury who wants to manage his own bank account and finances, or a young woman with a developmental disability who wants to socialize unaccompanied in bars with the aim of finding a boyfriend. In these situations, the autonomy principle appears to come into conflict with our professional responsibility to preserve our client's safety. We feel that we are not acting in the person's best interests if we do not prevent them from doing something that we feel has **risk**: a high probability of working out badly for them. And yet, this protective instinct is often interpreted by clients as patronizing and paternalistic.

From a legal rather than an ethical perspective, professionals have a "duty of care" — that is, an obligation to adhere to a reasonable standard of practice. That reasonable standard includes safeguarding the welfare of clients. Professionals often feel that they are violating the duty of care if they permit their client to undertake potentially dangerous behaviour. And yet, opposing that duty of care is the idea of "**dignity of risk**", or the right to be self-determining with regard to potentially risky behaviour. Being permitted to make one's own determination of what is or is not within the bounds of reasonable risk is essential for the integrity of the individual. Foreclosing on the client's choice in making such decisions runs the risk of compromising dignity and autonomy.

Rock (1988) identifies five factors that are essential for independence, whether we are talking about people with disabilities acquiring new skills, young people learning to function on their own, or anyone entering a new situation. The first is risk-taking, or the ability to try things that could fail and have negative consequences. Taking risks and pushing the boundaries is critical for any new learning. The other four factors needed to pursue independence are privacy to try things without an audience, choice about how one wishes to proceed and what the priorities are, organization and control of the parameters of the process, and encouragement to believe in oneself and the possibility of success.

Self-determination

We have mentioned the idea of self-determination in the preceding discussion. Deci and Ryan (1985, 1995) and Ryan and Deci (2000) define **self-determination** as the degree to which an individual's behaviour is self-motivated — that is, guided by three innate, universal needs: competence, autonomy, and relatedness. Competence refers to being able to control outcomes and experience mastery. Autonomy (according to Deci and Ryan) refers to being a causal agent, and acting in harmony with personal integrity. Relatedness refers to connecting with, interacting with, and caring for others.

On the basis of these three qualities, individuals can be situated along a continuum from self-determined to controlled. Motivational interviewing is used to ascertain where the individual falls along the continuum and to assess opportunities for intervention (Patrick &

Williams, 2012). This continuum is anchored by endpoints that sound very much like another important idea — locus of control (Rotter, 1966).

Locus of control

Locus of control refers to the extent to which one believes that one's destiny lies in one's own hands, or in the hands of others. Internal locus of control refers to a situation much like self-determination, where the individual believes that his or her own efforts are the most important factor in determining success or failure. External locus of control means a belief that one's fate lies in the hands of external forces, specifically fate, chance, or powerful others. Internal locus of control is obviously more compatible with independence, but both extremes are somewhat dysfunctional.

Capacity

Another idea from the legal arena is capacity, and it is important in talking about making choices, being autonomous, and exercising free will. Capacity is particularly an issue when an individual experiences a cognitive impairment — for example, when someone has a brain injury, dementia, developmental disability, or mental illness. Every legal jurisdiction has its own specific definition of *capacity*, but in general, **capacity** refers to the ability of individuals to make decisions for themselves (Kerzner, 2006). It usually includes the ability to understand the options, to process information needed in evaluating the options, and to appreciate reasonably foreseeable consequences (Ontario *Substitute Decisions Act, 1992*).

Since the 14th century, the Crown has assumed responsibility to act in the best interests of those who it was judged could not make decisions on their own behalf — a legal principle called *parens patriae*, literally meaning "in place of parents" (Kerzner, 2006). However, since the United Nations (2015) *Universal Declaration of Human Rights* in 1948, the pendulum has swung in favour of individual rights and autonomy. Some of the areas where there is legal concern around decision-making include consenting to health care, managing personal property and finances, making a will, allocating a power of attorney, driving a car, living independently, and even ending one's own life.

When a legitimate finding of incapacity exists, the law typically outlines several options for substitute decision-making. The individual can designate a power of attorney to act as his or her proxy. In the absence of a designated attorney, the court can appoint a guardian or trustee. When no surrogate is designated, especially in the case of health-care decisions, there is an explicit ordering of substitute decision-makers: spouse, adult child, parent, adult sibling, adult grandchild, close friend.

Also under the law, the court can assert that an individual cannot be held responsible for his or her actions due to mental capacity. The *Criminal Code of Canada* allows for a number of considerations when mental capacity is judged to be compromised. An individual may be judged not competent to stand trial, meaning that at the time of trial he or she is unable to adequately participate in his or her own defence. Alternatively, an individual may be judged to have been not competent at the time a crime was committed or a contract was entered into. This assessment frees the individual from responsibility for the crime or other breach, but does not liberate him or her from legal consequences.

This extremely complex area cannot be covered here with any degree of thoroughness, but it is important for those working in health and social services to have some awareness of the potential for a legal judgment of non-competence, thereby officially limiting an individual's autonomy. Some options for resources in your jurisdiction might be

- the government website in your province or state,
- advocacy and legal aid organizations in your region, and
- professional regulatory bodies governing the conduct of professionals.

Conclusion

This chapter has grappled with the very pervasive but troublesome issue of independence. In it, we have defined *independence* as a somewhat concrete idea — one closely related to competence and typically norm-referenced in terms of expectations of adults in Western society. In contrast, we have offered the idea of autonomy as an alternative to independence. We have *discovered* that autonomy is the ability to assume agency and responsibility for one's own life and decisions, even in the absence of the explicit ability to perform certain tasks or functions. Autonomy is an expression of choice and free will, and an essential aspect of self-determination. Upholding autonomy is the foremost ethical principle in human relation-ships — a component of basic human dignity.

The chapter also introduced several legal ideas — the idea of legal capacity, guardianship, substitute decision-making, duty of care, and dignity of risk. These ideas often have particular meanings in different jurisdictions, and may be important for health and social services professionals to understand.

Leipoldt (2006) encourages us to reconsider the notion of inde-pendence, and to instead *dream* of interdependence. He invites us to ask ourselves if any of us is really independent, or if independence is an illusion. Who among us could really survive, let alone flourish, without any support or assistance from anyone? And even if we could, what sort of life would that be?

As we *design* and *deploy* services to people with disabilities, these questions are particularly meaningful. They bring us face to face with hard choices about how we as individuals and as a society expend resources. These resources could include the personal resources of time and energy — should they be spent to independ-ently complete rather pedestrian tasks like dressing or toileting? Is it possible to accept a degree of dependence and let someone else help with those tasks in order to save energy for more important func-tions like spending time with valued others? What are the costs of accepting that increment of dependency — personal, interpersonal, financial? What is the cost of not accepting it?

Chapter 9

Health care and health maintenance

Introduction

What do we mean by **health**, and where do we draw a line between health and disability? The classical definition of *health*, and the one that most people would cite if asked, is that it means freedom from illness or injury. In 1948, the World Health Organization advanced the definition that "Health is a state of complete physical, mental and social well-being, and not merely the absence of disease or infirmity" (WHO, 1948). A more modern definition of *health* comes from the *Ottawa Charter for Health Promotion* (WHO, 1986): "Good health is a major resource for social, economic and personal development and an important dimension of quality of life." This definition situates health as a resource for living. Like other resources, it is presumably expendable, in limited supply, and has both intrinsic value and also value in terms of the things it permits one to do.

Maintaining one's health is a critical aspect of self-care, and arguably even more important for people who live with disabilities. While we all recognize that our health is one of the most valuable resources we have, for people with disabilities, health is even more important as a resource for everyday life.

The health of people with disabilities

People with disabilities experience what DeJong et al. (2002) refer to as "a thinner margin of health" (p. 267). While they are not ill

119

(necessarily), if they become ill, the consequences are potentially greater and may even persist after the illness is resolved. People with disabilities often cannot afford to lose a further increment of functioning due to illness, because of the impact on their overall independence. Imagine someone already struggling with fatigue due to a progressive neuromuscular condition. Something as simple as getting the flu could have significant consequences for his or her ability to work, maintain routines, or participate in relationships. Even a brief period of bed rest may have significant long-term effects in terms of de-conditioning, skin integrity, and assistance required.

Health maintenance is typically thought of as a series of four levels of prevention (summarized in Table 9.1):

- Primary prevention refers to those services and programs that target the whole population and try to prevent them from exposure to risks known to impact health.

Table 9.1: Health maintenance — the four levels of prevention

Level of prevention	Targets ...	Goal to prevent ...	Examples
Primary	... the entire population	... exposure to risk factors	immunization, fitness/exercise, water treatment, screening, stress management
Secondary	... those at risk	... illness	smoking cessation, weight loss, cholesterol management
Tertiary	... those who are ill or injured	... disability	acute treatment, emergency intervention, pharmacological & surgical interventions
Quaternary	... those who are disabled	... social disadvantage	rehabilitation, social programs, community resources

- Secondary prevention targets those already at risk, and tries to prevent them from becoming ill.
- Tertiary prevention targets those already diagnosed with a particular condition, and tries to prevent them from being impeded in their daily activities by their health condition.
- Quaternary prevention targets those who already have a disability, and tries to prevent the disability from resulting in social disadvantage, marginalization, or inequity.

Health maintenance is challenging for people with disabilities for a number of reasons (DeJong, Palsbo, Beatty, Jones, Kroll, & Neri, 2002):

- People with disabilities often don't have the same opportunities for health maintenance and prevention as non-disabled people, such as physical activity.
- The balance of their health can be more fragile and easily disturbed.
- Due to the multi-factorial nature of disability, people with disabilities are often managing more than one health condition.
- People with disabilities may be taking numerous medications, each with side effects and complications.
- People with disabilities tend to experience earlier onset of chronic conditions associated with aging, such as cardiac and arthritic changes.
- Functional consequences of illness or injury are more significant, such as bed rest, wound healing, or chest congestion.
- Disability may cause illness to be prolonged and complicated, and treatment of illness or injury may be more complex.
- There are often multiple providers and agencies involved, with greater need for communication and coordination.

People with disabilities experience the typical health concerns for their age, gender, and background — issues like infectious diseases, degenerative conditions, environmental exposures, and pathological processes. However, they may also experience issues directly related to their disability (McColl, Arnold, Charlifue, Glass, Savic, & Frankel, 2003):

- issues related to the underlying health condition with which their disability is associated,

- secondary complications of the disability, and
- administrative and system issues associated with disability.

For example, an individual with a visual disability associated with diabetes may also experience secondary complications of long-standing diabetes, such as peripheral neuropathies, skin ulcers, cardiac issues, or even amputation. Furthermore, they may need assistance claiming insurance benefits to cover equipment, supplies, and aids. They may need physician confirmation of their disability in order to access pension and tax benefits. In any given year, the person with a disability might need any of the following categories of health maintenance and health care:

- age and gender-related screening for chronic diseases;
- standard disease prevention, monitoring, and immunizations;
- treatment for normal infectious and acute conditions;
- health promotion and lifestyle interventions;
- monitoring of disability status;
- monitoring and treatment of secondary conditions (e.g., overuse syndromes, fatigue, injuries, bowel, bladder, skin conditions);
- social and mental health issues;
- eligibility for disability benefits, such as pensions, tax credits, insurance claims, other social and welfare benefits;
- caregiver issues and relief; and
- referral to specialists, diagnostics, and institutional services.

We have referred several times to the issue of aging with a disability, and the potential for complications that accrue through a lifetime with disability. Many disabilities have fairly predictable secondary conditions that arise over time. For example, a number of neurological and mental health conditions have predictable physical, cognitive, and personality changes associated with aging. Wheelchair users experience common conditions like shoulder damage, back/neck pain, and skin breakdowns — all secondary complications related to paralysis. People with disabilities seem to fall into three groups as they grow older (McColl, Shortt, Gignac, & Lam, 2011):

- those who appear to be aging earlier than their non-disabled contemporaries, because of early onset of degenerative, sensory, or pathological processes;

- those who appear to be aging with more difficulty because of the layering on of multiple complex conditions. This group is sometimes referred to as experiencing double jeopardy, because those multiple conditions have not just an additive but a multiplicative effect when they occur simultaneously; and

- those for whom the experience of aging is attenuated; in fact, aging brings them more in line with their contemporaries. This is referred to as the age-as-leveller effect, since non-disabled people begin to acquire the disabilities that disabled people have lived with for some time — sensory changes, musculoskeletal changes, organ system changes. Thus, the experience of disability becomes more normative as the entire cohort ages.

Utilization of health services

The literature shows unequivocally that people with disabilities are high users of health services of all types. Using population-based data for Canada, our research showed that people with disabilities used the following two to three times more than their non-disabled contemporaries: primary care, hospital care, specialist care, allied health services, home care, attendant care, and alternative/ complementary care (McColl & Shortt, 2006). Self-rated health (excellent, good, fair, poor) was the only factor that was more important than disability in predicting who would use health services (McColl, 2005). The impairments that were most predictive of health service use were pain (37.8%), cognitive problems (29.4%), emotional problems (9.7%), and mobility impairments (7.5%). With each additional chronic condition, a 50% increase in utilization was seen.

Despite this excess utilization, three times as many people with disabilities reported unmet needs as the non-disabled cohort — 17.5% of disabled people reported an unmet need in the past year compared to 5.2% in the general population. In particular, people with disabilities were significantly more likely than non-disabled people to report an unmet need for emotional or mental problems (15.1% vs. 9.5%).

Unfortunately, those with the most severe needs also experienced the greatest number of unmet health needs (McColl, Jarzynowska, & Shortt, 2010). Even after controlling for the effects of health and chronic disease, disability still represents a significant source of health need (McColl et al., 2011). With restrictions in most family practices on the number of issues that can be raised in a single appointment (usually between one and three), it can readily be seen how the number of annual visits would exceed the average, and how people with disabilities might leave the office feeling that their needs had not been met.

The main reason for unmet needs among disabled respondents was cost — a surprising finding in Canada, where health care is meant to be free from economic barriers. Direct costs for health care were three times greater among disabled vs. non-disabled Canadians (McColl et al., 2011). These included costs for transportation, parking, attendant care, insurance, prescription co-payments, administrative services, and expendable supplies that are not insured (Godfrey et al., 2011). Given that disabled people are among the most economically disadvantaged in the country, costs that to others might be inconsequential can be impossible to overcome for some.

Access to health services

Access to health care is a key determinant of successful health maintenance for people with disabilities. Access to health care has become a highly politicized issue, and the term *access* is used very broadly. When the popular press refers to access issues, it typically means impediments caused by wait times, geographic maldistribution, and under-supply of health human resources (especially physicians). These issues affect access for disabled and non-disabled people alike; however, there are also other issues that impede, or even prevent, access to health services for people with disabilities (McColl et al., 2008).

Access to any health services can be impeded at three points in attempting to secure service (McColl, 2005; McColl & Shortt, 2006):

- finding a doctor and getting an appointment;
- getting into the practice and using the facilities, particularly examining, diagnostic, and treatment spaces; and
- receiving a reasonable standard of care.

At each of these junctures, four types of barriers can interfere with access:

- physical barriers, such as door widths, stairs, manoeuvring room, signage;

Table 9.2: Places where access can be impeded for disabled patients

	Physical barriers	Attitudinal barriers	Informational barriers	Systemic barriers
Finding a doctor				
Getting in				
Receiving care				

- attitudinal barriers, such as unwillingness to provide needed services or make accommodations for people with disabilities;
- informational barriers, such as lack of knowledge of disability-related considerations, complications, and resources; and
- systemic barriers, such as inadequate provisions for disability in health system planning and implementation.

The matrix in Table 9.2 shows the many different places where access can be impeded for disabled patients. The following discussion details the barriers that arise at each interface.

Finding a doctor and getting an appointment

Primary care is the sector of the health care system that tends to be our first contact. Primary care is located in the community (rather than in institutions), and patients usually have a long-standing relationship with a doctor, nurse practitioner, or other health-care professional or staff (McColl & Dickenson, 2009). As mentioned above, over 90% of Canadians have a relationship with a primary care setting, and the same is true for people with disabilities. Good access to primary care has been shown to be the key to a healthy population and to efficient use of the health services and resources (Starfield, 1997).

Physician shortages have been an issue in many communities, and the press has reported difficulties finding a family doctor. Our research shows that people with disabilities are as likely as those without to have a family doctor and to be able to get an appointment (McColl, Aiken, & Schaub, 2015). We surveyed a provincial program in Ontario tasked with helping people to find a doctor in their area, and found that disabled people were slightly more successful in finding a doctor once registered with the program, and waited the same amount of time for a successful match (approximately 65 days). Program staff, however, revealed that *attitudinal and systemic barriers* made it more difficult to link disabled patients with a doctor. Physicians were often reluctant to accept new patients if they had a disability, particularly a disability associated with pain or mental illness (McColl, Aiken, & Schaub, 2015).

Attitudinal barriers: People with disabilities constitute a small subset of the typical primary care caseload (Wallace and Seidman, 2006), and yet they can consume a disproportionately large share of the practice's resources. Although only about 6% of the average caseload have complex chronic conditions and disabilities, they consume about 33% of primary care resources (Wallace & Seidman, 2006; Rosen, 2007). With an average primary care caseload of 1000 to 1500 patients, this means that 60 to 90 patients consume fully a third of the practice's time and resources — about the same amount as the 700 to 1100 (72%) patients who have no chronic conditions. The top 6% require intensive management, including a high degree of coordination among multiple providers and agencies, in addition to frequent contact, coaching, and support. This level of service may be intermittent, but when a health problem arises, it is typically complicated. (See Figure 9.1.)

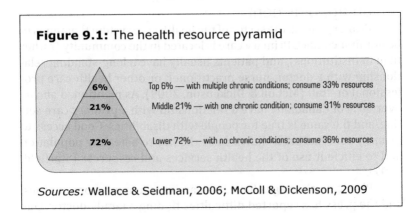

Figure 9.1: The health resource pyramid

6% Top 6% — with multiple chronic conditions; consume 33% resources

21% Middle 21% — with one chronic condition; consume 31% resources

72% Lower 72% — with no chronic conditions; consume 36% resources

Sources: Wallace & Seidman, 2006; McColl & Dickenson, 2009

When asked about their experiences serving patients with disabilities, the most common theme raised by family doctors was that they took more time than their non-disabled patients. For people with physical disabilities, slower movements, more time to get around, the necessity to move furniture, difficulties with dressing/undressing, and positioning to be examined all contributed to requiring more time. For those with mental or cognitive disabilities, memory and comprehension issues sometimes required additional time. Communication difficulties — either hearing, comprehension, or expression — could also take time. Physicians pointed out that they were not compensated for any additional time taken to accommodate the needs of individual patients (McColl et al., 2008).

Systemic barriers: Taking more time is incompatible with the financial incentives inherent in the compensation system for physicians, and patients who consistently require more than the standard 10- to 15-minute appointment represent an economic liability. Volume-driven compensation systems, whether fee-for-service or capitation, have been shown to lead to a practice known as cream-skimming or cherry-picking — that is, deliberately selecting patients based on a cost-benefit analysis, systematically excluding those most likely to represent a financial burden on the practice (Barros, 2003). Thus "the very patients who are most likely to benefit [from health care] ... are least likely to be welcomed into a practice" (Kasperski & Ontario College of Family Physicians, 2005).

In our health-care system currently, health professionals are granted the privilege of autonomous self-governance, including structuring their practice in whatever way they see fit. Professionals are trusted to uphold a high standard of professional ethics and to put patient care ahead of their own personal gain. Strictly speaking, it would be possible for a physician to construct his or her practice in such a way as to exclude patients with disabilities. They could simply say that they hadn't the expertise or other practice qualities or configuration to serve a particular patient, and thereby exclude someone with a disability.

The current system of physician compensation has been called "perverse" since it renders the most needy patients the least attractive to a prospective provider (Chisholm & Stewart, 1998). Medical professional associations are well aware of the practice of differential selection of patients, and in recent years has gone on record against profit maximization at the expense of patient equity (Kasperski & Ontario College of Family Physicians, 2005; Canadian Medical Association, 2004). Limiting access to medical services on the basis of disability is an explicit violation of human rights. Further, it undermines the public trust in the health-care system. It also tends to exert an undue burden on physicians who *do* take all comers — often younger physicians seeking to set up a practice. Although complaints have been brought against individual physicians who have refused to accept a disabled patient, this form of discrimination is subtle, and a systemic response to this issue has not been advanced. Provincial governments and medical associations say that they trust physicians to manage their practices equitably, and they have not made explicit requirements.

The only payment model that overcomes this disincentive is the salary model. Currently only about 10% of physicians choose to be paid this way, and there is no inducement to encourage physicians to choose this payment option. It has been shown, however, to result in better care for disabled patients in primary care. Using a chart review method, our research showed that the quality of care for selected complaints (e.g., hypertension, urinary tract infections, diabetes) and for preventive health care among people with disabilities was significantly worse when physicians were paid by capitation or fee-for-service than it was for physicians paid by salary (McColl et al., 2010).

On the other side of this issue, our research with family physicians shows that many go to extraordinary lengths to serve their patients with disabilities — visiting them in their homes, seeing them outside of office hours, having telephone visits with them, and renewing prescriptions and ordering tests over the phone. One family doctor reported that she routinely saw her patient in his car to save him the inconvenience of transferring and coming up to the office (McColl et al., 2008).

Although many primary care settings now run after-hours clinics or provide 24-hour on-call services, many people with disabilities use the emergency room of a hospital as their first point of contact. Its advantages are that it is reliably accessible, it usually has accessible parking and reasonable public transportation, and it is a one-stop venue where prescriptions can be filled and diagnostics/imaging can be done all in one location if needed. The research shows that people with disabilities use emergency rooms at a greater rate than the general population, often as a source of primary care (Knott, 2013; Guilcher et al., 2013).

While this setting is the ideal location for casualties or potentially life-threatening situations, it is not the best venue for primary care for people with disabilities. For people with complex conditions, there is little attention to complexity or co-incident issues. The goal in the emergency department is to treat the presenting urgent condition, and get the person back out as promptly and efficiently as possible. Thus for someone with a long story to tell or a multi-faceted problem, there is little opportunity for the full picture to emerge and a comprehensive, sustainable plan to be developed. Furthermore there may be little understanding or knowledge about disability — how to assist, how to transfer, and the need for special vigilance for particular issues, like skin care, bowel and bladder management, and positioning. The culture in the emergency room is at the opposite end of the spectrum from the culture of rehabilitation or social services for people with disabilities. With its focus on acute care, it is entirely at odds with good disability self-management and health care.

For people with disabilities, specialist care is another important aspect of health care. Specialists may be rehabilitation doctors (or physiatrists), or they may be neurologists, urologists, surgeons, dermatologists, rheumatologists, psychiatrists, internal medicine specialists, or any number of other experts. Because of the complexity of their conditions, many people with disabilities have more than one specialist with whom they interact at least annually. Our research with people with spinal cord injuries showed that 97% had a family doctor, 58% had a rehabilitation specialist or physiatrist, and 56% had both a family doctor and a rehabilitation specialist. Many had also made additional visits to specialists in the preceding year (Donnelly et al., 2007; Smith, McColl, Aiken, & McColl, 2014).

The challenge for people with disabilities is to be the "quarterback" of the health-care team — to know what kinds of problems to take to which doctor, to know what information that doctor will need, to coordinate communication among the health professionals, to make sure they all have information about what each one is doing, and to confirm that treatments from one don't conflict with those from another. In an ideal world, especially with the state of electronic communication, all of the necessary information would be exchanged automatically; in our less-than-perfect world, however, people with disabilities must play an active role in managing multiple health-care providers and ensuring that they all know what each other is doing. This requires highly effective communication skills and health literacy, supreme diplomacy and tact, and a significant degree of knowledge about how the system works. It also requires relationships with providers that are respectful of this role that individuals must play, and of the knowledge of the patient about his or her own condition and experience with disability.

Donnelly and colleagues (2007) show that people with disabilities develop complex rubrics for navigating their personal health-care systems.

Entering and using the facilities

Being able to enter the building, access the reception area, manoeuvre in the exam room, and use the examining table and other equipment is the second interface where access to health care may be impeded for people with disabilities. Access at this level is constrained by physical, attitudinal, and informational barriers.

Physical barriers: The most straight-forward reason for difficulties with access to health services is physical barriers — stairs, narrow doorways, obstacles, cramped spaces, clutter, and inaccessible counters, racks, shelves, surfaces, and tables. These are arguably also the easiest to remedy, and yet they remain a significant problem. As surprising as it may seem, many health-care settings are unaware of what to do to make their practices and processes more accessible to people with disabilities (McColl et al., 2008; Sullivan et al., 2011). Only half of doctors in a Canadian survey were compliant with guidelines for universal access (Jones & Tamari, 1997), and only 15% of practices had an accessible examining room with an exam table that would accommodate someone with a mobility disability (McColl et al., 2010).

Patients and physicians don't always agree about accessibility. Twice as many physicians as patients reported that their offices were accessible; a third of patients were unsatisfied with the accessibility of their physician's office (Shankardass, 2003). Despite receiving the majority of their operating budgets from public funds, physicians' offices have historically been classified as private sector premises, and have thus not been subject to the accessibility requirements of the public sector. Physical barriers not only delay or inconvenience attempts at access, but they can actually prevent it. These barriers send a further message that the practice may be inaccessible in more subtle ways.

Attitudinal barriers: Attitudinal barriers to accessing health-care facilities and equipment typically take the form of unwillingness to provide needed equipment or to accommodate atypical ways of doing things. As we have said before, some physicians went to extraordinary lengths to accommodate their disabled patients, but others quite simply stated that it was not their job to assist with transfers, dressing and undressing, or communication issues. Nor did they feel it was their job to ensure there was anyone in the practice who could assist. Rather, they felt that it was patients' responsibility to find their own ways to overcome access issues, such as bringing someone with them to fulfil all of these support and access functions (McColl et al., 2008).

Informational barriers: Knowledge barriers also keep disabled people from accessing health care. While physicians are clearly experts in health care, they themselves confess that they need more information about disability in order to treat their disabled patients optimally (McColl et al., 2008). The literature shows that physicians have relatively little exposure to disability in medical school (Claxton, 1994; Burge, Ouelette-Kuntz, Issacs, & Lunsky, 2008) and virtually no training in how to relate to or assist someone with a disability (McColl et al., 2008; Ruddock, McColl, Benecki, & Wilson, 2007). They are unaware of the correct manner to relate to disabled patients, and they face not only personal discomfort but also potential professional liability if an incident occurs, such as a fall.

In response to this informational barrier, four strategies have been identified that people with disabilities tend to invoke in order to maximize expertise in primary care (Bowers, Esmond, Lutz, & Jacobson, 2003):

- Some find an agreeable family doctor and for the sake of their good relationship, they endure inadequacies in the medical-technical aspects of care.

- Some become educators about disability for their doctors, and take it as part of their patient role to provide information about the latest developments regarding their own disability to their doctor.

- Some become managers or coordinators of their own care. They develop and manage the network of service providers, each chosen for expertise on certain key complaints or health issues.

- Some become researchers, and substitute their own research for the perceived lack of provider expertise.

The other type of informational barrier that exists for some disabled patients is not being able to receive important health information in a manner that is accessible. For patients who are deaf or hard of hearing, this means having interpreters or amplification devices available. For patients who are visually impaired, it means having signage and information available in large-print, Braille, or other high-contrast formats. For patients with cognitive or emotional issues, it means giving a thought to writing information down so it can be consulted later or shared with caregivers.

Receiving a reasonable standard of care

Research substantiates that people with disabilities often receive an inferior standard of health care. They are not properly assessed, they do not receive guideline-level care, they are overlooked for screening and prevention, and they feel dismissed and disrespected by health professionals (Booth & Kendall, 2007; McColl et al., 2008; Wullink, Veldhuijzen, Lantman-de Valk, Metsemakers, & Dinant, 2009). Thus, even if patients can gain access to the practice, they are at risk of a poorer standard of care, particularly if their doctor operates on a volume-driven compensation system. The literature substantiates this finding, reporting that disabled patients routinely report feeling rushed, dismissed, and devalued by service providers, resulting in a lack of confidence in the process of care (Iezzoni, 2002; Veltman, Stewart, Tardif, & Branigan, 2001). The main barriers against receiving excellent care are attitudinal and informational.

Attitudinal barriers: There are a number of attitudes that have been observed in the health-care system that are incompatible with good health care for people with disabilities. Particularly troubling in this regard is the fact that many providers don't recognize or acknowledge attitudes that may be counterproductive and, in fact, they would be highly resistant to the idea that there is anything wrong in their attitude toward disability (Sanchez et al., 2000; Antonak & Livneh, 2000).

Negative attitudes that have been observed among health professionals can take several forms. The simplest is the view that a person's disability is a bad thing — a negative trait or an abnormality (Office for Disability Issues, 2006; McColl & Bickenbach, 1998; Tervo, Azuma, Palmer, & Redinius, 2002). Even when the intent is benevolent, the view of disability as an undesirable characteristic is an impediment to good health care. To the individual with a disability, it is an inexorable condition of life — in the same category as other traits that they can do nothing to change. No judgment is required about whether it is good or bad.

Another difficult attitude among health professionals is the persistent claim that disability is a form of illness. In fact, there is an important distinction to be made between disability and illness, and it has to do with how we think about a person who is ill.

According to Parsons (1961), when we think about someone who is ill, we attribute to them "the **sick role**". We automatically afford them two freedoms; and in return, we expect two responsibilities:

1. We afford them the freedom from any blame for their illness — the illness is a misfortune that is beyond their control, and they can't be held accountable for it.
2. We afford them freedom from responsibility for normal duties and role functions. We permit someone who is ill a high level of temporary dependency. We don't expect people who are sick to go to work, to make our meals, to participate in social situations, or even to uphold normal standards of social propriety, such as dress or manners.

In return for these two freedoms, we ask of people who are ill only two things:

1. that they try to get better, and
2. that they cooperate with those who are trying to help them, particularly health professionals.

The sick role assumes that illness is temporary, and that normal conditions will be restored in due time.

It should be obvious that this role definition is not going to work when talking about disability. Disability is not illness; it is not usually a temporary condition, and it is not typically expected to go away so that the previous order can be restored. Instead, disability requires people to be in a new kind of relationship with one another. While we do hold disabled people blameless for their condition — usually because it is associated with an underlying illness or injury — we do not exempt them from all social responsibilities, nor would they wish us to. What they want and need from health professionals, and from society in general, is the same thing we all want — to be appreciated for our skills and talents, and for the contributions we can make. While all of us would welcome the opportunity to be dependent when we are ill, a steady state of dependency undermines a person's autonomy, agency, and integrity. It denies the value of the full person. It doesn't work for people with disabilities to live with perpetual dependency.

The other condition of the sick role that doesn't work when talking about disability is the expectation of cooperation with people who are trying to help. This condition assumes that health professionals have more relevant information than their patients, and that their expertise is paramount. That may be a reasonable expectation when one is temporarily ill, but it isn't tenable over the long run. When we are ill, we are usually quite happy to turn over decision-making and responsibility to a benevolent other. But imagine being expected for the rest of your life to accept that others know better than you do about what is best for you, and to be expected to go along with whatever they say. Layer upon that the fact that disability is a highly personal experience that relatively few people share, and fewer still understand. It is clear that this expectation of meek cooperation becomes even more unreasonable. Layer upon that further the many misconceptions about disability that prevail in society, and the disempowering reality of having someone else controlling your destiny. No matter how benevolent the other, it simply doesn't work to be that cooperative for the rest of your life. While illness and disability may (and often do) co-exist, the two call for quite different responses from clinicians (Paris, 1993; Jorgensen, 2005). Illness calls for a curative response, whereas disability calls for a collaborative problem-solving approach.

Misunderstandings and discordant expectations also exist between physicians and disabled patients regarding the patient's overall health, potential for recovery, and even life expectancy (Iezzoni, Davis, Soukup, & O'Day, 2003). Disabled patients expect to be treated as aggressively as anyone else, and expect to recover from new conditions rather than to simply add them to existing conditions. They don't view their health as an inevitable downward trajectory, and have the same expectations as anyone in the population about receiving the best that the health-care system has to offer. In Canada, this is virtually a defining characteristic of our culture — that all citizens are entitled to the highest standards of health care available, regardless of their ability to pay.

Another factor that may interfere with receiving a reasonable standard of care for people with disabilities is attribution. In Chapter 5, we talked about under- and over-attribution, and nowhere is that tendency more prevalent than in health care. Under-attribution refers to failing to take adequate account of the disability, while over-attribution refers to the tendency to attribute everything to the disability, and therefore not explore new complaints as thoroughly as warranted. In the absence of sound knowledge about how the disability affects particular systems or conditions, the professional invokes one of these two response sets. On the one hand, the professional pretends the disability does not exist and simply treats the patient as he or she would any other patient, without regard for the potential complications that may result from the disability (under-attribution). On the other hand, the professional throws up his or her hands and says there is nothing that can be done, and that the patient has to expect to live with a certain amount of symptomatology because he or she is disabled (over-attribution). A similar phenomenon has been reported in literature on health care for elderly people.

Informational barriers: Knowledge about disability and under-lying disabling conditions is one of the most challenging barriers to accessing good quality health care for people with disabilities. Many disabilities are the result of relatively rare conditions, and perhaps only one or two patients in a given practice experience that condition. In addition to specialized, condition-specific knowledge, there are particular issues that are typically not well addressed for people with disabilities, specifically psychological health, sexual and repro-ductive health, lifestyle, and prevention (Donnelly et al., 2007). Issues like depression, anxiety, and substance abuse seldom receive treatment consistent with clinical guidelines, and can significantly reduce quality of life, and even lead to excess mortality (Fann et al., 2011; Findley, Banerjea, & Sambamoorthi, 2011). One frequently overlooked area of care for people with disabilities is the area of sex-ual and reproductive health.

Oshima, Kirschner, Heinemann, and Semik (1998) note that physicians are typically not prepared for the special issues associ-ated with sexuality and disability, or with specific sexual, gynaeco-logical, or obstetric needs.

Figure 9.2 describes two programs offered by Special Olympics Canada aimed at ensuring a reasonable standard of care for disabled individuals.

Conclusion

Maintaining good health is a critical aspect of self-care for people with disabilities — perhaps even more important than for the gen-eral population, because of the many health challenges that can

Figure 9.2: Special Olympics Canada — an example of reasonable standard of care

Healthy Athletes is a program of Special Olympics Canada. Being healthy is more than just being physically active, and the Healthy Athletes program offers free health exams in areas that might need further attention, such as vision care, podiatry, audiology, dentistry, health promotion, sports medicine, and physical therapy. Because of these exams, Special Olympics has become the largest global health organization dedicated to serving people with an intellectual disability.

Healthy Communities is a model program made possible by the Golisano Foundation. The program addresses the severe health disparities faced by people with intellectual disabilities. A Healthy Community is a location officially recognized by Special Olympics for creating year-round access to quality health care. Through partnerships, fitness and wellness programs, dozens of Special Olympics locations throughout the world are paving the way for inclusive health.

Source: http://www.specialolympics.ca/learn/special-olympics-programs/healthy-athletes

accompany disability. In this chapter, we have *discovered* that health maintenance can be seen as a number of different levels of prevention, some of which individuals themselves take responsibility for, and some of which they rely on health professionals for.

We have also *discovered* that people with disabilities are unquestionably high users of the health care system, and yet they report unmet needs at higher levels than most. Accessing the right health professional at the right time is a challenge for people with disabilities. It involves getting to see a doctor or other health professional, using the facilities of the health care setting, and receiving a reasonable standard of care. Each of these access points can be impeded by physical, attitudinal, informational, or systemic barriers.

The literature is unequivocal that one of the best assurances of good health for people with disabilities is having a good relationship with a family doctor. The *design* of health-care programs and systems is based on the assumption that every patient is linked to a family doctor, and that the family doctor acts as the hub for incoming and outgoing information about personal health. Despite the best of intentions, however, family physicians are constrained in terms of the amount of time they can spend on a visit. Particularly for patients who routinely attend with five or six issues (of which perhaps only two or three can be addressed), it is little wonder that complex patients often leave with unmet needs, regardless of the quality of care that is delivered in the standard, brief interaction.

The *dream* for primary care for people with disabilities is to incorporate a team of providers in the primary care setting — individuals such as pharmacists, social workers, and occupational and physical therapists — who have specific expertise about disability. Good access to specialists is also essential, to ensure a high degree of expertise specific to their condition. A multi-disciplinary team is ideal to adequately manage the array of health and social concerns that may arise for people with disabilities in managing their long-term health.

When thinking about how to *deploy* multi-disciplinary services to people with disabilities in the community, six models have emerged in the literature, each with advantages and disadvantages (McColl et al., 2009;): clinic, outreach, self-management, community development, shared care, and case management (McColl & Dickenson, 2009). The key issues in considering these models are the need for structured communication, lines of accountability and responsibility, and methods of compensation.

Chapter 10

Spirituality and disability

Introduction

In Chapter 6, we talked about the fact that self-care included more than simply activities of daily living, like bathing, dressing, and toileting. It also included emotional, cognitive, and, perhaps somewhat surprisingly, spiritual self-care. In this chapter, we explore more fully what is meant by spiritual self-care, and why we might assume that having a disability affects a person spiritually.

Defining *spirituality*

Before proceeding further, we must confront the thorny issue of defining *spirituality*. Sinclair, Pereira, and Raffin (2006) surveyed numerous articles pertaining to spirituality and observed that different authors treated the issue of defining *spirituality* differently:

- Some authors resisted defining *spirituality* altogether, claiming that defies definition because it is so abstract and personal. Instead, they invited readers to invoke their own experiential and intuitive definitions of *spirituality*.

- Some authors defined the word broadly and intentionally ambiguously, leaving room for interpretation by readers. These authors were inclined to say what spirituality is like or what it is related to, but they steered clear of saying what it is. It is like meaning, or connection, or sacredness, but it is impossible to say exactly what it is.

- Other authors attempted a clear and precise definition, recognizing that it may be contrary to what some readers think spirituality is, but at least it allows the reader to know what the author means.

In this chapter, I take the latter approach. I recognize that the definition I offer will leave some readers questioning, but I offer this definition in part to stimulate that thought process and to encourage, rather than to shut down, the debate about what spirituality is.

In proposing a definition, I default to etymology — the study of words and their origins. Etymologically, *spirituality* is a three-part noun:

- The suffix *–ity* means "a state or condition". For example, *solidity* means the state or condition of being a solid; *spirituality* means the state or condition of being spiritual.
- The suffix *–ual* means "of or related to". For example, *sensual* means of or related to the senses; *spiritual* means of or related to the spirit.

The root word *spirit* derives from the Latin *spirare*, meaning "to breathe", or *spiritus*, meaning "breath". Like breath, spirit interacts with living things and creates a bond between living things. Unruh, Versnal, and Kerr (2002) suggest that there are three ways that we typically understand the notion of spirit.

1. *Religious:* Some people understand *spirit* according to the doctrine of a particular religion or faith tradition. Spirit is a force entirely outside of human beings, with a particular name. For example, the three major monotheistic religions (Judaism, Christianity, and Islam) call that force Yahweh, God, or Allah, respectively.

2. *Sacred:* Some see *spirit* as beyond our understanding and beyond the reach of our five senses, but not aligned with a particular institutionalized form of religion. They acknowledge that spirit is eternal, divine, and sacred, but there is no agreed upon way for humans to refer to it.

3. *Secular:* Finally, some people believe that *spirit* is something that humans possess. It exists entirely within human beings, and is explainable according to the science and laws that govern the universe. We may not know how it works yet, but it is within the potential of humans to understand and discover. It is the product of human will, emotion, and intelligence.

One of my favourite explanations of *spirit* uses the metaphor of the Magic Eye puzzles that readers may be familiar with (Peloquin, 1997). These are the puzzles that used to appear in the entertainment section of the newspaper — there is a box filled with various colours and shapes but with no perceptible form. Readers are instructed to bring the picture to the end of their nose and stare at it until their eyes become unfocused. When you slowly move the paper away from your nose, an image appears. However, as soon as you try to focus on the image, it disappears back to its imperceptible form. Spirit is like this, too. If we free our mind and our senses, we can sometimes capture a glimpse of spirit, but as soon as we try to objectify it, to define it or pin it down, it eludes our grasp.

If **spirit** is, as the dictionary defines it, "the force that animates living things", then the most obvious definition of *spirituality* arises when we put all three of the parts back together. *Spirituality* is "a state or condition / of being related to / the force that animates living things". I have tried to smooth that awkward definition out, resulting in the following (McColl, 2011):

> **Spirituality** *is the sensitivity to or desire for the presence of spirit.*

In other words, spirituality is the human capacity for experiences that are beyond what our senses or our intellect can process. It is a quality that permits humans to experience connections with others and with unseen forces that cannot be quantified or measured.

Spiritual themes associated with disability

Spirituality is a part of the condition of being human. From the beginnings of human history, we have been fascinated by a layer of existence that is beyond the grasp of our intellect and our senses.

Humans have always venerated invisible powers that they felt were responsible for the world unfolding as it does. Our unique ability to reflect on our own existence leads us to ask questions, like "Why are we here?", "Who's in charge of how things happen?", and "What happens when I am no longer here?" The fear of death and the unknown is at the root of much of humans' seeking for answers that lie in the spiritual realm.

People with disabilities have been shown in many cases to have an even more profound experience of spirituality. Kim, Heinemann, Bode, Sliva, and King (2000) offer the following observations:

- Approximately one-third of people with disabilities experience a spiritual epiphany. As a result of their disability, they are awakened to their spirituality, are more inclined to seek answers to spiritual questions, and more certain that the disability has spiritual meaning.

- One-third of disabled people experience disability as a spiritual crisis. They experience a loss of faith and a sense of alienation from their spiritual core.

- The remaining one-third see no particular relationship between the disability and their spirituality, and are disinclined to interpret the disability in any spiritual way.

As health and social service professionals, it is not essential that we be equipped to have spiritual conversations with the people we serve, but it is important that we are able to recognize when spiritual issues are present. For clients or patients who are dealing with a profound existential challenge, other issues may seem trivial. They may be unable to engage in any other part of therapy or treatment until the existential or spiritual crisis is addressed.

Here are some examples of the kinds of questions that arise for people in the midst of a spiritual crisis (Cunningham, 2000; Curlin, 2008; Stienstra & Ashcroft, 2010):

- Why did this happen to me?
- What does it mean to be human? Am I still human?
- What does this mean for my relationship with God?
- Is there meaning in suffering?
- How is a single life valued?
- To whom does my life belong?

- When does life begin and end?
- Should I fight this or accept it as my destiny?
- How are people connected to each other? Responsible for each other?
- How does this affect others in my life?

The following discussion is offered to equip us with ideas, words, and themes that can alert us to the fact that our client or patient may be asking for understanding.

Finding meaning with disability

Eiesland (1994) says that the search for meaning in the face of disability leads many people to conclude that they have a unique relationship with their spirituality, and also with the world and with a higher power. She proposes that there are six ways that people with disabilities find meaning in the experience of disability through spirituality. A review of the literature shows that similar themes arise in research on meaning attributed to illness, pain, and suffering (McColl, 2011).

1. *Disability as an expression of the will of a higher power:* One of the most common meanings attributed to disability, according the literature, is the idea that disability can be interpreted as an expression of the power of a divine or supreme will. Disability is a reminder that there is a power governing the universe that is greater than humans. There is no way for humans to understand why things happen. The only role for humans is to submit. This explanation goes hand in hand with a belief that a supreme power participates in everyday life on Earth and has a direct hand in what does and doesn't happen. This belief is at odds with most contemporary theology, as it undermines human autonomy and agency. It is also certainly at odds with the increasingly secular nature of contemporary society.

2. *Disability as punishment for sin:* A second theme in the search for meaning in disability is the idea that disability is somehow a punishment for sin — either a sin of omission, a sin of commission, or simply a lack of faith. Looking at it logically, the idea that a deity is keeping a report card on each person seems archaic, superstitious, and illogical. And yet, it contin-

ues to be invoked as a way of describing the relationship between spirituality and disability. Even people with no professed religious belief will express the idea that the disability occurred because of something (unrelated to any actual cause or pathology) that they did or didn't do. This interpretation casts disability not as the incomprehensible will of a supreme power, but rather as a deliberate moral judgment and punishment. This attribution suggests an egotistical, vengeful deity that would intentionally cause human suffering as a way of satisfying its own agenda.

3. *Disability as a reminder of embodiment:* A third theme found in the literature on disability and meaning is the idea that disability is a reminder of the fragility of human beings, the transience of our experience on Earth, and the ultimate mortality of humans. This view reinforces the duality of mind/body and spirit. Disability occurs only in the mind or body, and not in the spirit. It distances people from the material dimension of their lives (the mind and body), objectifies their corporal experience, and undermines the connection between body and spirit. It sends the embodied self to the background, and may even lead people to despise their embodiment and to fail to care for the body or mind.

4. *Disability as an opportunity for redemption:* The fourth way of finding meaning in disability is to view the disability as a test, or an opportunity to prove one's worthiness. Life with a disability is a burden to be borne stoically and virtuously, as an indication of one's moral superiority and fitness for ultimate reward. According to this view, individuals are meant to embrace their circumstances, and to consider them a means to a higher purpose. Many religious traditions offer models of sacrifice and martyrdom, where individuals are ultimately redeemed by their faith, and rewarded for past suffering with eternal life. This approach to understanding what it means to live with a disability denies the complexity and full humanity of people with disabilities. It suggests only one way of being — the path of meekness and forbearance. It denies the essential struggle — what Barnard (1995) refers to as the "existential paradox" — the tension between resistance and acceptance, between struggling mightily to have a full life and accepting that some limitations cannot be overcome.

5. *Disability as mission:* The fifth way of finding meaning in the experience of disability is to portray it as an opportunity for mission — either by others toward people with disabilities, or by people with disabilities toward others. Either way, the purpose in life with a disability is found either by giving or receiving charity. According to this view, any prior designs on a career or life path should be abandoned, because the disability has rendered these plans obsolete. The new path is one of mission and service, of doing for others, or of accepting the good works of others. Virtually every faith has a tradition of service, but only a few adherents devote their lives entirely to service. This way of finding meaning in disability situates people with disabilities among those virtuous few, or as the charitable recipients of their efforts.

6. *Disability as a condition of life:* The final theme expressed by Eiesland (1994) is a reaction to the preceding five. According to her view, the most constructive approach to finding meaning in disability is to strip away all the metaphors and images and to view disability simply as a condition of life. It is neither positive nor negative. It offers neither an advantage nor a disadvantage — it simply is. While Eiesland acknowledges the oppression and alienation that people with disabilities have experienced both currently and historically, and the challenges and difficulties they struggle with every day, she also notes that disability can offer a unique perspective on the world that can be duly valued. She suggests considering a person's ability or disability in the same category that we would consider their age, their sex, the colour of their hair, or any of the other conditions of life that individuals can do nothing about. This emotional neutrality permits people with disabilities the freedom and latitude to have the kind of life they construct, rather than a culturally pre-determined path.

Talking about spiritual themes with people with disabilities

Several years ago now, I was fortunate to work with an interdisciplinary group looking at how people who acquired a sudden-onset disability thought about spirituality (McColl, Bickenbach, Johnston, Nishihama et al., 2000; McColl, Bickenbach, Johnston, Schumaker et al., 2000). We asked 18 people who had acquired a brain injury or a spinal cord injury in the past two years to tell us what they thought had happened to their spirit when their body or their brain had become disabled. Many of them described themselves as "not a religious person". They very often prefaced their responses with qualifiers like, "I'm not sure how to say this", or "I hadn't really thought about that before". And yet, their responses to our questions were remarkably rich and insightful.

The qualitative data from those interviews were coded and classified. The resulting five themes echo many of the ideas above. Although these themes apply to a particular experience of disability (specifically, a traumatic onset of physical or cognitive disability), their resonance with experience and with other literature leads us to believe that they have broader application to different types and situations of disability. Again, they are offered here to alert readers to how people might express a spiritual issue.

- *Awareness:* Many of our participants said that they had a greater awareness of something beyond their everyday experience since the onset of their disability. They felt more of a sense that there was a spiritual presence in their lives. Sometimes that awareness was positive and sometimes it was negative. Sometimes people were comforted by the awareness of a larger reality, but sometimes they were confused, alienated, or angry to think that spirituality could exist alongside trauma, suffering, and death.

- *Intimacy:* Another theme expressed by our research participants with regard to their spirituality was an altered sense of closeness, not only to family and friends, but also to the world, to nature, and to a divine being. Again, closeness could be altered in either a positive or a negative direction. Some people said that they felt a trans-personal kind of closeness — to all of humanity, particularly others who were dealing with difficult circumstances, and also to a divine being. Others said they felt abandoned, alienated, distanced from the world and from what formerly they believed. Whether or not they had previously believed in a "god", the experience of disability had led them to experience a loss of faith and connection.

- *Trust:* Disability had brought our participants into a different kind of relationship with others, often one that entailed a degree of dependency. In this respect, it required them to trust others in a different way. This pertained not only to their interpersonal relationships but also to their trans-personal relationship with humanity in general, and with their deity. Dependency either deepened their relationships or destroyed them. If they were able to believe that the world, humanity, and their higher power were essentially good and trustworthy, dependency created new opportunities for connection. On the other hand, if there was a feeling that others (including their god) could not be trusted, then trans-personal relationships broke down.

- *Mortality:* The onset of a disability created in our participants a greater awareness of death — of the permanence and proximity of death. It also led them to question what happens after death and the possibility of a life beyond death. Several respondents explored with greater intentionality the theme of what happens when we die. To some, this brought comfort; to others, distress.

- *Purpose:* The final theme that was expressed in our research with people experiencing the onset of a disability was an increased awareness of purpose in their lives. Some were thinking for the first time about their lives in the context of a larger plan, perhaps a divine plan. They sought to understand where they fit and what their life was meant to be about. Some found a sense of purpose, even if they were not yet sure exactly what that purpose was. Others lost purpose — they lost the sense that their life was important and meaningful. For some, purpose was expressed in relation to specific others — often family — while for others, purpose was experienced in relation to all of humanity, to the world, to other disabled people or other marginalized people.

Several other observations arose out of the very rich opportunity presented by this research. First, many of our participants were not the typical demographic of religious participants, and so therapists, nurses, and other professionals might have concluded that spiritual issues were not on their agenda. This assumption would have proved to be false — not only were some very unlikely characters thinking about spiritual things, they were willing and able, perhaps even anxious, to talk about them.

Secondly, we were cautioned that some of our participants with cognitive impairments might be incapable of talking about issues as abstract as spirituality. Again, those assumptions proved to be false. Participants with severe cognitive limitations were able to share with us thoughts and insights as nuanced and profound as those with no obvious cognitive impairments.

Thirdly, many of our participants expressed a feeling of inadequacy regarding their vocabulary and fluency in talking about spiritual issues. Particularly if they were not versed in the language of a certain religious tradition, they had no other basis for finding words. The lack of words, or the discomfort with using the wrong words, had prevented them from talking about these issues to anyone else. Once invited to use whatever words made sense to them, they were off to the races, with plenty to say.

Clients or patients are not the only ones to feel this inadequacy in communicating about spirituality. Therapists told us a similar thing — that although they wished to offer their clients the opportunity to talk about spiritual concerns, they didn't know how to bring it up (McColl, 2011). They were concerned that they might use language incorrectly and inadvertently offend their clients. They worried that they might be perceived as imposing their own beliefs on their clients. They didn't want to intrude on the client's privacy — they thought spirituality might be too personal to be discussed in their environment. Or they felt that spirituality was too emotional and might upset the patient, or that they themselves might become too emotional. Finally, they worried that they wouldn't know what to do if their client did raise a spiritual issue.

Addressing spiritual issues in practice

The main reason for the preceding discussion is to offer health and social service professionals an opportunity to recognize when a client with a disability has a spiritual concern that they might like to discuss with someone. The evidence in the literature is robust that spirituality is a bridge to health (McColl, 2011), but how do we begin our journey across that bridge? There are three options available when a patient or client wishes to pursue a spiritual issue — refer them to a qualified spiritual health practitioner, deal directly with the spiritual issue yourself, or provide opportunities for the client to indirectly address the issue.

The first option is the easiest. Acknowledge that the person appears to have something important and profound on his or her mind, and ask if you can help find someone to talk with — a leader in the person's faith community, a spiritual counsellor, a multi-faith chaplain, or other spiritual health professional.

The second option — dealing directly with spiritual issues — probably only appeals to those who have had some additional preparation, either through their own life of faith or through supplementary credentialing. Direct spiritual interventions include prayer, meditation, worship, spiritual counselling, pilgrimage, and religious rituals or blessings, to name a few. In many jurisdictions, spiritual or pastoral care is a licensed profession, and care needs to be taken not to trespass on professional boundaries.

Here are four questions to ask yourself, to ascertain if you can offer direct spiritual care (Farah & McColl, 2011):

1. Is it clear that there is a spiritual issue that the client wishes to address?
2. Is the client receptive to the idea of spiritual intervention?
3. Is the therapist equipped — both personally and professionally — to provide spiritual intervention?
4. Would the workplace support the use of spiritual intervention as part of the professional's role?

If the answer to all four of these questions is yes, then there is no actual impediment to offering direct spiritual care.

The third alternative is to offer the opportunity for indirect spiritual experiences. The literature shows that there are a number of everyday activities that can take on spiritual meaning for individuals if pursued thoughtfully and deliberately. Several examples include storytelling and narrative, symbols and rituals, creative expression, movement and dance, exploration of nature, and even some aspects of work, especially where it involves service or commitment to others. Participation in these activities can offer the potential to produce wonder and awe, communication and deep connection, transcendence of worldly experience, and resonance with universal stories and myths, truth and beauty (McColl, 2011).

Forster, McColl, and Faradella (2007) and Forster, McColl, Paterson, and Oullette-Kuntz (2009) offer a model of transformational rehabilitation as a way of addressing spiritual issues with clients with disabilities. The transformational model is based on the collected works of Jean Vanier (1995, 1997, 1998) and on a rare opportunity to work directly with Vanier. The model has as its focus the transformational relationship between a therapist and a person with a disability. This relationship is characterized by commitment, compassion, and cooperation. It is explicitly reciprocal, recognizing that working with each client is a privileged opportunity for growth for the therapist as well as the client. The transformational process is one of increasing awareness and acceptance of self, leading to greater maturity, agency, and authenticity.

Conclusion

This chapter addresses spirituality as a part of overall self-care. In the chapter, we *discover* some of the spiritual questions that arise, and themes that are expressed, among people with disabilities. Spiritual issues warrant special consideration in disability studies because we *appreciate* the magnitude of the disability experience as one that defies commonplace, everyday explanations. This chapter explored what the literature says about spirituality and disability and what our own research has shown about how spirituality is experienced by those living with disability. It is offered in this section along with the *dream* that self-care be considered in its broadest interpretation, including spiritual self-care.

In *designing* ways of engaging with our clients on a spiritual level, the chapter offers some language to try out, some concepts and themes to listen for, some questions to contemplate, and some activities that offer the possibility of spiritual conversations. It is not essential to know what to do about a spiritual issue or crisis in order to be an effective professional, but it is necessary to be able to recognize when a spiritual issue is being brought forward, to be able to acknowledge that you have heard it, and to have some strategies to deal with it.

As we think about *deploying* the knowledge gained in this chapter, it is important to be honest with ourselves about the extent to which we are comfortable having conversations about spirituality. Few health professionals will be prepared to deal with spiritual issues directly; however, all should be able to take at least one of the other two approaches to responding to spiritual issues: helping the person find someone qualified to talk to, or offering the person further opportunities to explore and discuss spiritual themes through activity. The chapter offers some guidance for assessing when it is suitable to incorporate spiritual issues in the overall care plan for self-care.

Chapter 11

Sexuality and disability

Introduction

The final chapter of this section on self-care addresses the issue of sexuality and disability. **Sexuality** refers to a human capacity for sexual feelings, and also to one's sexual orientation and activity. Humans are hard-wired for sexuality (Isler, Beytut, Tas, & Conk, 2009). Sexuality and reproduction along with basic survival are the two biological imperatives that drive human beings at their most fundamental level. Sexuality is a basic quality of human beings, and it has been linked with numerous tangible health benefits and with overall quality of life (McCabe, Cummins, & Deeks, 2000; O'Dea, Shuttleworth, & Wedgwood, 2012).

Sexuality is a multi-factorial entity that, like disability, is partly biological and partly socially constructed (Sakellariou, 2012). Just as the impairment part of disability can be specifically located in biology, so too there are parts of human sexuality that are objectively found in the body — sexual organs, hormones, and processes (Wunsch, 2014). The human organism is programmed for sensory, physiological, developmental, and psychological experiences associated with sexuality.

Equally important in thinking about both sexuality and disability is the way society shapes how we think and act. Our social and cultural experiences have a profound impact on how we view ourselves, and how we conduct ourselves relative to others. From earliest childhood, we are indoctrinated into the cultural script of what is normative for us, and expectations of conformity are imposed (Sakellariou, 2012). Healy, McGuire, Evans, and Carley (2009) suggest that nowhere is the discourse about "normality" more prevalent and polarized than when talking about sexuality and disability. We are instructed about the boundaries between private and public behaviour, the expectations we may have and those that others may have of us as sexual partners, and the interpretation of floods of emotion and sensation accompanying sexual activity to name but a few. Sexuality and disability is a broad and varied topic, and in this book we will be able only to scratch the surface of this highly personal issue.

Barriers to sexuality

People with disabilities encounter a number of barriers in their attempts to experience sexuality and express themselves as sexual beings — some within themselves and some external, located in our society, our attitudes, and our institutions. In this chapter, I will not only try to identify some of those barriers, but also to appreciate how the sexual aspect of humans is a vital and generative force that is equally alive in people with disabilities as in those without (Altuntug, Ege, Akin, Kal, & Salli, 2014). People with disabilities have sexual and reproductive needs similar to those of members of the general population. As health and social service professionals, the question arises as to how we can nurture and honour this aspect of our clients while maintaining their privacy, safety, and personal integrity.

Person-level barriers

There are a number of factors that may present unique challenges for people with disabilities in experiencing the full range of sexual and reproductive experiences. Some of these are within the person and are directly or indirectly affected by the disability itself. Different disabilities obviously present different challenges, but there are a few of the disability-related factors that affect full sexual functioning (Elliott & McBride, 2014):

- mobility, whether due to paralysis, limited flexibility, or joint range;
- spasticity or other positioning difficulties;

- cardiovascular complications, such as autonomic dysreflexia or cardiac insufficiency;
- pain or fatigue;
- specific sexual dysfunctions, such as erectile or ejaculatory dysfunction;
- hormonal imbalances that alter sexual appetite or performance;
- incontinence of bowel or bladder that require special attention prior to sexual activity; and
- iatrogenic or collateral effects of treatments, such as drug side effects or interference of medical devices or prosthetics.

Although they are many and varied, these issues may be the easiest to deal with, with the assistance of specialized clinics and professionals. There has been considerable attention in recent years, and a broad array of options developed, not only to enhance sexual participation (including such issues as positioning, achieving orgasm, erection, ejaculation, vaginal lubrication, masturbation, sexual devices, and adaptive aids), but also to assist in reproduction (including fertility, conception, pregnancy, delivery, and genetic counselling).

There may also be cognitive, emotional, or social person-level barriers to sexual functioning. Cognitively, one of the key barriers that has been documented in the literature is the ability to understand the subtleties and complexity of sexual behaviour, sexual responses, and sexual relationships (Parchomiuk, 2012). Emotionally, a certain level of maturity is required to participate as a partner in a sexual experience. Socially, there are skills and attitudes that are part of a sexual encounter, all of which facilitate a satisfying, mutual experience, as opposed to one that is upsetting, oppressive, or even abusive.

For people with some types of disabilities, such as intellectual disabilities, an adult body may not coincide with the cognitive ability to understand sexual functioning, with the emotional maturity to handle a sexual relationship, or with the social skills to manage one's sexuality in socially accepted ways. It is inappropriate, however, to deny the sexual maturity and sexual autonomy of disabled adults, regardless of their development in other areas. It is a source of enormous conflict and disenfranchisement to assume that disabled adults exist in a state of "suspended adolescence" or "perpetual childhood" (Azzopardi-Lane & Callus, 2014; Altuntug et al., 2014).

Development of human sexuality

The literature on the cognitive, emotional, and social aspects of sexuality among people with disabilities tends to focus on the field of developmental or intellectual disability. An appreciation of the developmental perspective on human sexuality is helpful in understanding this literature.

Human sexuality typically develops over four phases across the lifespan. It is often mistakenly assumed that babies and children are asexual, but thanks to Freud and others in the early 20th century, we know that this is not so. Sexual responses are present from birth, and progress through various exploratory phases up to the age of about 12 (DeLamater & Friedrich, 2002). During this time, the ability to form secure attachment develops, and many important messages are internalized about sexuality.

At adolescence, changes associated with puberty lead ultimately to sexual maturity and the ability to reproduce. Sexual organs mature, and new levels of hormones result in the development of secondary sex characteristics (such as body hair, muscles, and breasts), along with a surge of interest in sexuality. Psychologically and emotionally, adolescents are separating from their family of origin and developing unique identities, including gender identity, meaning the sense of culturally mediated affinity with being a man or a woman, and sexual identity, meaning a sense of both one's attraction and attractiveness to others.

By 19 or 20, young people typically enter the adult phase of their sexual lives. This phase is associated with partnering, and in many instances, reproducing, raising children, and launching those children toward independence. Sexual lifestyle is usually consolidated in this period, and depending on the surrounding culture, can be more or less conventional.

The final phase of sexual development is ushered in by menopause in women or andropause in men. Hormonal changes at midlife (usually around 50) cause changes in fertility and may also cause changes in sexual activity and satisfaction. Both men and women can remain sexually active virtually to the end of their lives, depending on their circumstances (DeLamater & Friedrich, 2002).

Social barriers

Stereotypes about sexuality among disabled people are the foremost social barrier to a healthy and satisfying sexual experience. Stereotypes are often based on inaccurate assumptions about the relationship between sexual functioning and other areas of functioning. Isler and colleagues (2009) describe a number of paradoxical stereotypes that exist in relation to people with disabilities and their sexuality.

The most common mistaken assumption is that people with disabilities do not experience sexual feelings, or that those feelings are somehow less important or less intense than among non-disabled people. By contrast, another surprisingly common stereotype is that people with disabilities are "over-sexed", uncontrolled, or somehow deviant in their sexuality. These characterizations are based on false beliefs, prejudices, and oversimplified judgments (Parchomiuk, 2012).

One of the most troubling aspects of these stereotypes is the way they contribute to making an already difficult situation more troublesome. Negative attitudes toward the sexuality of people with disabilities compound the inherent challenges discussed above in pursuing intimate relationships. Reflected attitudes can undermine an individual's sexual identity, self-esteem, and self-confidence. At worst, they validate the individual's worst fears that they are not considered a suitable sexual partner, that they are not attractive to others, or that they are perceived as some sort of asexual or deviant being (Altuntug et al., 2014).

Over the past century, a number of flagrant human rights violations have been perpetrated based on stereotypes like these. On the assumption that people with intellectual disabilities are unable to control their sexual impulses, they have been perceived as a danger both to themselves and potentially also to others. In response, those who care for them try to create environments that ensure their safety and protect them from difficult or dangerous situations. These environments, however, tend to be highly restrictive, focusing on rules and prohibitions (Azzopardi-Lane & Callus, 2014; Frawley & Bigby, 2014). Environments can also be restrictive in terms of the lack of private space in some living environments.

A situation that arouses particular tension when talking about disability and sexuality is the possibility of procreation. Becoming pregnant, giving birth, and raising children have been regarded by some as "impossible", "unnecessary", or "forbidden" for people with disabilities (Parchomiuk, 2012). Historically, people with developmental disabilities and severe mental illness were often sterilized to avoid this possibility. However, a landmark human rights case ended that practice in Canada — the case of *Eve v. Mrs. Eve* (1986). Eve (a pseudonym) was a developmentally disabled young woman whose mother sought to have her sterilized to protect her from unwanted pregnancy. The case went all the way to the Supreme Court of Canada, where the court unanimously upheld Eve's right to autonomy over her body — that is, not to be sterilized against her will.

Another way environments can create barriers is through inaccessibility. Think about the kind of venues where people can meet and get to know one another. Imagine being in your favourite bar or club, and being deaf, blind, or easily distractible. Imagine encountering everyone at their belly-button level if you were in a wheelchair. These may seem like trivial considerations, but along with entrenched attitudes about the suitability of disabled people as sexual partners, they can significantly impact the ability of people with disabilities to experience and express their sexuality.

A significant social barrier to sexuality for people with disabilities is the lack of information available to them (McCabe et al., 2000). Parents and carers have been notably reluctant to even discuss sexuality with disabled adults or young people, for fear of "putting ideas into their heads" (Healy et al., 2009; Taleporos & McCabe, 2003). Health and social service professionals have also proved less than forthcoming with information about sexual issues, options, and possibilities. The most benign explanation is that they don't have adequate up-to-date information to share with their disabled clients, or that they are themselves uncomfortable talking about sexuality (Parchomiuk, 2012; Valvano et al., 2014). More troublesome explanations include some of the very attitudinal restrictions we have been discussing above — they don't consider disabled people as legitimately sexual, they don't think sexual issues will arise for their client, or they don't want to facilitate the possibility of a sexual encounter for their client (Meaney-Tavares & Gavidia-Payne, 2012). For disabled people who identify as gay, lesbian, bisexual, transgendered, or queer, the challenges are multiplied.

And yet, a lack of information and discussion about sexuality leaves disabled people inordinately vulnerable to sexual abuse and sexually transmitted diseases (McCabe et al., 2000; Vaughn, Silver, Murphy, Ashbaugh, & Hoffman, 2015). Whether because of physical limitations that render them less able to avoid unwanted advances, or mental/emotional limitations that make them less discerning of unscrupulous motives, there is considerable evidence that people with disabilities are at increased risk of abuse and sexually transmitted diseases. Estimates run as high as 50% for people with intellectual disabilities who have been victimized at some point in their lives. Questions arise as to the ability of people with cognitive or developmental disabilities to give consent to sexual overtures. Because of difficulties interpreting social cues, people with intellectual or emotional disabilities may also inadvertently be perpetrators of sexual abuse (Meaney-Tavares & Gavidia-Payne, 2012).

Conclusion

In this chapter, we have *discovered* a definition of sexuality and noted how potentially problematic it can be to talk about the two concepts of sexuality and disability together. Both are socially constructed phenomena, and both have certain discomforts and taboos associated with them. In delving into this topic as part of disability studies, we *dream* of a world where people with disabilities are encountered in their full humanity, including their sexuality.

Professionals and service organizations have been identified as a key barrier to disabled people who are attempting to have a full life, including an intimate relationship. As we *design* programs and services, I hope some of the ideas contained in this chapter will be helpful. For example, as we design living spaces for people with disabilities, it should not be assumed that privacy can be compromised in favour of security considerations, staff efficiency, or convenience. Privacy for sexual encounters is an expectation that any adult would be entitled to in selecting a home, and disabled people should be entitled to the same privacy.

Some readers will find themselves in a position to *deploy* services that directly affect the possibility of a sexual dimension in the lives of their clients. While there are undoubtedly some personal challenges (physical, cognitive, or emotional) to be confronted in assisting clients with a disability to pursue a sexual relationship, by far the bulk of the challenges are social. Negative stereotypes about disabled people, limited information about the possibilities and options available, and restrictive environments are just some of the social barriers encountered by disabled people seeking a sexual life. Perhaps most troubling of all is the reflected impact of these barriers, making people with disabilities question their own sexual nature and identity, and adding to their vulnerability and exclusion.

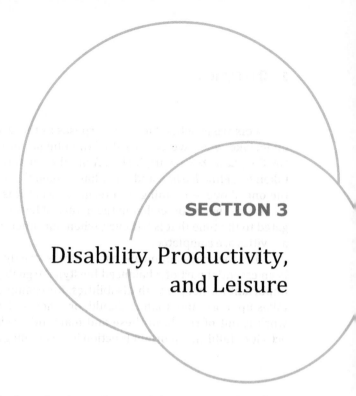

Disability, Productivity, and Leisure

As discussed in the introduction to Section 2, Sections 2 and 3 of this book correspond to the three major domains of life: self-care, productivity, and leisure. We now turn our attention to productivity and leisure.

Productivity is made up of activities one undertakes during the main part of one's day. Productivity usually occupies a considerable portion of a person's time — often as much as a third to a half of the hours in the day. Productivity is typically characterized by some degree of obligation. That obligation may take the form of a formal employment relationship (full-time or part-time); it may involve contractual work; or it may simply be an understanding between two people.

Productivity may include one or more of the following:

- work (whether remunerative or not),
- parenting or other caregiving,
- homemaking and home maintenance,
- civic and organizational engagement, and
- voluntary roles.

Productivity also includes activities that help prepare for future productive roles:

- education and training,
- vocational rehabilitation, and
- other rehabilitation.

Leisure is defined for our purposes as those activities that we undertake when we are freed of the obligation to be productive (McColl, Law, & Stewart, 2015). A number of authors have undertaken to define *leisure*, and most have taken the same approach as the one above — defining it in terms of what it is *not*, rather than what it is. This is somewhat in the nature of leisure — that it is relegated to the time that is left over, when our other less discretionary activities are completed.

But that does not mean that leisure is strictly a luxury. Leisure is an essential part of a balanced lifestyle. Arguably it is even more important for people with disabilities, for example, when self-care takes up more time than it should, or when satisfying productive work is out of reach. In these and many other situations, leisure activities fulfil an important function in assembling a meaningful life.

Chapter 12

Disability and work

Introduction

According to Lysaght, Ouellette-Kuntz, and Lin (2012), it is in the nature of humans to want to work. Productive roles fulfil a number of important functions for people (Leiulfsrud, Ruoranen, Ostermann, & Reinhardt, 2016; Potts, 2005; McColl, Law, & Stewart, 2015):

- They represent our participation in society and give us a stake in the larger enterprise of our community.
- They afford us a network of contacts and colleagues, sometimes referred to as "social capital".
- They shape our identity and offer us a degree of social recognition.
- They afford us the opportunity to be autonomous and self-sufficient.
- They alleviate the sense of being a burden to our family, our community, or our society.
- They structure our time and provide shape and definition to our days.
- They permit us to use our talents and abilities.
- They allow us to make a contribution.

Perhaps most importantly for disabled people, productive roles are a symbol of our integration, or reintegration, in the world. They are a tangible indication of full participation.

Drawing on data from both the United States and Canada, the following tables offer some statistics about the types and amounts of productive activity undertaken by disabled and non-disabled citizens (Wilson & McColl, 2017). The tables feature eight types of productive activities, ordered in terms of the amount of time spent by disabled Canadians. Note that the data are featured in numbers of minutes spent in a typical day in each activity.

Table 12.1 shows that non-disabled Canadians spent a total 429 minutes, or 7:15 hours, in productive activities in a typical day, while non-disabled Americans spent an average of 415 minutes, or 6:55 hours. Disabled Canadians spent 5:39 hours in productive work — about 90 minutes less than their non-disabled counterparts. Disabled Americans spent only 3:56 hours in productive activities — 3 hours less than their non-disabled counterparts. Disabled Canadians spent more than twice as much time as disabled Americans in paid work (121 vs. 52 minutes), as well as more time in virtually every other category of productive activity.

Table 12.2 shows the Canadian results for men and women, and several notable observations can be made regarding productive occupation according to sex. Disabled men and women spent more time than non-disabled on all but three of the productive activities listed in the table. They spent less time on paid work (men 103; women 63 minutes less), education (both about 22 minutes less), and childcare (men 10; women 17). Disabled men and women spent notably more time than non-disabled on housework (men 18; women 20 minutes more).

Disabled men spent an average of about 1½ hours less on paid work than non-disabled men, while disabled women spent about 1 hour less than non-disabled women in paid work. Both disabled men and women spent about 20 minutes less on education, compared to non-disabled.

Paid work

Among productive roles, perhaps the most sought-after is **employment** or paid work. In addition to the benefits conferred by any productive role, work has the added benefit of being the most socially recognized affirmation of "participatory parity" — that is, being on an equal footing with non-disabled peers with regard to participation (Solstad Vedeler & Schreuer, 2011). Quinlan and associates (2009) suggest that for many people with acquired

Table 12.1: Minutes spent in productive activities by Canadians and Americans with and without disabilities (2010)

	Canada		United States	
	Not disabled	Disabled*	Not disabled	Disabled
Paid work	206.3	120.9	205	51.6
Light housework	84.1	102	86.4	98.7
Shopping & services	30.9	32.6	27.7	28.1
Heavy housework	27.2	32.4	23.8	25.3
Civic, voluntary	16.1	19.5	17.3	15
Childcare	27.4	14.5	25	9.6
Education	34.8	12.4	28.6	4.6
Adult family care	2.5	4.4	1.2	1
Total (/ 1440 min per day)	429.3	338.7	415	233.9

* Ordered according to column labelled "Disabled" in Canada

Source: General Social Survey 2010 (Statistics Canada, 2011), American Time Use Survey (U.S. Bureau of Labor Statistics, 2017)

Paid work	• regular work, jobs, and handicrafts produced for sale; looking for work
Education	• full-time and part-time programs, homework; personal study
Light housework	• most indoor chores and tasks
Heavy housework	• most outdoor and garage tasks
Childcare	• household children
Adult care	• household adults
Shopping, services	• purchasing goods, use of commercial and professional services outside of home
Civic, voluntary	• community organizations, voluntary help to non-household persons or causes

Table 12.2: Minutes spent in productive activities by disabled and non-disabled Canadian men and women (2010)

Activity*	MALES			FEMALES		
	ND	D	(D – ND)	ND	D	(D – ND)
Paid work	239.3	136.3	–103.0	172.6	109.3	–63.3
Light housework	51.6	56.6	5.0	117.3	136.1	18.8
Heavy housework	35.8	48.8	13.0	18.4	20.0	1.6
Shopping/ service	25.5	29.8	4.3	36.5	34.7	–1.8
Civic/ voluntary	14.2	20	5.8	18.1	19.1	1.0
Education	32.8	11.4	–21.4	36.8	13.2	–23.6
Childcare	17.5	7.1	10.4	37.4	20.2	17.2
Adult care	2.5	3.5	1.0	2.4	5.2	2.8
Total Time per Day	419.2	313.5	134.8	439.5	357.8	81.7

ND: Non-disabled; D: Disabled

* See definitions in Table 12.1.

Source: General Social Survey 2010 (Statistics Canada, 2011)

disabilities, returning to work is equated with recovery. They are no longer a patient; rather, they are again an adult, a citizen, a contributor.

Paid work may take on a number of forms, and some may be more suitable than others at different ages and stages of life, or at different levels of ability. The normative standard in North American society is competitive employment. This means functioning in a competitive environment in an existing job — sending in a resumé and cover letter, having an interview, obtaining a job, reporting to a supervisor, meeting a standard of performance in order to retain the job, and hopefully progressing through the ranks toward one's full potential. This type of competitive employment, if full-time, entails about 40 hours per week, with limited latitude for special consideration.

There will be some disabled people who seek to return to or to assume this level of responsibility; however, for many others, a more flexible approach to work may make more sense:

- Contract work or part-time work, for example, may be more realistic, especially when the rigours of morning self-care and commuting present a challenge. Alternately, working from home or self-employment may be suitable alternatives.

- Supported employment that includes technical aids, equipment, or personal support services in the workplace is an option for others (Torjman & Makhoul, 2016). These accommodations are usually provided by funded programs in the community.

- Sheltered employment, for some, may be an appropriate alternative, although there is always a concern over exploiting disabled people's labour in sheltered environments.

- Microbusiness and social enterprise are also options for employment for some disabled individuals.

Rates of work participation

The statistics provided in Table 12.2 clearly show that disabled people spend less time on paid work than their non-disabled counterparts (Wilson & McColl, 2017; Wilson, McColl, & Parsons, 2015). To re-iterate from Table 12.2,

- disabled men spent about 1.5 hours less in paid work than non-disabled men;
- disabled women spent almost 1 hour less than non-disabled women in paid work; and
- disabled men spent about half an hour more than disabled women at paid work.

According to the latest national statistics on disability (Statistics Canada, 2012), 45% of the working-age population with disabilities (aged 25 to 64) are employed, compared to 79% of the general population of the same age. Five percent (5%) of working-age disabled Canadians were "unemployed", meaning they were available and actively looking for work, but unable to find work. The remaining 50% were "not in the labour force", meaning they were neither working nor seeking work, including those who had taken early retirement.

Among the 50% who are not in the labour force, 18% were classified as potentially employable, meaning that they planned to look for work in the coming year, were currently students or had been previously employed. About half of these had been out of the labour force for more than two years while the other half had actually worked in the preceding two years. Obviously, the longer that someone is out of the labour force, the more difficult it is to return.

Among the 45% who are disabled workers, 35% were considered full-time workers (meaning that they worked 30 or more hours per week), while 10% stated that their disability limited the number of hours they could work.

The employment rate for disabled Canadians is comparable to the rate reported for all 28 OECD countries, which was 44% (OECD, 2010b). The OECD notes that the global economic crisis and changing population demographics have resulted in fewer clerical, service, sales, and agricultural jobs. Among developed countries, such as Canada, more of the available work is part-time and temporary, shiftwork, and evening and weekend work. When economic trends like these affect the overall workforce, their effects are more pronounced and detrimental among disabled workers and other economically disadvantaged sectors (Till, Leonard, Yeung, & Nicholls, 2015).

Factors affecting work participation

Employment of people with disabilities is affected by factors both within the person and in the environment.

Person factors

One of the key personal factors affecting employment is disability severity (Till et al., 2015). Severity of disability is calculated based on the number, intensity, and frequency of activity limitations the person experiences. The more severe the disability, the greater limitation it appears to impose on the ability of individuals to work. Only 26% of those with very severe disabilities and 42% of those with severe disabilities were able to work. Rates were somewhat better for those with moderate (54%) or mild (68%) disabilities, but still below the non-disabled rate of employment of 79% (Statistics Canada, 2012); thus, there are clearly other factors at play.

Employment is also affected by the type of disability. Those with physical disabilities were more likely to be employed, whereas developmental, cognitive, mental, or emotional disabilities posed more difficulties when seeking employment (Till et al., 2015).

Another personal factor that affected employment was age at onset of disability. Those with disabilities acquired at younger ages had better employment prospects than those injured in adulthood (Livermore, Goodman, & Wright, 2007; Escorpizo, Miller, Trenaman, & Smith, 2014). Presumably, these young people have an opportunity to tailor their educational and career plans to their disability context. Disabilities acquired at older ages had greater negative effects on the potential for employment (Till et al., 2015). Of course, there is also some legitimacy related to giving up work at older ages that makes the decision not to actively pursue work more normative for those injured in midlife or beyond (Leiulfsrud et al., 2016).

A highly significant determinant of employment is education. Higher levels of education help disabled individuals overcome many disability-related employment problems (Till et al., 2015). For those with a university education, the rate of employment was similar between those with mild or moderate disabilities and those without disabilities — 77% vs. 83% (Statistics Canada, 2012). Even those with severe or very severe disabilities were employed at significantly greater rates if they had a university education (59% vs. 34% without university education). This may have to do with the type of work sought by those with higher education — typically white collar or professional. A university education often enables individuals to work in their chosen field; however, the statistics show that disabled workers were less likely to be in management roles — 12% vs. 20%, compared to non-disabled workers with similar qualifications.

For those with less than high school education, often the types of jobs available had higher physical demands. The rate of employment was only 20% for those with less than high school education and severe or very severe disabilities, compared to 65% in the general population.

Interestingly, having a disability negatively affects the work prospects of disabled men more than it does for disabled women. Also, the effect of having a disability is considerably greater for Americans with disabilities than it is for Canadians with disabilities. This finding is surprising given the expectation that the *Americans with Disabilities Act* (U.S Department of Justice, 2000; 2008) provides legislated protection for disabled workers (Wilson & McColl, 2017).

Environmental factors

There are also numerous environmental factors that affect the employment prospects for people with disabilities. Like many scarce resources, when jobs are hard to come by in the general population, the situation is exacerbated for disadvantaged populations like people with disabilities (Till et al., 2015). Many are discouraged from looking for work due to some of the following factors (Statistics Canada, 2012; Livermore at al., 2007):

- lack of locally available jobs;
- inadequate training or experience;
- previous unsuccessful attempts to find work;
- couldn't make as much working as on disability pension;
- discrimination in the workplace in the past;
- employers wouldn't give them a chance;
- loss of fringe benefits, such as drug coverage;
- accessibility issues; and
- transportation/commuting issues.

Particularly troubling among these deterrents are the allegations of discrimination in the workplace. About half of disabled workers felt they had been discriminated against in the workplace (51%): 17% felt they had been denied an interview when applying for a job, 23% felt they had been denied a position for which they had interviewed, and 13% felt they had been denied a promotion because of their disability (Till et al., 2015). In all, 46% of disabled workers reported that they had had difficulty advancing in their career because of their disability (Statistics Canada, 2012).

Workplace accommodations

Workplace accommodations are an essential topic to understand when talking about employment and disability. **Accommodations** refer to considerations afforded in the workplace to ensure that no discrimination takes place on the basis of "race, national or ethnic origin, colour, religion, age, sex, sexual orientation, gender identity or expression, marital status, family status, genetic characteristics, *disability* [or] conviction for an offence for which a pardon has been granted or in respect of which a record suspension has been ordered" (*Canadian Human Rights Act,* 1985). Discrimination occurs when someone is denied a job or other opportunity because he or she possesses one of these characteristics.

In order to understand workplace accommodations, it is necessary for us to discuss *bona fide occupational requirements* (or BFORs). These are the actual capabilities that are required in order to perform a particular job. In theory, every job can be explained in terms of BFOR, and these capabilities are obviously what an employer is seeking when hiring. If the disability interferes with a BFORs of the job in question, then the employer is justified in not hiring someone who cannot perform this function. For example, commercial pilots must have a certain degree of visual ability — this is a BFOR. It would not be considered discriminatory to refuse someone with a visual impairment a job as an airline pilot, whereas it might be discrimination to refuse someone an airline ground staff job with the same disability. If the applicant is able to fulfil the BFORs and suspects that the disability has been used as an excuse not to hire him or her, then there may be grounds for a claim of human rights infraction.

An accommodation is a measure that is taken to allow a disabled worker to be able to use his or her skills to fulfil the BFORs of the job. Forty-two percent (42%) of disabled workers need one or more accommodations in order to be able to perform their job effectively. Below is a list of accommodations that are seen most commonly for disabled workers (Till et al., 2015):

- modified hours (23%),
- special chair/backrest (17%),
- modified duties (13%),
- special workstation (12%),
- human support (4%),
- accessible elevator (4%),
- adapted computer (3%), and
- accessible parking (3%).

Many of these accommodations represent either no additional cost to the employer or minimal cost, and 80% of disabled employees report that their accommodation needs are met in the workplace (Statistics Canada, 2012). Those most likely to be unmet are communication aids, specialized computer technology, and human supports. In approximately half of the cases where accommodation needs are unmet, the employee admits that he or she did not ask for the accommodation, and the employer did not know that it was required.

Whether or not to disclose

You might wonder why an employee would not ask for something to which the law clearly states he or she is entitled. The answer, at least in part, lies in the previous discussion of feelings of discrimination and disadvantage among disabled workers. Gerber, Price, Mulligan, and Shessel (2004) found that almost half of their sample of people with learning disabilities encountered negative reactions from employers when they disclosed their disability, and a quarter experienced negative reactions from co-workers. Discrimination, labelling, and stigma have been identified as the greatest impediments to employment for disabled individuals (Shier, Graham, & Jones, 2009).

The literature offers several tangible examples of how discrimination happens in the workplace. Henry, Petkaukos, Stanislawzyk, and Vogt (2014) showed that interviews between prospective employers and disabled versus non-disabled applicants differed significantly in their content. Interviews with disabled job applicants tended to focus on what the candidate could *not* do, while those with apparently non-disabled candidates focused on what they could do. Scheiber (2015), in a study featured in *The New York Times*, sent resumés and covering letters in response to hundreds of advertisements for various levels of employees. In some he disclosed the presence of a disability — anything from Asperger's syndrome to a spinal cord injury. In others, he featured the same qualifications and experience, but no mention of disability. Twenty-six percent (26%) fewer of his fictitious disabled candidates were granted an interview, compared to their matched non-disabled candidates. The type or extent of disability disclosed did not appear to make a difference — the same degree of disinterest was present among employers regardless of the nature of the disability.

Of course, some disabilities are evident to employers — but many are not. Typically physical or sensory disabilities are more likely to be evident, whereas mental health issues, cognitive or learning disabilities (often called "invisible disabilities") may be concealed from employers or prospective employers initially. Workers may feel (and apparently with some justification) that the disability will affect their chances for employment or advancement.

Henry and colleagues (2014) have shown that employers do display some reluctance to hire people with disabilities, especially those with mental or emotional disabilities. Here are some of their concerns:

- They worry about work-related issues, such as lower productivity, higher absenteeism, and increased need for supervision.
- They worry about social issues, such as resentment or discomfort among their employees.
- They worry about financial consequences, such as the costs of accommodations.

Finally, employers worry about human rights issues — their own ignorance and discomfort with disability, their lack of knowledge of the rights and entitlements of disabled employees, and the possibility of saying the wrong thing or having their intentions misinterpreted.

All of these issues can lead to a subtle form of discrimination that is difficult to pin down, but that nonetheless results in foreclosed opportunities for people with disabilities (Gewurtz, Langan, & Shand, 2016). In short, employers consider it an "unnecessary risk" to hire someone with a disability (Henry et al., 2014).

What those employers fail to understand is that they forgo a number of significant benefits when they automatically eliminate disabled candidates or employees from consideration. Job retention has been shown to be high among disabled workers (Henry et al., 2014; Torjman & Makhoul, 2016). Diversity in the workplace benefits everyone, by creating a more humane and caring culture that carries tangible as well as intangible benefits (Lysaght et al., 2012). Not only does inclusive hiring increase the talent pool available, it also results in improved brand recognition, growth in leadership among managers and employees, and enhanced customer loyalty (Henry et al., 2014; Grant, 2015).

The decision about whether or not to disclose the presence or extent of a disability, and the attendant need for accommodation, is one of the most difficult decisions faced by individuals seeking employment. Whether at the stage of applying for a job, interviewing for a job, starting a new job, or changing status within an existing job, the question arises as to whether or not to make the disability a part of the discussion (Gewurtz et al., 2016; Gerber et al., 2004).

Recent privacy legislation in most jurisdictions protects disabled people from having to disclose details of a health condition when seeking employment or accommodations; however, this does not necessarily make the process more smooth and transparent. The research shows that employment and accommodations work out best when candour and transparency prevail, when the employer is engaged in a collaborative process, and when the employee feels like he or she retains some degree of control over the conditions of work (Henry et al., 2014; Meredith & Chia, 2015; Solstad Vedeler & Schreuer, 2011).

Barriers to employment for people with disabilities

The *World Report on Disability* (World Bank & WHO, 2011) itemizes the eight most significant barriers to full participation, equity, and opportunity for people with disabilities as follows. Note that none of these eight factors has anything to do with the underlying health condition of the person.

1. Policies and standards that fail to adequately deal with the situation of people with disabilities or to meet their basic needs;
2. Negative attitudes about disability;
3. Lack of services, lack of funding, lack of access to needed supports;
4. Problems with delivery of services, such as sparse geographic distribution, economic barriers, provider inadequacies, and inaccessibility;
5. Inadequate funding for basic essentials of life, as well as for special needs associated with disability;
6. Inaccessibility of the built environment, and failure to take account of the situation of people with disabilities in space planning and assignment;
7. Lack of consultation with disabled people, and the absence of any process to engage disabled people in public debate; and
8. Lack of data or evidence to substantiate the scope and magnitude of needs and resources for people with disabilities.

Gruhl (2012) used the metaphor "stuck in the mud" to describe how people with disabilities feel about their prospects in the labour market, based on qualitative research with people with serious mental illness. Barriers can be classified as physical, procedural, or attitudinal (Torjman & Makhoul, 2016).

Physical barriers to employment refer to those aspects of the physical environment that impede access for people with disabilities. Simply being able to enter the building and get to the right floor and the correct office can exclude some workers. Inadequate signage, lack of information and other communication failures can create an inaccessible environment. Not only the office but also the washrooms, the food service and social areas, the passageways, and the workstation itself need to be considered for accessibility. Finally, transportation, commuting options, and parking can be very significant barriers to pursuing employment (Schur, Kruse, & Blanck, 2005; Cook et al., 2006; Solstad Vedeler & Schreuer, 2011; Leiulfsrud et al., 2016).

Procedural barriers to employment refer to policies and procedures in the workplace that systematically disadvantage workers with disabilities. Most often these barriers are inadvertent — they result from failure to consider the needs of disabled employees; however, sometimes procedural barriers are more malign and intentional. They can involve everything from how a job is advertised, how applications are adjudicated, how candidates are contacted and interviewed, how decisions are made about offering the job, how compensation is calculated, how new employees are oriented, how co-workers are introduced, how accommodations are handled, how expectations are communicated, how opportunities are (or aren't) presented, how difficulties are treated, and how achievement is recognized and rewarded (Bahm & Forchuk, 2009; Iwasaki & Mactavish, 2005; McGinn, Gahagan, & Gibson, 2005). Each of these aspects of the employer–employee relationship has the potential to represent a barrier to employment. Some of these barriers are subtle and others are blatant. Some result from misunderstandings about disability, some from lack of knowledge about human rights and entitlements of disabled workers, and some from sheer ignorance and disregard (Draper, Hawley, McMahon, & Reid, 2012; Gewurtz et al., 2016). Whatever the cause, employees are in a disadvantaged position to pursue any sort of redress in terms of power in the relationship.

Finally, *attitudinal barriers* have been identified as the greatest impediments to employment for people with disabilities (Shier et al., 2009). We have discussed attitudes toward disability in several places in this book, but we highlight them here as they are such an important factor in trying to think about how to improve the employment prospects of people with disabilities. Attitudinal barriers consist of false assumptions, unsubstantiated beliefs, generalizations, and all forms of stereotypes about disability. These can relate to disabled people in general, their performance, their potential, their skills and experience, and their ability to fit in with the workforce.

Approaches to enhancing employment for people with disabilities

So, what can we do to overcome the barriers and obstacles to meaningful employment discussed above?

According to Gruhl (2012), employment strategies tend to fall into one of two camps: place-and-train or train-and-place. *Place-and-train strategies* situate the individual in a work setting and provide on-the-job training and support in situ as needed. These strategies have the advantage of providing real-world experience, adding to the individual's resumé, and confronting real problems in a timely manner as they arise. They do not depend on transferability of learned skills, as the learning is direct and situational. They have the disadvantage, however, of being heavily dependent on an existing job opening and a committed employer who is willing to demonstrate flexibility and support. The culture of such a workplace typically flows from the top, and so must start with an enlightened chief executive officer (Grant, 2015; Henry et al., 2014).

Train-and-place refers to employment strategies that start with off-site skill development, practice, and role-playing. Once "work readiness" is attained, the program assists with job placement and support. These programs have the advantage of offering participants a low-risk, high-support environment in which to learn and develop skills; however, they have a number of disadvantages as well. The downfall of these types of programs generally lies at the back end. They are heavily dependent on the availability of jobs in the open labour market, and on the ability of individuals to compete in a work setting that has not necessarily been prepared to accept and support them. Considerable frustration and ultimately loss of interest can result if the program does not lead to employment, and yet that stage is completely out of the hands of the program and its personnel.

Strategies to enhancing employment for disabled people

Based on current literature, there are five different strategies that promote satisfying work participation for disabled people and effective job placement for employers.

1. **Vocational or pre-vocational rehabilitation programs**
    Train-and-place programs usually look like traditional vocational or pre-vocational rehabilitation programs — a staple of 1970s-style rehabilitation that is enjoying a renaissance in the contemporary literature (Dowler & Walls, 2014). Vocational rehabilitation programs typically take place in a multidisciplinary environment, and they can be part of an in-patient, out-patient, or community rehabilitation program (Escorpizo et al., 2011). Several authors stress the importance of early intervention to optimize success in vocational rehabilitation and prevent loss of skills and confidence (OECD, 2003; McGinn et al., 2005). Vocational rehabilitation is strengths-based, rather than deficit-based, and focuses on skill development (Gruhl, 2012). It is usually offered to candidates less than 45 years of age, with the prospect of a new or renewed career (OECD, 2003). It usually begins with basic skills and progresses to social skills, job search strategy, and job retention skills. According to Escorpizo and associates (2011), vocational rehabilitation focuses not only on remediation of impairments but also on overcoming activity limitations and participation restrictions. Other names for this type of program include work readiness, work hardening, employment/job preparation, and work-role development. They have been shown to have a high benefit-to-cost ratio, and yet vocational rehab programs are difficult to find (McGinn et al., 2005) — "too little, too late", according to the international Organisation of Economic Co-operation and Development (OECD, 2003).

The remaining four strategies that we will discuss fall under the place-and-train approach. The consensus in the literature is that these types of programs are generally more effective than train-and-place programs at securing sustained employment (Gruhl, 2012). They are normally operated under the auspices of a community disability organization, and they depend on skilled community workers with trusting relationships with employers in their own community.

2. **Individualized placement and support**
   Also called customized employment, job coaching, or supported employment, individualized placement and support is
   a community-based program that supports an individual to
   obtain the position of his or her choice, and then intervenes
   in the workplace — with the employer, employee, and co-
   workers — to ensure appropriate supports in the workplace
   and a receptive environment. Agency staff may also provide
   or arrange for on-the-job supports as needed to optimize
   work performance and promote job retention (Dowler &
   Walls, 2014). This approach is obviously highly individualized, and must be delivered on a one-on-one basis; thus, it is
   relatively costly (Riesen, Morgan, & Griffin, 2015). However, it
   has shown the highest probability of achieving and retaining
   employment, and of earning more than the minimum wage
   (Dowler & Walls, 2014). It is considered a "best practice"
   according to a review by Gruhl (2012).

3. **Diversified placement strategy**
   Also called transitional employment (Gruhl, 2012) and cooperative programs (Lysaght et al., 2012), diversified placement
   approach (Dowler & Walls, 2014) entails rotating the prospective employee through a series of work placements, with
   the expectation that he or she will not only learn a wide range
   of skills through performing a variety of different jobs, but
   also discover aptitudes, suitability, and preferences for particular types of work. In an ideal world, the candidate would
   encounter an employer who was willing to take him or her on.
   While that can only happen in a minority of cases, the candidate does obtain experience that can feature on a resumé, and
   potentially he or she may also find employers who are willing
   to provide a reference. In some cases, placement employers
   can even make introductions to other possible opportunities.
   This approach does not necessarily situate the candidate in a
   new job at the conclusion of the program, but it does vastly
   increase the probability of finding a job by providing
   diversified real-world experience.

4. **Sheltered workshops**
   This is an increasingly uncommon strategy for employment of
   people with disabilities (particularly those with cognitive and
   social disabilities). This category can include microbusiness,

social enterprise, and work enclaves. Sheltered employment typically entails simple repetitive work that is relatively easily mastered — often job lots or piecework that would be a poor use of time for skilled employees. The work environment of a sheltered workshop offers some of the features of a regular workplace, such as expectations about attendance, comportment, and performance, but compensation is typically below labour force standards and allowances are made for virtually all types and manifestations of disability. This approach is based on the assumption that people want and need to work, regardless of the presence of a disability, and that working for pay carries with it particular benefits. The distinguishing feature of this approach is that the entire workforce is usually disabled (sometimes with the exception of supervisors), and the enterprise is designed to provide work for people who might otherwise not be able to obtain *any* work. Sheltered employment has been questioned in recent years for exploiting the labour of disabled people and taking advantage of workers who have relatively few options (Kober & Eggleton, 2005). While this may be true, sheltered employment has also been shown to offer significant benefits to workers, such as high levels of quality of life, empowerment, and social belonging — especially when the alternative is to have no work.

5. **Wage subsidies**
   This final strategy for enhancing employment among people with disabilities is another controversial one. Wage subsidies refer to funding programs aimed at overcoming the typical objections of employers regarding hiring disabled employees, such as these:
   - It could take longer for them to be oriented and become productive employees.
   - They may be less productive than regular employees.
   - They may take more time off and not be able to function to full capacity due to illness.

Even though these assumptions have been shown to be inaccurate (Torjman & Makhoul, 2016), where they persist wage subsidies offer employers a financial incentive to give a disabled employee a chance. Often that chance results in the employer discovering that his or her preconceived reservations were unfounded, and that the disabled employee is a good business decision even without the subsidy.

The controversy, of course, revolves around the fact that it is against the law to discriminate against disabled workers, and employers should not need to be incentivized to adhere to the law. The other side of the coin, however, is that wage subsidies bring results. They do render employers more willing to overcome their reluctance to take on their first disabled employee. That experience in turn leaves them somewhat more enlightened about the relative ease of accommodating a disabled employee. It also increases their awareness of the benefits of an inclusive workplace, and makes them more inclined toward hiring disabled employees in future (Henry et al., 2014).

Conclusion

In summary, employment for people with disabilities is a complex issue. There are a number of reasons that people with disabilities often struggle to secure employment. Some of these reasons are attributable to the employer; some to the workplace, the broader system, and society; and some to the person him- or herself. Employers have been found to be reluctant to employ disabled individuals, mostly due to misunderstanding and ignorance. Workplaces can be inaccessible in a number of ways — physical barriers, non-inclusive attitudes, and lack of flexibility, to name a few. Systems contain disincentives to work, and often fail to demonstrate the creativity that could overcome these issues. One of the most commonly encountered barriers at the system level is the inability to organize attendant care and transportation that is reliable and timely. As for the person him- or herself, we must be honest that some disabilities make some individuals more or less suited to certain types of employment (Iwasaki & Mactavish, 2005). Thus, the job of assisting disabled clients to find jobs is highly individualized and skilled.

We have *discovered* that work is a fundamental part of being an adult, and that people with disabilities desire and expect to work just as all adults do. We have certainly *discovered* that workforce participation is not equitable for people with disabilities in Canada. There is quantitative evidence that people with disabilities are unemployed and under-employed at greater rates than their non-disabled counterparts.

These two observations together lead us to *dream* of a society where these inequities are overcome, and attitudes and stereotypes about disabilities do not foreclose on the opportunities of disabled people to have productive and meaningful work lives. The proof that this dream has become a reality would be if people with disabilities no longer feared disclosing the presence of a disability to a prospective employer. Instead, they could readily be truthful about the way they were able to be most successful in their work, knowing that the necessary accommodations would be provided without judgment.

We have examined several approaches to *designing* programs and strategies to promote productive engagement for people with disabilities, and we have considered the pros and cons of each.

In terms of *deployment*, there have been some suggestions that disability organizations figure prominently in any prospects for improved employment for people with disabilities. Consumer organizations have a unique opportunity to increase awareness of the talent pool among their members, and to showcase successful employment of disabled workers (Henry et al., 2014). They have a potential role in developing relationships with employers in their community, connecting workers with opportunities, and advising on improving accessibility and furnishing accommodations (Gewurtz et al., 2016).

Figure 12.1 is a story that illustrates many of the points discussed in the chapter. This story was written by Joanne Smith, TV journalist and broadcaster. It is the story of Mark Wafer, Toronto businessman and entrepreneur (Smith, 2017).

Figure 12.1: Story of Mark Wafer (by Joanne Smoth)

Mark Wafer is deaf, and he fully understands the challenge of trying to find gainful employment with a disability. He decided the best thing for him to do, to avoid the prejudices of trying to get hired, was to open his own business. In 1992, he opened his first Tim Hortons coffee shop in Scarborough. Over the next five years, he opened another shop each year, eventually owning six franchises for 25 years.

In the early days, Mark realized he couldn't keep up with the demands of all his businesses. He reflected on his own determination, and decided to do something different. He hired an employee with Down's syndrome, named Cliff.

Mark was so dedicated to ensuring the success of this new employee, he enlisted the help of Community Living Toronto to coach this young man in his job, and show him how to take the bus to and from work. Once trained, Cliff became one of Mark's best employees. He arrived for work early each day. He had to be persuaded to take breaks. And, he had to be encouraged to go home after the end of each shift.

Seeing the value of hiring individuals with disabilities, Mark went on to employ almost 200 individuals with disabilities — all types of disabilities, including those who were deaf, blind, or physically or cognitively disabled, with mental health issues and learning disabilities. They worked in all areas of the business, including management — even his director of operations.

Mark's statistics are a testament to the value of hiring individuals with disabilities. Over 25 years, Mark's employees with disabilities:

- were more productive and innovative than their non-disabled counterparts. Mark said his employees with disabilities had 20% higher productivity. Why? "Because to them their job is precious. It took a long time to get that job."
- were rarely late or sick. The absentee rate for employees with disabilities was 55% lower than for employees without disabilities.
- required little or no supervision.

continued....

Figure 12.1 continued

- worked in a safer manner. Mark never had to file a workplace injury claim for any worker with a disability over the 25-year period.
- demonstrated incredible loyalty, and rarely left. His annual employee turnover was 40% — versus an industry average of 100%.

Even more interesting, his non-disabled worker turnover was also only 55%. He said this was because inclusion benefits everyone in the workplace. Overall employee morale was enhanced. He said, "When a business builds capacity with workers who have disabilities, it also affects the non-disabled workers' ability to communicate and respond to various needs in the workplace." This was especially true for managers and supervisors, who became far more aware of how they spoke to employees who may or may not have had a disability. When determining if an employee with a disability had the capability to do a task, they included the person in the discussion, rather than making the judgment call without them. Simply put, Mark said inclusion makes for better management.

Mark mentioned he often had new job applicants ask if he was the Tim's guy who hired people with disabilities. When he said he was, he also asked them what type of disability they might have and how he could best make the accommodation they needed. The response was often, "Oh, I don't have a disability, but I want to work in an inclusive workplace."

Mark also reported that customer feedback was 100% positive. He said once customers have the experience of interacting with servers with disabilities, they want to shop at retail outlets that represent the fabric of their community, and that includes workers with disabilities.

Another interesting point he made was that his group of six restaurants out-performed the average in sales and transactions because customers would tell him they bypassed other Tim Hortons locations to come to his. This makes a compelling economic case for inclusion.

Mark didn't know the decision to hire Cliff over 25 years ago would transform his business and help him make

continued....

Figure 12.1 continued

positive attitudinal changes in his community. He says the myths and misconceptions about employing people with disabilities remain the greatest barrier to a more inclusive workplace. For example, many people assume hiring someone with a disability is associated with big expenses. For him, the average accommodation cost was $500, but in most cases it was 0.

For Mark, changing attitudes was just a matter of doing it — simply hiring an individual with a disability and letting that person's performance, dedication, and productivity speak for itself. In doing so, he changed hundreds, if not thousands, of his colleagues' and his customers' attitudes.

Mark recently sold his businesses in order to, as he says, "become a full time advocate, activist, and trouble maker". He has now co-founded a company called Canadian Business Sense-ability to move the agenda forward at the corporate level. By working with other businesses on how they can do what he did, he has helped find work for over 1,000 individuals with disabilities in meaningful and competitively paid jobs.

And a follow-up note on Cliff — Mark is proud to say that Cliff still works full-time at the Tim's where Mark first hired him. He's married and owns his own condominium, and continues to tell everyone about how great his job is.

Source: Smith, 2017.

Chapter 13

Disability and education

Introduction

The evidence is clear that the best assurance against unemployment and poverty for people with disabilities is education, in particular post-secondary education. And yet that goal is not within reach for many disabled people, and there are "persistent achievement gaps" in the area of education between disabled and non-disabled people (Government of Ontario, 2017).

In this chapter, we focus on elementary, secondary, and post-secondary education, and explore differences between disabled and non-disabled students. We also look at the educational system and how it has developed, both practically and ideologically, over the past 40 years. Finally, we focus on inclusive education and universal design for learning as tools for ensuring equity in access to education.

The Participation and Activity Limitation Survey (Behnia & Duclos, 2003; Government of Canada, 2011; Statistics Canada, 2008) found that 4.6% of Canadian children aged 5 to 14 years of age have a disability — 5.7% for boys and 3.4% for girls. In terms of education, 56.7% of disabled children attend regular neighbourhood schools, while 43.3% attend some form of **special education**. Full-time special education programs, either a separate classroom in a regular school or a separate school altogether, account for 16.4% of disabled children. The remaining 26.9% are involved in part-time special education, meaning that they receive some courses separately and some with their non-disabled peers (Statistics Canada, 2008).

The majority (85%) of parents say that their own child's disability is being accommodated by their school; however, children attending regular schools report that their participation is restricted in physical education (45.7%), play at recess or lunch (41.7%), school outings or trips (23.6%), and even in the classroom (28.9%).

According to parents, 42% of children who need special education are not getting it. Special education options are significantly more available in urban settings; thus, many areas simply don't have special schools or can't attract trained staff (Kohen, Uppal, Guevremont, & Cartwright, 2001; Loreman, 2014). Most children in special education have severe or very severe disabilities — 78% of disabled students. The most common disabilities seen in special education are learning disabilities (89.6% of children in special ed.); communication disabilities (54.3%); developmental disabilities (53.0%); and psychological, emotional, or behavioural disabilities (52.2%). Approximately 10% each are accounted for by physical, hearing, and visual disabilities.

Focusing specifically on post-secondary education, in 1992, 6.2% of all post-secondary students identified themselves as disabled, while by 2010 this percentage had risen to 7.5% (Wilson, McColl, & Parsons, 2015). That represents a rate increase of about 40% over 18 years, or about 3.7% per year. Over the same period, the overall enrolment rate in post-secondary education increased by 2.3% per year. In other words, enrolment in post-secondary education increased considerably more steeply for disabled than for non-disabled students.

A right to education

Human rights codes at the provincial, national, and international levels all specify the right to education for all citizens, regardless of disability. The United Nations *Convention on the Rights of Persons with Disabilities* (UN, 2006) perhaps states it most eloquently in Article 24 — that participating nations must ensure "an inclusive education system at all levels ... [toward the development of] human potential, dignity and self-worth, ... personality, talents, creativity, mental and physical abilities, ... effective participation in a free society". It entreats nations to ensure access, reasonable accommodations, support as needed, and qualified educators.

In Canada, education is administered at the provincial/ territorial level, with each jurisdiction having authority over the particulars of its educational system. Typically elementary and secondary education are governed by one ministry within the provincial or territorial government, and post-secondary education (colleges, universities, training programs) is governed by a separate ministry. This fact is a function of ideological and cultural differences between the two sectors. For the subsequent discussion, it is important to understand this difference. Whereas elementary and secondary education are guaranteed to every citizen, post-secondary education is a competitive sector where one needs to earn a place and maintain a high standard of achievement. Post-secondary education itself is not a right, but equal treatment within the post-secondary environment is. So, while disabled people are not guaranteed access to post-secondary education, they are guaranteed equity in consideration and participation in post-secondary education if they qualify for entrance.

Over recent decades, case law has clarified the rights of people with disabilities with respect to education, mirroring the evolving ethos regarding education and young people with disabilities. In 1997, the Eaton family sought extensive medical accommodations for their daughter Emily, a 12-year-old girl with severe cerebral palsy, to allow her to attend school in an integrated classroom (*Eaton v. Brant County Board of Education*, 1997). The Supreme Court of Canada ruled that different treatment was warranted by Emily's individual circumstances, and special education in a segregated classroom was in her best educational interests. Despite protests from a number of disability groups seeking to uphold the value of integration over segregation, the Court expressly acted in what it felt to be the best interests of the child. The disability community interpreted the verdict as a setback in the struggle for inclusion.

Fast-forward to 2012, when the Supreme Court of Canada found that it constituted discrimination to deny Justin Moore, a young boy with a severe learning disability, a remedial program that enabled his participation in school. The rationale was as follows:

> ... a healthy democracy and economy require[s] educated contribution. Adequate special education, therefore, is not a dispensable luxury. For those with severe learning disabilities, it is the ramp that provides access to the statutory commitment to education made to all children. (*Moore v. British Columbia*, 2012)

This case exemplifies the shift from an individual, compassion-based approach to education, compatible with the charitable or medical model of disability, to a systemic approach based on human rights and freedoms, consistent with the social model of disability (Carr, 2016).

Inequalities in education
And yet inequalities persist. The *Canada Survey on Disability* (Statistics Canada, 2012) offers evidence of the differences in educational attainment between disabled and non-disabled Canadians; see Table 13.1.

There is a lot of information in this table, so let me unpack it:

1. Looking at the first two columns (numbers in italics), we can see that significantly *more* people with disabilities attain the lower levels of education (less than post-secondary comple-

Table 13.1: Educational attainment by disability status (adults 25–64 years of age)

	Disability					
	Non-disabled	*All disabled*	*Mild*	*Moderate*	*Severe*	*Very severe*
Less than high school	*11.4*	*20.0*	15.7	22.8	21.6	25.7
High school completed	*23.7*	*26.6*	26.3	24.4	28.1	32.7
Some post-secondary	*38.2*	*39.5*	36.3	35.9	38.0	32.7
Post-secondary completed	*26.7*	*13.9*	21.4	17.6	12.3	8.9
TOTAL	100.0	100.0	99.7	99.9	100.0	100.0

Post-secondary includes college and university, as well as specific training programs.

Source: Canadian Survey on Disability, 2012

tion), while *fewer* attain the highest level, compared to non-disabled peers.

2. About *twice as many* disabled people do not complete high school, while about *half as many* complete post-secondary education (compared with non-disabled).

3. It is evident from the table that severity of disability has a significant effect on educational attainment. There is a persistent *increase* in the proportion not completing high school as severity increases from mild to very severe.

4. Similarly, there is an *increase* in the proportion not completing post-secondary education as severity of disability increases, just like high school.

Although it is not shown in the table, there were no significant differences between disabled men and women in educational attainment.

Disabled adults who had had their disability while they were in school were asked about the nature and quality of their educational experiences (Statistics Canada, 2012):

- 34% said they had to take fewer courses on account of their disability;
- 30% said it had taken them longer than their non-disabled peers to achieve their educational objectives;
- 30% reported that they had discontinued their studies because of difficulties associated with their disability; and
- 23% reported significant interruptions in their educational career because of their disability.

Socially, there is evidence that school can be a difficult experience for disabled children as well (Jamieson et al., 2009). Forty percent (40%) of the national sample reported feeling excluded or avoided, and 27% experienced physical and verbal bullying (Statistics Canada, 2012). In a qualitative study of young people transitioning from elementary to secondary school, Doubt and McColl (1997) found that both extrinsic and intrinsic factors limited the participation of disabled youth in the school environment. Extrinsic factors included lack of peer and staff support, negative reactions, and inaccessible activities. Intrinsic factors included self-protection strategies, such as self-exclusion, hiding the

Table 13.2: Average time (minutes) spent in education* for Canadian and American adults (18 to 65), disabled and non-disabled

	Canada		United States	
	Non-disabled	Disabled	Non-disabled	Disabled
Male	32.8	11.4	28.1	4.9
Female	36.8	13.2	29.0	4.3
All	34.4	12.3	28.5	4.6

* Includes full- and part-time studies, homework, and personal study.

disability, finding a niche, making fun of the disability, and needing to educate peers. In a particularly evocative statement, one young man described how he had found a way to be "one of the guys", but he recognized that he would always be "a secondary guy".

Wilson and colleagues (2015) made an interesting comparison between Canada and the United States in terms of educational participation among disabled adults. Using data on time use, from the Canadian General Social Survey and the America Time Use Survey (see Table 13.2), they found that non-disabled Canadians spent an average of 34.4 minutes per day on education, while Americans spent 28.5 minutes — that is, about 6 minutes more for Canadians. A slightly more pronounced difference exists between disabled Canadians and Americans — 12.3 minutes for Canadians with disabilities versus 4.6 for Americans with disabilities, which is about 8 minutes difference. The difference between disabled and non-disabled is about the same in both countries — 22 minutes in Canada and 24 minutes in the United States. These data pertain to all adults from 18 to 65, so many will not be involved in education at all, while a small proportion are involved in full-time or part-time post-secondary education.

Wilson and colleagues use time use as an indicator of the extent to which disabled and non-disabled people participate equally in various sectors of society. Looking only at students enrolled in post-secondary education, they examined the time spent in 18 essential, everyday activities. They found that disabled students spent more time than non-disabled students in an average day on

- screen time (primarily computer; 38 minutes more than non-disabled);
- active leisure (37 minutes more);
- personal care (18 minutes more); and
- travel, including commuting (18 minutes more).

Conversely, disabled students spent less time on

- sleep (27 minutes less than non-disabled students) and
- social activities (19 minutes less).

These findings suggest a somewhat more stressful experience in post-secondary education for young people with disabilities versus those without.

Furthermore, Wilson and colleagues (2015) have shown that dissimilarity between time use profiles of disabled and non-disabled students suggests a systematic inequity of some type — either access to opportunities or resources. When examined over time, convergence of time use toward greater similarity suggests increasing equity. That is, time use patterns of disabled and non-disabled samples becoming more and more alike is a sign that the environment supports their participation more equitably. In their research looking at access to post-secondary education, they were also able to compare Canada in 1992 with Canada in 2010. Despite the increased enrolment of disabled students in post-secondary education, noted above, there was no convergence of time use between disabled and non-disabled students in 2010 compared to 1992. In other words, disabled students are *not* looking more like non-disabled students as time goes along. They still experience the same differences in how they spend their time that they did in 1992, suggesting that the environment did not change all that much in the intervening 18 years.

Segregation, integration, inclusion

I alluded above to an evolution in the approach to educating disabled young people over the past 50 or so years. Historically, philosophies regarding the education of disabled children evolved in much the same way as those governing disability in general. At the beginning of the 20th century, education was considered a charitable good dispensed to disabled children (mostly those with sensory impairments, such as deafness and blindness) through religious and benevolent organizations. Disabled children were shielded from potential exploitation, and offered special tuition in "schools" that catered to what they needed to know for the life that was expected to be ahead of them (OECD, 1999).

From there, the conceptualization of disability moved to the medical model, where diagnosed issues were "treated" by professionals and education was folded into the health-care plan for the child — often in an institution or long-term care home. Education for disabled children was outside of the mainstream educational system, and was offered mostly in segregated settings.

By the 1970s, the "normalization" movement saw education as a way to draw disabled young people in from the margins, which was compatible with the sociological definition of disability (Ravaud & Stiker, 2001). Rather than being identified by their diagnosis or medical conditions, disabled learners were classified according to their special educational needs — that is, their need for special tools, supervision, or assistance. Different levels of special education were designed to cater to the needs of children with a variety of different types of disability.

In 1994, the Salamanca Statement reflected the changing views of society toward the education of disabled children. The United Nations Educational, Scientific and Cultural Organization (UNESCO) held its annual conference in Salamanca, Spain, and reaffirmed the right to education for all, regardless of individual differences. The Statement pointed to meeting the needs of every child within the regular educational system as the way to "combat discrimination, create welcoming communities, build an inclusive society, achieve education for all, [and] improve efficiency and cost-effectiveness of the entire education system". This was meant to be achieved through "child-centred education", focusing on the individual child and his or her special needs. In other words, disabled children were still considered a minority in the educational environment; their special needs still required tailored interventions to permit them to assimilate.

In the early years of integrated education, disabled children were "shoe-horned" into regular classrooms, while everyone tried to figure out what was needed in order to make the enterprise successful. But co-location did not necessarily achieve integration. As Ravaud and Stiker (2001) put it, "mechanical inclusion does not guarantee organic inclusion." Neither the physical space, the resource materials, the teachers, the administration, nor the students were equipped to respond to the challenges that occurred (Kauffmann, Anastasiou, Badar, Travers, & Wiley, 2016).

Inclusive education

In the intervening 20-plus years, as the social model of disability has taken hold, a new way of thinking about educating disabled children has evolved, with a focus on the environment and its capacity to respond to diversity. This approach has come to be known as inclusive education. **Inclusive education** attempts to remove barriers to participation in education by offering alternatives in the learning environment and by practising inclusion. It represents a system-focused approach rather than an individually focused approach. It focuses not on relocating and rehabilitating the child, but rather on transforming the educational system to welcome all learners. It creates a community in the classroom that is a microcosm of society, where children learn to relate to one another and to authority figures in a manner that guarantees the rights of all (Thompson, Lyons, & Timmons, 2014). Inclusive education has been shown to have positive effects not only for disabled children but significantly also for non-disabled children in terms of learning to function in a diverse world and developing positive attitudes, social skills, and leadership capacity.

According to Porter (2014), three things are needed for a successful transition to inclusive education:

1. teachers and parents who are committed and prepared;
2. spaces and resources that are conducive to inclusion; and
3. peers that understand the culture of inclusion.

Teachers are key to the success of inclusive education. There is no question that inclusive education places requirements on teachers that would not exist with a more homogeneous student body. Although inclusive education is considered a moral imperative, not everyone is on side, and misconceptions persist about what inclusive education means (Schneider, 2015). In order for teachers to be able to function optimally in an inclusive environment, they need professional development, training, coaching, support, and incentives. On a more practical level, they need favourable teacher–student ratios, skilled educational assistants and volunteers, and educational materials in hard copy and online that are compatible with what they are trying to achieve (Thompson, Lyons, & Timmons, 2014; OECD, 1999). There are obviously resource implications of many of these requirements, necessitating the commitment of administration, board, and government to the enterprise of inclusive education.

In the previous chapter on work, we discussed the concept of individual accommodations to enable participation and to create equity in access to opportunities. Specific accommodations are equally important in the education setting to allow students to optimize their engagement in education. Some of the most common accommodations sought in educational settings are alternate-format text materials, extra time on assignments or exams, help from an educational assistant, specialized technology for accessing course materials, and note-taking or recording of classes. These accommodations are usually prescribed as a result of an individualized assessment, and, like the work environment, there is an expectation that they will be provided and facilitated by instructors. According to national statistics, 23% of students need accommodations during their education, and 7% actually require structural changes to the educational environment to be able to access school (Statistics Canada, 2012).

Another key feature of the current model of inclusive education is the availability of special resource persons to work with teachers and children to ensure the needs of disabled children can be met. Often these resource persons are health professionals, and represent an intersection of the health and education systems. Using data from Ontario, the most common professional was occupational therapy, seeing almost half (49.7%) of the children referred in a given year (2008/9; Deliotte & Touche, 2010). Speech-language pathologists saw about a third of children referred (35.3%), physical therapists saw 11.6%, and nurses saw 3%.

Universal design for learning

With regard to curriculum, one of the ways to achieve inclusive education is through **universal design for learning** (UDL). UDL is an educational framework that uses insights from neuroscience to permit learners to perceive, comprehend, organize, express, and engage in education in multiple ways. It seeks to use a variety of means of representation, expression, and engagement to produce resourceful, motivated learners who are strategic and goal-directed in their approach to learning. It involves an overhaul in the way we think about the relationship between teachers and students, and recasts the teacher's job as optimizing access to learning in a highly complex environment rather than simply "teaching".

Figure 13.1 provides guidelines for representation, expression, and engagement according to the UDL framework:

- Representation includes offering information in a variety of formats, being deliberate and precise in the use of language, and consolidating key points and applications.
- Expression includes optimizing access to assistive technology, providing tools for communication, and increasing effective time and resource management.
- Engagement includes optimizing choice, fostering collaboration, and facilitating coping

Conclusion

I hope this chapter has helped us to *appreciate* the importance of education for opening doors for people with disabilities. We have *discovered* that educational inequities exist — some due to the disability itself, but many due to societal restrictions and barriers that hold disabled students back. A key barrier is attitudes — of society in general, teachers, administrators, parents, and other students. Poor attitudes can result in an unwelcoming environment for disabled children, outright bullying, and low expectations. Other societal barriers include a lack of supply of trained educators and inadequately equipped facilities.

There has been considerable ideological progress in the area of education — from segregation of disabled children in special schools and programs to integrated education, where disabled students are co-located with non-disabled children in the mainstream school system, to inclusion, where the educational system is re-*designed* to accommodate and celebrate diversity. It is still somewhat of a *dream*, but perhaps it is becoming more visible on the horizon that disabled children will participate alongside their peers in fully accessible educational programs. While we can't necessarily single-handedly re-*design* the educational system, we can all *deploy* the attitudes and aptitudes of inclusive education and universal design for learning in our practice and advocacy. As Barton and

Figure 13.1: Guidelines for universal design for learning, version 2.2 (2018)

Universal Design for Learning Guidelines

Provide multiple means of **Engagement**	Provide multiple means of **Representation**	Provide multiple means of **Action & Expression**
Affective Networks The "WHY" of learning	Recognition Networks The "WHAT" of learning	Strategic Networks The "HOW" of learning

Access

Provide options for **Recruiting Interest** (7)	Provide options for **Perception** (1)	Provide options for **Physical Action** (4)
• Optimize individual choice and autonomy (7.1) • Optimize relevance, value, and authenticity (7.2) • Minimize threats and distractions (7.3)	• Offer ways of customizing the display of information (1.1) • Offer alternatives for auditory information (1.2) • Offer alternatives for visual information (1.3)	• Vary the methods for response and navigation (4.1) • Optimize access to tools and assistive technologies (4.2)

Build

Provide options for **Sustaining Effort & Persistence** (8)	Provide options for **Language & Symbols** (2)	Provide options for **Expression & Communication** (5)
• Heighten salience of goals and objectives (8.1) • Vary demands and resources to optimize challenge (8.2) • Foster collaboration and community (8.3) • Increase mastery-oriented feedback (8.4)	• Clarify vocabulary and symbols (2.1) • Clarify syntax and structure (2.2) • Support decoding of text, mathematical notation, and symbols (2.3) • Promote understanding across languages (2.4) • Illustrate through multiple media (2.5)	• Use multiple media for communication (5.1) • Use multiple tools for construction and composition (5.2) • Build fluencies with graduated levels of support for practice and performance (5.3)

Internalize

Provide options for **Self Regulation** (9)	Provide options for **Comprehension** (3)	Provide options for **Executive Functions** (6)
• Promote expectations and beliefs that optimize motivation (9.1) • Facilitate personal coping skills and strategies (9.2) • Develop self-assessment and reflection (9.3)	• Activate or supply background knowledge (3.1) • Highlight patterns, critical features, big ideas, and relationships (3.2) • Guide information processing and visualization (3.3) • Maximize transfer and generalization (3.4)	• Guide appropriate goal-setting (6.1) • Support planning and strategy development (6.2) • Facilitate managing information and resources (6.3) • Enhance capacity for monitoring progress (6.4)

Goal

Expert Learners who are...

Purposeful & Motivated	Resourceful & Knowledgeable	Strategic & Goal-Directed

Armstrong (2001) aptly put it, "inclusive education is not an end in itself, but a means to an end, ... an inclusive society" (p. 708).

To conclude, in Figure 13.2, I offer another story from Joanne Smith, freelance journalist and disability advocate (Smith, 2017).

Figure 13.2: Story of Kira (by Joanne Smith)

Almost 20 years ago, I did a story on a reverse-integrated kindergarten program — a unique program that enabled non-disabled children to attend school alongside disabled children at the Bloorview Rehabilitation Centre. The goals of the program were: to promote confidence, self-esteem, self-advocacy and inclusion for children with special needs. And it did just that.

In this story, I featured a little girl (who I'll call Kira) who had cerebral palsy. She was an incredibly bright, outgoing, social, happy 5-year-old who gushed with confidence. She loved her school and her friends — both those with and without disabilities. The program's fully integrated approach and environment helped create a limitless perspective. She was ready to take on the world.

As I said, the goals of this program were to promote confidence, self-esteem, self-advocacy and inclusion for children with special needs; but amazingly, at the same time, this program's accepting and completely inclusive environment promoted a sense of understanding, equity, empathy, fair play and diversity for the non-disabled children as well — so much so that when parents realized the positive impact the program was having on their children, a huge wait list grew for non-disabled children to attend this school. Imagine that — a huge demand by non-disabled people to attend programs designed for people with disabilities!

I continued to see Kira after the story aired at various events, and every time she exuded the same self-confidence and joy as the first time I met her.

Then two years later, I got a call from Kira's mother. She had been transferred to a new school — a regular pub-

continued....

Figure 13.2 continued

lic school. There were no other children with disabilities in her class, so there wasn't the same level of contact and co-participation as she experienced at her old school. During the first week of school, a group of classmates had pushed her in her manual wheelchair up a hill — she thought they were going to play — then let her go backwards down the hill. She was injured badly and ended up in hospital. She eventually recovered from the physical injuries, but the emotional ones were more devastating. This once self-assured girl's spirit was broken, and it was heartbreaking to see. Sadly, my next story with Kira was about bullying, and the direct impact of not *being in an environment that fostered understanding, acceptance, equity and fair play.*

On a follow-up note on Kira ... I recently learned that she graduated from teachers' college and doesn't have a full-time job yet. She did land a job substitute-teaching; however, she can't take it. It entails working at different schools, often at the last minute, and she doesn't have reliable transportation to be able to get where she needs to be with short notice. She can't rely on Wheel-Trans, which requires her to book trips days in advance. It's an unacceptable situation.

Source: Smith, 2017.

Chapter 14

Disability and income

Introduction

Although this chapter is titled "Income", it deals with a number of indicators of economic prosperity. The content of this chapter is significantly affected by the issues addressed in the previous two chapters, that is, employment and education.

One way of thinking about economic prosperity is in terms of capital (Robson & Nares, 2006). **Capital** is usually considered from four perspectives:

- **Human capital** — the education, skills, health, and other personal resources of the individual; his or her personal ability to participate in the economy;

- **Physical capital** — the tangible assets that the individual possesses that enhance his or her productivity, such as housing, transportation, or business assets;

- **Social capital** — the networks, connections, and personal relationships that contribute to the welfare of the individual; and

- **Financial capital** — the actual income and liquid assets the individual has at his or her disposal.

We will consider all four of these briefly in this chapter, but we focus on the latter.

Without a doubt, the situation of people with disabilities is complicated by being associated with poverty. In Canada, the p-overty rate for people with disabilities is double what it is for non-disabled Canadians. More than a third (35%) of Canadians with disabilities live in poverty, compared to 18% of non-disabled Canadians, and compared to an average of 22.5% in other OECD countries. Put another way, approximately a third (33%) of Canadians with disabilities have incomes below 60% of the national median income (OECD, 2010b).

In Canada, we don't designate a specific "poverty line", as they do in the United States, which reflects only household income. In the United States, 19% of disabled people live below the poverty line — almost twice as many as the 10% of non-disabled people who live below the poverty line. Instead, we tend to use "material hardship indicators", meaning the ability to afford a standard basket of goods and services; however, the results are about the same.

Poverty in Canada means the inability to afford fresh fruit and vegetables, a warm winter coat, and an inexpensive gift for a child's birthday (Notten & Mendelson, 2016). These modest articles conform with our expectation of a minimum standard of living in a prosperous, developed country like Canada. One measure of poverty used in Canada is the LICO, or **low-income cut-off** (Tweddle, Battle, & Torjman, 2017). The LICO refers to the threshold beyond which more than 63% of after-tax revenues are spent on necessities, such as food, shelter, clothing, and personal needs, leaving only 37% to cover health, education, transportation, recreation, and all other expenses. People with disabilities have a 1.6 times greater risk of experiencing stress over their ability to pay for housing, and a 1.9 times greater risk related to paying for food (Smith, 2013).

Regardless of how one measures or characterizes poverty, disabled people in all but a very few countries in the world are significantly worse off than their non-disabled counterparts. This intersection of disability with social and economic vulnerabilities — lower school participation, lower educational attainment, lower employment rates, less full-time work, poorer working conditions, lower wages, lower incomes from all sources, less asset ownership, poorer living conditions, higher costs for health care, greater expenditure on disability-related goods and services, increased likelihood of living alone — all contribute to a double jeopardy situation, where multiple disadvantages have multiplicative rather than simply additive effects. The *World Report on Disability* (World Bank & WHO, 2011) rates the five most significant impacts of disability as follows:

(1) less economic activity, employment, saving, spending; (2) lower education; (3) greater poverty; (4) less community and civic participation; and (5) poorer health.

Economic inequality

We have talked in the previous two chapters about inequalities in education and employment for people with disabilities. Those deficits in education and employment ultimately play out in terms of *financial capital*. People with disabilities have significantly less financial capital — that is, fewer economic resources at their disposal — compared to non-disabled Canadians. In 2010, the National Household Survey, conducted by Statistics Canada, showed that people with disabilities are considerably worse off than their non-disabled counterparts (Statistics Canada, 2012).

- Among working-age people, those without disabilities had on average 50% more income than those with disabilities ($31,160 annual income for non-disabled aged 15–64 vs. $20,420 for disabled). Furthermore, there is a gradient in terms of severity of disability. Those with mild disabilities made only about $1,000 less per annum than those with no disability ($29,950 vs $31,160), while those with more severe disabilities made considerably less: $21,620 for those with moderate disabilities, $16,810 for those with severe disabilities, and $14,390 for those with very severe disabilities.

- Within the labour force, disabled workers made considerably less than their non-disabled counterparts. For those who were university graduates, disabled males made about $23,000 less per year than their non-disabled peers ($69,200 vs. $92,700), and disabled women only a few thousand less ($64,500 vs. $68,000). Among all workers, disabled men made $9,500 less than non-disabled, and disabled women made $8,800 less (Strombolopolous, 2013).

- Among seniors, the discrepancy is not quite so marked. Disabled seniors had incomes averaging $21,450, compared to non-disabled seniors at $24,920. This is attributed to two factors — the higher prevalence of disability in older age, and the greater reliance of seniors on pension and public-source income.

Income is an important indicator of economic well-being, but so too is the possession of "wealth" (Sherraden, 1991). **Wealth** is defined as not only the presence of income, but also the ownership of assets. **Assets** most commonly include real property (home and land), business assets, savings, and securities (Parish, Grinstein-Weiss, Yeo, Rose, & Rimmerman, 2010). Assets are often classified as short-term (or liquid) assets, such as bank accounts and investments, and long-term, such as real estate and retirement savings (Rothwell & Goren, 2011).

Assets are at the root of social stratification, and are considerably more influential than income for determining who will flourish and who will not (Sherraden, 1991). The ownership of assets permits individuals to think about the future, to take risks, and to make commitments (Boshara, Cramer, & Sherraden, 2006; Soffer, MacDonald, & Blanck, 2010). Assuming that younger people will be net borrowers while older people are net savers, asset-holding permits families to smooth out lifetime consumption and ensure a stable standard of living (Buckland, 2010; Robson & Nares, 2006; Williams, 2006). Assets mitigate economic strain; they provide a cushion against economic disruption and a degree of security against future extraordinary expenses. They act both directly and indirectly to affect individual well-being and family functioning (Conger, Rueter, & Rand, 2000; Rothwell & Goren, 2011). Assets provide individuals and families with a stake in the economy and a sense of economic agency and self-sufficiency.

Individuals and families affected by disability experience "asset poverty" at greater rates than their non-disabled counterparts. **Asset poverty** occurs when a family's total assets minus total debts are not sufficient to meet their basic needs for three months or more (Haveman & Wolff, 2005). Asset poverty among families affected by disability is a result of lower incomes, higher out-of-pocket costs, and lost productivity, rendering many families unable to afford basic household goods and services, let alone to save for the future (Putnam et al., 2005; Seltzer & Krauss, 1994, 2001).

Asset poverty rates were found to be two to four times greater for families affected by disability compared to other American families (Parish et al., 2010; Rank & Hirschl, 2010). Families affected by disability had only about one-third as many assets as those without disabilities (Emerson & Hatton, 2009). Almost half (46%) of households with a member with a disability had no savings at all; they were 68% more likely than their non-disabled peers to be entirely without financial assets.

Dufflo, Gale, Liebman, Orszag, and Saez (2007) showed that people with incomes less than $40,000 are very unlikely to be able to save. Given an average income of about $20,000 for people with disabilities, it is clear that saving would be a particular challenge (Statistics Canada, 2012). Families that experienced income poverty were 60% more likely to transition into asset poverty in the subsequent year, and less likely to transition out of hardship in the future (Seltzer & Krauss, 2001). A number of other factors aside from income also affect the ability of disabled individuals and families to save. These include both micro-economic factors (those particular to the individual, such as his or her disability and other personal circumstances) and macro-economic factors (issues like the political and economic climate and attitudes toward debt) (McColl & Schaub, 2013).

High asset poverty rates were pervasive across age cohorts. Fifty-five percent (55%) of parents under 45 with disabled children experienced asset poverty, compared to 38% of all American families. Forty-two percent (42%) of parents with disabled children remained in asset poverty into their retirement years, compared to 11% of all American families (Rank & Hirschl, 2010; Parish et al., 2010).

Parish and colleagues (2010) found that mean asset accumulation was on average 15% lower for families with at least one working-aged adult (18 to 64) with a disability than for a comparison group of families where no adults had a disability. Net worth was lowest for households where the head of household was a member of a visible minority, did not have a high school diploma, or was a single woman.

In terms of debt, Emerson and Hatton (2009) found that families in the United Kingdom with a child with a disability were more than twice as likely to be in debt and to have trouble paying off debts compared to the reference group. They also had approximately 50% more total debt than other families.

People with disabilities are also disadvantaged in terms of *physical capital*. Differences in physical capital lead to structural economic inequalities that are deeply rooted in society. Take, for example, home ownership — perhaps the most basic indicator of economic security. Robson and Nares (2006) note that housing is the most significant asset owned by most Canadian families, representing 38% of all assets. (Second is retirement savings, accounting for 12% of wealth.) According to Emerson and Hatton (2009), only 55% of families with a disability in the United Kingdom were able to own their own home, compared to 72% of other families. In the United States, only 4% of disabled adults own a home, compared to 70% of non-disabled adults (Soffer et al., 2010). In the absence of relatively lucrative paid employment, the costs of home ownership are simply out of reach.

Buckland (2010) notes the difficulty for low-income families to obtain bank credit of any kind, particularly a mortgage. Instead, they are often forced to rely on "fringe credit", such as private loans and cheque cashing services. These financial agencies are notoriously expensive and unregulated. Similar deficiencies are evident when exploring the ability of people with disabilities to raise capital for business enterprises, to pursue advanced or professional education, and to save for retirement.

With regard to *social capital*, Soffer and colleagues (2010) refer to "gateway assets" to describe the social connections and relation- ships that contribute positively to economic security — assets like personal and family contacts, expert advice, private transportation, excellent health care, and health maintenance. These supports permit individuals to obtain advanced education, to be socially and geographically mobile, and to obtain optimal employment — in short, to be well off. Putnam and associates (2005) note that people with disabilities are less likely to have opportunities that lead to the development of social capital. They refer specifically to advanced education and employment experiences, and the subsequent development of beneficial contacts and connections.

Costs associated with living with a disability

In addition to the usual costs of living experienced by each of us, peo- ple with disabilities incur a layer of extraordinary costs associated with living with a disability. Here are some examples of these costs:

- housing costs — accessible housing, renovations, modifications for accessibility, safety, convenience, efficiency;
- transportation — vehicle adaptation, accessible taxis, inability to use public transit (thus need for a private vehicle);
- adaptive devices — orthotics, prosthetics, mobility devices and accessories, continence supplies and other expendables, computer, and peripherals;
- medications, supplements, dietary specialities;

- health care costs — complementary treatments, non-insured services; and
- assistance/supervision — at home, at work, housekeeping, meal preparation, attendant care.

Some of these costs are easy to itemize and quantify, whereas others are hidden and more challenging to substantiate. For example, an individual with a disability may require a family member to miss work (or even give up work altogether) to provide either intermittent or regular assistance; the individual might need a particular type of costly clothing or accessory; the family may need a trained attendant rather than a babysitter in order to be able to go out (Witt et al., 2011; Edwards, Higgins, Gray, Zmijewski, & Kingston, 2008; Emerson, Shahtahmasebi, Lancaster, & Berridge, 2010; Parish, Rose, & Swaine, 2010; Torjman, 2017).

The additional costs associated with living with a disability can be estimated in a number of ways, but the most common is to simply ask people with disabilities to report their costs (e.g., direct survey approach, expenditure diary approach, budget standards approach). The following estimates are not comparable with each other because they differ on a number of important factors, including what expenses were included, the year of the study, the country and currency, and the type of disability considered. However, they paint a graphic picture of the extraordinary costs that accrue as a result of daily living with a disability.

- The Centers for Disease Control (2004) in the United States found that the average lifetime medical and non-medical costs (assistive devices, home and automobile modifications, special education, losses to employment income) were $1,014,000 for persons with intellectual disabilities, $921,000 for persons with cerebral palsy, $417,000 for people with hearing loss, and $566,000 for people with visual impairments. The cost of special education alone could range between 42% and 82% of the total direct costs incurred by families caring for a child with an intellectual disability.

- Sobsey and Calder (2006) observed that in Canada, the economic impact of the extraordinary costs associated with disability is mitigated by government programs, private insurance, and services from charitable organizations. Further, they note that some of the typical costs of child-rearing are reduced when a child grows up with a disability; for example, post-secondary education and car insurance.

- A study in the United States (Ganz, 2007) included costs for home modifications, special education, and employment supports. This study estimated lifetime costs at $3.2 million US, and found that non-medical costs were much higher than medical costs.

- An Australian study estimated the cost of disability at 29% of household income for families with any person with a disability, and 37% for households where the head of household experienced disability (Saunders, 2007). The study also found that each point in a four-point severity scale accounted for approximately an additional 10% in the cost of disability to households. The cost of a moderate restriction was estimated at 30% of household income, a severe disability at 40%, and a very severe disability at 48%.

- Between 1995 and 2001, the cost of disability in Ireland increased from 20% to 30% of disposable income (Stapleton, Protik, & Stone, 2008).

- A Canadian study using data from the 2001 Participation and Activity Limitation Survey estimated the overall average outlay for disability-related costs at $1,159 per year (Burton & Phipps, 2009). When multiplied by the average life expectancy of 83 years (Styan, 2012), the average lifetime out-of-pocket cost of disability in Canada is $96,197. This conservative estimate only includes direct out-of-pocket costs and truncates costs at the top end.

- Knapp, Romeo, and Beecham (2009) found that the lifetime cost of caring for an adult with autism spectrum disorder (ASD) in the United Kingdom was £796,050 for those with no co-morbid intellectual disability and £1,234,044 for those who also had an intellectual disability. These costs included special education, health and social care, respite care, accommodation costs for children not living with their families, and foregone employment income. They did not include informal care or foregone employment income by family members.

- Recent Canadian estimates of the lifetime cost of spinal cord injury (Kruger, 2011) estimated $1.6 million for people with paraplegia and $3.0 million for people with tetraplegia. This study included direct costs (i.e., health care and prescription drugs, equipment and modifications, long-term care) and indirect costs (i.e., morbidity, premature mortality, unpaid caregiving costs).

- Based on differences in standard of living between households, Cullinan, Gannon, and Lyons (2011) estimated the cost of disability in Canada in 2001 at 22.8% of average family income. This translates to $7,634 per year, or $633,628 over a lifetime. For families with a child who has "some limitation", lifetime costs were estimated between $564,151 and $842,058. For those with a severe limitation, lifetime costs were estimated between $908,755 and $1,036,592.

- American estimates of the lifetime cost related to traumatic brain injury came in between $85,000 and $3 million US, depending on severity. This study included medical costs, foregone employment income, and costs related to the care of the individual post injury (Brain Injury Institute, 2012).

It is clear that there are significant extraordinary costs associated with living with a disability — costs that can consume between one-quarter and one-half of annual household income. Extraordinary expenses attributable to disability have been estimated between $100,000 and $3 million (CAD) per capita, depending on the severity of disability and the subsequent requirements for personal care, health care, and specialized housing and equipment.

Sources of income for people with disabilities

We have already discussed (in Chapter 12) that only about 45% of people with disabilities are employed and earning wages. Ideally, this means a living wage plus benefits; however, it can also be part-time work, contract work, self-employment, or piecework. These latter options often don't furnish enough income to make ends meet.

So, where does the money come from to support people with disabilities if they are unemployed or under-employed? There are a number of sources, and those for which one qualifies depends on at least three factors:

- how one became disabled — whether or not the disability was incurred as a result of military service, a work accident, an automobile accident, as a victim of crime or other personal violation

Table 14.1: Sources of income for people with disabilities

Employment income	Non-employment income	
	Yes	No
Yes	20%	31%
No	37%	12%

(for example, victims of a tainted blood transfusion or of maternal thalidomide are eligible for compensation);

- the severity and duration of disability;

- whether or not one contributed to the pension or insurance plan through employment deduction or private contributions.

Among working-age people (15 to 64), 37% receive only income from benefits and sources other than employment; 31% receive only their employment income; 20% receive some employment income supplemented by other sources; and 12% receive no income (see Table 14.1).

Other sources that typically make up the revenue streams that support people with disabilities include the following:

1. *Pensions:* A **pension** is a fund into which one makes regular contributions, usually through employment, in order to ensure an income stream when one ceases working, typically due to retirement. The Canada Pension Plan / Quebec Pension Plan — Disability (CPP-D/QPP-D) pension supports about 19% of people with disabilities in Canada with a monthly pension that is 75% of what the individual's retirement pension would have been. (At age 65, it converts to the regular Canada or Quebec old age pension.) The maximum pension obtainable is about $1,100 per month, and the average is about $800 (OECD, 2010b). In order to qualify for the CPP-D, one must have a "severe and prolonged" disability, and must have contributed to the program through employment-related deductions. The CPP-D is a program of the federal government, and it has a very stringent eligibility standard —

57% of applicants are denied coverage on initial application, and 35% of those are ultimately accepted pending appeal.

2. *Welfare:* The next most common source of revenue for people with disabilities in Canada are provincial social assistance or "welfare" programs, supporting about 15% of disabled people (OECD, 2010b). **Social assistance** programs are administered by each province, and they are considered the income program of "last resort", meaning that all other options must be exhausted before they kick in. Social assistance is based on a means test that assesses both household needs (including food, shelter, clothing, and other basic necessities, including special needs), and available financial resources (including both income and assets). Typically exempted are assets that would support possible future employment, such as a residence, vehicle, or other work-related equipment.

Both of these programs also have a number of other benefits associated with them, such as coverage for prescription drugs, health services, and medical and technical equipment. These items can amount to substantial costs if not covered, and often make it difficult for individuals to transition off pension or welfare for fear of losing these benefits. Even if they could find work, they would be considerably worse off if they had to bear these disability-related expenses personally. This phenomenon is referred to as the "welfare wall", or the dependency created when income programs are structured in such a way as to make economic self-sufficiency unattractive (Torjman, 2017).

3. *Insurance:* Private insurance provides a revenue stream for about 10% of people with disabilities (Statistics Canada, 2012). Unfortunately, only about half of the workforce is covered by long-term disability insurance — probably because it is usually an optional benefit, and individuals can't (or don't want to) contemplate the possibility of becoming disabled (Meredith & Chia, 2015). Private disability insurance can be costly if not offered as part of a group employment benefit; yet, in the event that one does incur a disability that interferes with one's usual ability to earn a livelihood, it can mean the difference between maintaining something like one's usual lifestyle and not. Private disability insurance usually provides between 50% and 75% of one's prior income, and can be used to augment other programs, such as CPP-D.

There is also public insurance, operated by the federal government, against short-term absences from work due to illness or disability — specifically the Employment Insurance–Sickness Benefit (EI-SB). About 8% of disabled people at any one time are supported by the EI-SB. It is available only to people who have been employed and contributed through employment deductions. This is a short-term program to replace lost income during an illness of duration up to 15 weeks. EI-SB is a program of the federal government, and the expectation is that people with conditions lasting longer than 15 weeks will transition to the CPP-D, if they meet the criteria for severity.

Automobile insurance also provides an income stream for less than 2% of disabled people in Canada. Several provincial governments across the country have adopted no-fault public automobile insurance schemes that compensate individuals for disabilities incurred in motor vehicle crashes. Whereas previously the auto insurance sector was entirely private, some provincial governments in Canada have sought to reconcile inequities in coverage and premiums by regulating the sector to conform with provincial standards.

4. *Compensation:* Another important income stream is compensation schemes that replace lost revenue for people who acquire their disability through particular circumstances. The most common is workers' compensation. In Canada, workers' compensation is administered provincially and provides income and a variety of services to individuals whose disability arises from an injury incurred at work. About 8% of people with disabilities derive a revenue stream from workers' compensation. Workers' compensation programs have the explicit goal of returning workers to gainful employment, and so there is considerable focus on vocational rehabilitation and retraining.

   Also in the category of compensation are a number of specific pensions and funds provided by government for particular types of disabilities or groups of people. Here are a few examples:
   - The Government of Canada offers a veteran's pension to injured service persons who become disabled in the line of duty (less than 1%).

- Victims of crime are entitled to compensation for disabilities incurred as a result of an unlawful act.
- Victims of particular health-care episodes, such as tainted blood transfusions or thalidomide, are entitled to compensation.

About 75% of people with disabilities avail themselves of one of these sources of income; however, most programs provide inadequate coverage if only one benefit can be accessed (OECD, 2010b). The remaining 25% engage in the entirely legitimate practice of "benefit stacking". About 22% receive two sources of income, and 3% receive three or more, thus increasing the probability of deriving a reasonable standard of living for a small fraction of the population.

There are also a number of additional measures that federal and provincial/territorial governments use to try to put money in the pockets of people with disabilities. The federal government offers several options for tax relief and savings. Programs like the Disability Tax Credit, the Registered Disability Savings Plan, the Medical Expense Tax Credit, the Child Disability Tax Credit, the Disability Equipment Grant, and the Canada Student Loan Disability Program are all designed to offset the extraordinary expenses incurred by people with disabilities, to overcome social and economic inequities, and to encourage participation of people with disabilities. Unfortunately, tax measures only benefit people whose incomes are sufficiently large to require them to pay taxes, so as measures for alleviating poverty, they are limited (Torjman, 2017).

Provincial and territorial governments also operate programs within their areas of jurisdiction (e.g., health, education, transportation, childcare) to offset expenses associated with disability and thereby afford disabled people more disposable income. Although they vary by jurisdiction, programs are typically offered to subsidize housing, transportation, acquisition of adaptive equipment, health and social services, childcare, educational expenses, and attendant care, to name a few examples.

Conclusion

I hope it is evident from this chapter that income for people with disabilities, many of whom are impeded from working to their full capacity, is a very complex issue. We have *discovered*, sadly, that too often disability and poverty go hand in hand. Economic inequities persist, whether we look strictly at income or also consider assets and purchasing power.

The system of ensuring adequate income for people with disabilities in Canada has been criticized as being inadequate and incoherent (Torjman, 2017), and "restrictive, complex & difficult to access" (OECD, 2010b, p. 7) — in other words, not really a system at all (Every Canadian Counts, 2017). Because the system is highly decentralized — spread among federal and provincial/territorial governments and the private sector — it requires people with disabilities to be highly knowledgeable and sophisticated navigators of both public and private sector organizations. In addition, the fragmentation of the system contributes to a lack of good data on outcomes upon which to support the case for change (OECD, 2010b).

In a study of disability income across the 20 OECD countries, a report focusing on Canada shows that our system underperforms on just about every metric. For a prosperous country defined by its commitment to equitable access, Canada has a record of low benefit rates, low coverage rates, and low spending on disability benefits (OECD, 2010b):

- Benefit levels sat at about 20% of the gross average wage for an employee with comparable qualifications and experience across all 20 OECD countries.

- Disability benefits covered only about 4.5% of the working-age population, compared to the OECD average of 6%. This clearly misses more than half of the 10% who report a disability among those 15 to 64 years of age (Statistics Canada, 2012). Only Mexico, Korea, and Turkey have worse records.

- Canada contributed only 1.28% of gross domestic product (GDP) to disability benefits, compared with the OECD average of 2.4%. This placed Canada in the lowest category, along with Turkey, Korea, Mexico, Australia, and the United States. Six countries in northern Europe spent more than 3% GDP on disability benefits (Denmark, Germany, Netherlands, Poland, Sweden, and Norway).

How do we rectify this situation? We *dream* of a society where all people, including disabled people, have enough to ensure a reasonable standard of living and to live with dignity. The policy considerations of this dream are beyond the scope of this chapter, but there will be more on policy in Chapter 17. As professionals in the health and social services, however, we have a role in *designing* programs to maximize access to resources for our clients.

Perhaps the best we can do in the *deployment* of our services is to be realistic and aware of the economic situation of our clients. Many of our recommendations will have economic implications for clients — for example, acquiring equipment or supplies, transportation and parking for appointments, and childcare or attendant care considerations. To the extent that we take these into consideration, we increase the likelihood that our recommendations will be upheld, and that we can actually help our clients. We demonstrate that we are not simply privileged professionals who don't understand "real life". Instead, we show that we are sensitive to the multi-dimensional reality that our clients live with. When we *appreciate* the many factors that they balance in making everyday decisions, we show that we really care, as opposed to just pretending to care.

Chapter 15

Disability and leisure

Introduction

For our purposes, **leisure** is defined as activities that one undertakes when one is freed of the obligation to be productive (McColl, Law, & Stewart, 2015). Leisure activities typically share these qualities:

1. elective — we are not obliged to do leisure activities; we freely choose to spend our time in these particular ways;
2. intrinsically rewarding — we don't do them because they are remunerative or otherwise externally motivated; they are satisfying in their own right; and
3. characterized by positive affect — fun, relaxing, amusing, enjoyable.

Leisure is largely a subjective experience. It is defined partially by the way the activity is experienced. The same activity can be experienced as leisure, productivity, or self-care, depending on the circumstances. Challenge to readers #6 provides an example of cooking as leisure, productivity, and self-care. Can you think of any other examples of activities that could be all three?

Benefits of leisure

Leisure activities can confer a wide array of direct and indirect benefits (Krupa, 1998; Snir & Harpaz, 2002; Primeau, 2003; Martin, 2013; Shikako-Thomas & Law, 2015):

Challenge for readers #6

How would you characterize the activity of cooking a meal: self-care, productivity, or leisure?

- For a group of friends making a meal together on a Saturday night, enjoying a glass of wine and visiting at the same time, it is clearly leisure.
- For a professional chef in a busy kitchen with a 25-minute backlog in orders, it is obviously work, and stressful work at that.
- For a parent making a meal for his or her family, it is also productivity, but not remunerative work.
- For a student assembling a nutritious lunch and packing it in his or her knapsack to eat between classes (instead of buying from a vending machine), the activity is probably considered self-care.

- *Expression:* Leisure activities can provide a means of expression for ideas, emotions, or images that are deeply held and may not be expressed in the course of our other activities.

- *Creativity:* Leisure activities may bring out our gifts and engage our imagination; some creative activities, like art, music, or writing, result in unique or original products that may be beautiful, interesting, topical, innovative, or even controversial.

- *Skill development:* Leisure activities can be an opportunity to develop skills in physical, social, or cognitive areas. Sports participation, for example, can result in fitness, strength, endurance, flexibility, or agility.

- *Fun:* Leisure activities are often pursued because they are joyful experiences, like playing with children, listening to comedy, or playing a game with friends; they bring us delight and amusement.

- *Relaxation:* Some leisure affords an opportunity to recharge our batteries, to re-align our priorities, or to simply rest, such as meditating, watching TV, or napping.

- *Socialization:* Many leisure pursuits bring us into contact with others who share our interests, and who also enjoying spending time on particular activities.

- *Competition:* Some leisure activities are aimed at being better, and perhaps even the best! Sports and trivia are two examples of leisure activities whose motivation lies in pitting oneself against others, or against our own previous performance.

- *Challenge:* Other activities are inherently challenging without being competitive; they involve skill development or cognitive stimulation, such as doing crosswords, some kinds of reading, or discussion/debate.

Research has also shown that leisure participation has indirect benefits in the following areas (Duquette, Carbonneau, & Joudran-Ionescu, 2016; Sweet et al., 2013; Martin, 2013; Snir & Harpaz, 2002):

- social status and avoiding social stigma;
- positive affect, reduced stress, decreased depression;
- sense of mastery, self-efficacy, self-esteem, identity;
- development of social network;
- expansion of possibilities for the future; and
- overall quality of life — meaning the congruence between expectations of life and its actuality.

Categories of leisure

This long list of qualities suggests that we probably need a classification of leisure to help us in our discussion, and to ensure that we cover all bases. As in previous discussions, the *International Classification of Functioning Disability and Health* (ICF) provides a starting place (WHO, 2001). The ICF classifies recreation and leisure (d920) as play, sports, arts and culture, crafts, hobbies, and socializing.

Another option is provided by the Canadian Occupational Performance Measure (Law et al., 2014), which offers a simple classification of leisure as quiet recreation, active recreation, and socialization. Below are some examples of activities classified under each category:

- *Quiet recreation:* Listening to music, watching TV, reading, knitting or other handcrafts, hobbies, collections, creative arts, cards or board games; these activities tend to be sedentary, and many of them are individual solo activities;

- *Active recreation:* Sports, pet care, sightseeing, using parks or other recreational properties, visiting museums/libraries, travelling, attending sporting events, taking courses; and

- *Socializing:* Visiting friends/family, talking on the phone or Internet, hospitality, dining out, going to bars or nightclubs, attending group functions.

Time spent in leisure

The time use data to which we have referred in previous chapters employs five categories of leisure, and gives us an idea of how people with disabilities spend their leisure time compared to others (Wilson, McColl, Zhang, & McKinnon, 2017). Table 15.1 shows us that disabled Canadians spend a total of 42.1 minutes more than non-disabled Canadians on leisure, while disabled Americans spent

Table 15.1: Time use (in minutes per day) by Canadians and Americans (2010)

	Canada			United States		
Activity	*ND*	*D*	*(D – ND)*	*ND*	*D*	*(D – ND)*
Screen time	146.5	198.3	51.8	170.5	276.8	106.3
Social leisure	78.4	73.8	–4.6	49.1	46.0	–3.1
Travel	76.9	60.5	–16.4	73.6	46.8	–26.8
Active leisure	38.5	36.6	–1.9	33.1	31.5	–1.6
Passive leisure	21.7	34.9	13.2	22.2	45.6	23.4
TOTAL	362.0	404.1	42.1	348.5	446.7	98.2

ND: Non-disabled; D: Disabled

Screen time: watching TV, use of computers, digital devices; Social: socializing, visiting, entertainment, sport attendance, etc.; Travel: travel to, from, between activities; Active leisure: participation in sport, hobbies, crafts, amateur theater, music, etc.; Passive leisure: reading, listening to CDs, tapes, etc., writing letters

Source: Wilson et al., 2017

an hour-and-a-half more (98.2 minutes) than non-disabled Americans in leisure activities.

Here are a few noteworthy observations from this table:

- The biggest differences in time use between disabled and non-disabled people in both countries is accounted for by screen time (51.8 minutes more for Canadians and 106.3 minutes for Americans) and passive leisure (13.2 minutes more for Canadians and 23.4 minutes for Americans).

- The only leisure activity where disabled people spent significantly less time than non-disabled people was travel (16.4 minutes less for Canadians and 26.8 minutes less for Americans).

Table 15.2 compares Canadian men and women with regard to how they spend their leisure time. Disabled men spent about 48 minutes more in leisure than non-disabled men, while disabled women spent almost 43 minutes more in leisure than non-disabled women. Similar to Table 15.1, the main activities that account for those differences are screen time, travel, and passive leisure.

Table 15.2: Time use (in minutes per day) by Canadian men and women (2010)

Activity	Male ND	Male D	Male (D – ND)	Female ND	Female D	Female (D – ND)	(M – F) D
Screen	165.7	226.5	60.8	127	177.2	50.2	49.3
Social leisure	73.9	66.2	–7.7	83	79.5	–3.5	–13.3
Travel	79.7	62.8	–16.9	74.1	58.7	–15.4	4.1
Active leisure	43.4	41.7	–1.7	33.4	32.7	–0.7	9.0
Passive leisure	19.8	33.5	13.7	23.7	35.9	12.2	–2.4
TOTAL	382.5	430.7	48.2	341.2	384	42.8	46.7

ND: Non-disabled; D: Disabled

Looking at the differences between the sexes, disabled men spent about 47 minutes more in leisure than disabled women. This compares closely with the difference between non-disabled men and women, where men also spend about 42 minutes more at leisure than women. The main activity that accounts for the extra time is screen time, where disabled men spend 49 minutes more than disabled women. They also spend slightly more time at active leisure (9 minutes), while disabled women spend on average about 13 minutes per day more on social leisure than disabled men.

Relationship of leisure to work

A number of researchers have suggested that leisure and work are related to each other in terms of preferences, skills, aptitudes, and opportunities (Bundy, 2005; Christiansen, Baum, & Bass-Haugen, 2005). Apparently individuals choose leisure activities that prepare them for work, and that dovetail with other lifestyle choices (Christiansen & Townsend, 2004).

There are typically three ways to think about the relationship between leisure and work.

1. *Leisure as a spill-over from work:* Most researchers consider leisure to be made up of activities that express the same skills, interests, and aptitudes as those used at work (Snir & Harpaz, 2002). Furthermore, some see this relationship as reciprocal — not only do our leisure choices reflect our work choices, but our work can also reflect what we do in our spare time. We choose leisure activities that use the skills and inclinations that shape our work, *and* we may also (to the extent that we can) fashion a work life that embraces the things we like to do in our free time. For example, someone with an administrative job may find themselves using the same skills to run their children's sport league, or serve on the board of a charitable organization in their leisure time.

2. *Leisure as compensation for work:* A second option for the relationship between leisure and work is to think of leisure as a way to compensate for the inadequacies of work. Leisure permits expression of aspects of the self in ways that may not be permitted or welcomed at work. Someone who does a highly analytical job (an accountant or financial analyst, for

Table 15.3: Classification of work and leisure

		MOTIVATION		
		Intrinsic	*Both*	*Extrinsic*
CHOICE	Freedom of choice	Pure leisure	Leisure-work	Leisure-job
	Obligation	Pure work	Work-job	Pure job

example) might play in an amateur theatre group, or race off-road bikes in his or her free time.

3. *Leisure and work as independent:* The third option is that work and leisure are lived out independently of each other. The choices we make in how we earn our living are made on the basis of entirely different criteria from those we apply when choosing our leisure pursuits.

Two dimensions that are often considered in differentiating leisure from work are freedom of choice and the source of motivation (Sintas, de Francisco, & Alvarez, 2015). These two dimensions form a matrix that permits us to look at six different classifications of leisure and work; see Table 15.3.

- Pure leisure refers to activities undertaken purely by choice, and purely for intrinsic benefits they deliver — enjoyment, self-expression, self-efficacy, skill development, identity reinforcement.

- Leisure-work refers to activities that are freely undertaken, but that have elements of both internal and external motivation. For example, playing with one's children, while freely chosen, is done with the understanding that in addition to being fun, it is probably going to have some benefits for the child, and therefore is also part of the productive parenting role. There is a reason to do it beyond the fun involved.

- Leisure-job activities are those that are voluntary, but for which the motivation is supplied externally. Serving on a neighbourhood development committee might be an example of a leisure-job.

- Pure work is not voluntary; there is an element of obligation, but the motivation is primarily intrinsic. For example, an artist or creative person might describe his or her work as pure work. The motivation to create comes from within, and there is even some resistance to external validation that it is "good enough"; however, it is clearly work — it is undertaken for purposes such as making a living, contributing to home and society, and achieving one's potential.

- Work-job refers to activities that are obligatory and that involve both intrinsic and extrinsic rewards. Students in a professional education program often describe their time spent in their studies as work-job. Schoolwork is obligatory if they are to be successful, and the rewards are both intrinsic in terms of learning and achieving one's career goal, and extrinsic in terms of attaining good grades and making parents proud.

- Pure job refers to work undertaken strictly as an obligation and with no real intrinsic validation. This would include work that is done strictly for a paycheque or to meet external expectations, but from which no real satisfaction is derived.

At the very least, leisure is in a temporal relationship with work. By definition, leisure occupies a time slot that is circumscribed by work and self-care. Leisure is relegated to those hours left over when work and self-care are completed or otherwise set aside.

However, there is also a temporal relationship between work and leisure over the lifespan. The balance between work and leisure changes in predictable ways over the course of one's life in response to developmental demands. This pattern is labelled the work–play continuum (Shannon, 1970; Kielhofner, 1988). The pattern looks like a U-shaped curve with more leisure at the extremes and more work in the middle (see Figure 15.1). In childhood and older age, leisure plays a more prominent role in time use, while in youth and adulthood, a greater proportion of time is accounted for by work.

This idea of a dynamic tension between different types of activities introduces the notion of *balance* — an idea that has captivated researchers for decades (Pentland & McColl, 2008; Pentland & McColl, 2009). It is enticing to think that there is a perfect way to spend our time that will result in a balance of achievement and satis-

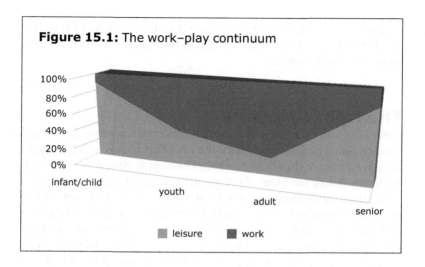

Figure 15.1: The work–play continuum

faction. But what does that balance look like and how do we achieve it? We all know what it feels like to experience an *imbalance* of time use — too much work for the time available, too little time to get ready for a forthcoming trip, time stretching out with nothing to do. These are all examples of an imbalance between activity and time, which feel, boring, frantic, distracting, or oppressive.

To the extent that leisure activities are the most discretionary, they are often the ones to be sacrificed when an imbalance is perceived. Most people would say they have insufficient leisure time, despite the fact that leisure time has been increasing steadily since the 1960s (Snir & Harpaz, 2002; Wilson et al., 2017). In 2010, non-disabled Canadians spent an average of 6:02 hours per day in leisure, up from about 4:50 hours several decades ago. Disabled adults, however, spent 6:44 hours in leisure (2010).

Does this additional half-hour of leisure mean that disabled people are happier with their leisure time, or that their lives are in a better balance? Not necessarily. People with disabilities have been shown to participate in fewer leisure activities overall, and in activities that are less active and less social (Shikako-Thomas & Law, 2015; Duquette et al., 2016). In the absence of work and the many benefits it confers (as discussed in the previous section), an increase of leisure time is not necessarily an indication of happier choices in how to spend one's time. Leisure is an important part of a balanced life, and for disabled people, it is often a route to integration and participation — a way to enter or re-enter the life of the community. It is not, however, a substitute for work and the many benefits that work confers (see Chapter 12).

The right to leisure

The definition of leisure as activities undertaken when free of the need to work may leave us with the idea that leisure is a luxury. In fact, in economic theory of the 19th century, leisure was portrayed as the exclusive purview of the wealthy, while the working classes toiled from dawn to dark. In contrast, leisure in the 21st century has been acknowledged as an essential part of a balanced lifestyle. The United Nations *Convention on the Rights of Persons with Disabilities* (2006) recognizes the right to leisure — specifically, to participate in all aspects of culture, recreation, leisure, and sport. Article 30 entreats nations to ensure access to media, culture, tourism, sport (both as participant and spectator), and recreation for all people regardless of disability.

The constraints on leisure participation are many and varied. They generally fall under the following categories (Hawkins, Peng, Hsieh, & Eklund, 1999; Darcy, Lock, & Taylor, 2017; Martin Ginis, Ma, Latimer-Cheung, & Rimmer, 2016; Martin, 2013):

- *Intrapersonal:* The disability itself; other illness, pain, or fatigue; fear of causing pain, injury, or exacerbation; lack of confidence; not enough time; lack of skill or experience; lack of knowledge of options and opportunities;

- *Interpersonal:* Lack of control over scheduling and decision-making; lack of family support; too busy with other responsibilities; lack of partner/co-participant; not accepted by other participants; or

- *Structural:* Costs; inaccessible facilities; need for special equipment; transportation not available; coaching/personnel lack expertise in disability issues.

Sports

Sport is an interesting special case of leisure participation. Sport has traditionally been an area where oppression and inequality have been challenged in both direct and symbolic ways (LeClair, 2011).

Race and gender equality issues have been repeatedly confronted on the sports field and, in recent years, so too have disability issues.

Perhaps the best example of sport as a means to overcome prejudice and limitation for people with disabilities is the Paralympic Games (International Paralympic Committee, 2003). In 1948, one of the pioneers of modern rehabilitation, Dr. Ludwig Guttman, began a movement to develop elite athletics among disabled veterans. The 1948 Stoke Mandeville Games were the first international competition of disabled athletes, with 16 injured servicemen competing. The Stoke games took place in England, just about 100 km away from London, where the fourteenth modern Olympic Games were occurring simultaneously.

In 1960, the Stoke Games became the first Paralympic Games, where 400 athletes competed from 23 countries. Since 1988, the Paralympic Games have occurred in the same city as the Olympics, typically immediately following the Olympics and using the same facilities. In 2010, former Olympic champion Sebastian Coe, as chair of the London organizing committee, stated that "We want to change public attitudes towards disability, celebrate the excellence of Paralympic sport, and enshrine from the very outset that the two Games are an integrated whole" (Gibson, 2010).

The Olympic commitment to equality is also expressed in the *Olympic Charter* (International Olympic Committee, 2010):

> The practice of sport is a human right. Every individual must have the possibility of practising sport, without discrimination of any kind, and in the Olympic spirit, which requires mutual understanding with a spirit of friendship, solidarity and fair play.

In 2018, the twelfth Winter Paralympic Games took place in PyeongChang, South Korea, alongside the twenty-third Winter Olympics. More than 500 disabled athletes competed in six events: alpine skiing, biathlon, cross-country skiing, ice sledge hockey, para-snowboarding, and wheelchair curling.

Another elite sport competition featuring disabled athletes is perhaps a more direct descendent of the Stoke Mandeville Games — the Invictus Games. In 2017, Toronto hosted the third Invictus Games, where 550 disabled veterans from 17 allied countries competed in 12 events.

Finally, a third international competition showcases excellence among athletes with intellectual disabilities — the Special Olympics World Games. The Special Olympics began in Chicago in 1968, and for 17 of its 28 meetings has been hosted by the United States. Although recognized by the International Olympic Committee, the Special Olympics focus to a greater extent on participation and fairness. They occur off-cycle with the Olympics and Paralympics.

Of course elite sporting competition involves only a small percentage of disabled athletes. By far the greater majority are recreational athletes and leisure-time fitness participants. Nonetheless, the question of integration versus segregation is highly relevant at all levels of sport or fitness participation:

- Is it better for disabled athletes to compete against other disabled athletes, or in open competitions?
- Are adapted sports equivalent to their original, non-adapted versions?
- Are specialized coaches, equipment, and facilities an advantage or disadvantage for disabled athletes?
- How does the level of financial support for disabled athletes or participants compare with that for non-disabled participants on a per capita basis?

These are just a few of the questions that persist when we talk about participation of disabled athletes. The discussion is exemplary of the integration–segregation debate in virtually every forum of participation.

In Canada, governments at all levels have decreed that, with a few historical exceptions, only integrated, equitable, accessible sport will be supported (Hoekstra et al., 2018). Ideologically, nothing less would be acceptable. But do disabled athletes and sport participants have an optimal experience when they operate as a minority among non-disabled participants? Integration can be enormously stressful if able-ist assumptions and environments go unchallenged (Schneider, 2015). While inclusion is clearly a moral imperative, there is some concern that it may result in inadequate attention to the particular needs of disabled participants (Beacom & Brittain, 2016).

Arts and culture

As mentioned above, leisure can also include activities that are creative and expressive — specifically, the arts. Participation in the arts can exist on a continuum from casual hobbyist to professional artist (in which case, incidentally, it is no longer leisure but rather productivity). Creative expression is usually pursued for its own intrinsic value, as well as for many other possible motives, including skill development, fund-raising, and social engagement. Think of everything from knitting to woodworking, jazz dancing, creative writing, improvisational theatre, and choral singing. The breadth and scope for artistic involvement is huge.

Barnes and Mercer (2001) define **disability arts** as cultural and media representations of disability issues. They distinguish disability arts from simply disabled people doing art, in that disability arts express the themes of the disability movement, such as rights to access, equality, and inclusion; the unique lived experiences of people with disabilities; and critiques of the social architecture that creates inequality. Whether expressed in visual arts, dance, theatre, comedy, literature, or music, disability arts are "educative, transformative, expressive and participative" (Barnes & Mercer, 2001, p. 529).

The arts permit expression of ideas and themes that might be less well received if expressed directly in words. Artistic media offer subtlety, sensibility, and suggestion — tactics that can be far more evocative and persuasive than dialectics. Imagine the difference between experiencing an art installation that permits viewers a first-hand look at exclusion and stigma compared to a position paper or speech on the same issues. The art installation almost certainly has the more lasting and penetrating effect.

Frazee (2006) characterizes disability arts as acts of resistance. They afford an opportunity to

- break into mainstream culture — to use expressive media to draw attention to disability issues;
- break from culture — to challenge the status quo and offer alternative representations of cultural ideals;
- dialogue with culture — to engage mainstream culture in discussions of issues that are challenging to confront directly, and for which it can be difficult to find an audience and a forum; and
- reflect on culture — to critique, analyze, or parody mainstream culture using media that permit perhaps a less strident and more inviting debate.

The sum total of artistic expressions about disability constitutes part of a disability culture — a shared identity among disabled people characterized by common interests, values, and beliefs. This culture includes as one of its central tenets an alternative aesthetic (Frazee, 2006). Disability culture resists the dominant culture's image of goodness, beauty, and grace, and instead participates in the assertion and dissemination of *the* disability perspective as one that is legitimate, worthy, and desirable.

The existence of a disability culture depends on the notion of a shared identity — of a core of shared experience that engages people with disabilities as a distinct and identifiable group. And yet, as we have discussed in previous chapters, the population of disabled people is characterized far more by heterogeneity than it is by homogeneity (Stamou, Alevriadou, & Soufla, 2016). It is made up of many different types of disability (physical, sensory, cognitive, emotional), to say nothing of the multiple intersectionalities with age, gender, ethnicity, social class, and other demographic characteristics (Prince, 2006b).

Is there a core of experience of confronting the world as a disabled person that unites disabled people with one another? That renders them a cultural entity? Do the difficulties faced by disabled people bring them together in solidarity? The research suggests they do not — that achieving unity and solidarity is a significant challenge for the disability community (Rioux & Sampson, 2006). When asked questions like those above, two-thirds of disabled people said they were not a part of a disabled community with shared values — 44% said there was no such thing as a disability community, and 22% said there might be a community, but they were not part of it (Ville, Crost, & Ravaud, 2003). Even among the one-third who said there was a disability community with a shared value system, the unifying experiences were typically expressed as medical experiences, like pain, incontinence, or dependence on others. These kinds of individual experiences are considerably more difficult to rally around than social experiences, like marginalization and exclusion (Prince, 2006b).

Arts and culture have been a forum for expressing not only disability solidarity, but disability pride. **Disability pride** is an awareness movement that began in Boston in 1990, and annually celebrates its mission with a parade and week of festivities, coinciding with December 3rd, the United Nations International Day of Persons with Disabilities. The disability pride movement has stated the following in its mission (Disability Pride Parade, 2013):

- to change the way people think about disability;
- to overcome "internalized shame" among people with disabilities; and
- to promote disability as a natural and beautiful part of human diversity.

Arts and culture are among the most effective media for promoting this agenda (Swain & French, 2000).

Play

Leisure can be divided into formal and informal leisure. Formal leisure is organized, governed by rules, oriented toward a goal, and hierarchical in terms of expertise and leadership. Some examples include organized sports, clubs, classes, and groups. Informal leisure, on the other hand, is spontaneous, unstructured, and initiated by the individual. Examples include hobbies, crafts, games, puzzles, socializing, reading, individual sport, fitness activities, and entertainment. A special case of informal leisure is play.

Play is defined in terms of five essential characteristics (Gray, 2008):

- Play is self-chosen and self-directed — individuals are free to quit at any time.
- Play is a process rather than an outcome — it is the activity that matters, not the product.
- Play has a structure — it is not free-form, but the structure emanates from the mind of the player, and so can be changed to ensure that the activity remains pleasurable.
- Play is located outside the mainstream of daily obligations and rituals; it is imaginative, "pretend", and non-literal.
- Play involves an active and alert level of consciousness, but is free from stress.

Play fulfils an essential developmental function in children, providing for them a forum for learning, trying, observing, practising, and rehearsing. According to Duquette and associates (2016), children derive social, psychological, and physical benefits from play, such as specific skills and abilities, social networks, role-related behaviours, identity, self-efficacy, and future possibilities, all of which build resilience.

Play is sometimes referred to as the main occupation of children, and even sometimes as their productivity (Deloitte & Touche, 2010). Wing (1995), however, makes it clear that children differentiate between their play and their work. They use a number of criteria for differentiating between work and play: the degree of obligation involved, the amount of effort required, the presence of authority figures such as parents or teachers, the necessity to finish rather than simply quit, the amount of fun involved, and the extent to which messiness is permitted. From the child's perspective, "Work is about what *you* want; play is about what I want" (Wing, 1995, p. 243).

Day (1979) itemizes five categories of play, differentiated from one another by their motivation:

1. Exploratory play is motivated by curiosity.
2. Creative play is motivated by the desire for expression.
3. Diversionary play is motivated by boredom or the need for distraction.
4. Mimetic play is motivated by the drive for mastery and competence.
5. Cathartic play is motivated by the need to release stress or tension.

The research shows that disabled children experience notably fewer opportunities for play and the many benefits it confers. They are more likely to engage in home-based play, individual rather than collaborative or team activities, and passive rather than active play, especially electronic media (Shikako-Thomas & Law, 2015). They have fewer play options from which to choose, and encounter more barriers to the things other children are doing (King, Petrenchik, Law, & Hurley, 2009). Disabled children are less likely to have the opportunity for unsupervised play; thus, they experience constraints on the playful nature of their activities (Wing, 1995). All of this results in less chance to develop self-efficacy, a sense of belonging with peers, and a healthy self-esteem (King et al., 2009).

Conclusion

In this chapter, we have *discovered* the many benefits of leisure participation and the importance of leisure not only as a way to occupy free time, but also as a part of a full and satisfying life, as a venue for skill development and personal growth, and as a means of engaging with others and developing a social network. We have *discovered* that there are notable differences in the leisure experiences of disabled and non-disabled people, both contemporaneously and across the lifespan.

As we *dream* of future possibilities for a world that is more accepting and accessible to people with disabilities, there are a number of movements that express this ideal. The Olympics express this dream in their mission statement. Disability arts and culture express this dream in their creative enterprises, and in resistance to the prevailing ideals of beauty and value. The UN *Convention on the Rights of People with Disabilities* expresses this dream in its expectations of nation states (United Nations, 2006).

What is required to *design* a world where these dreams can be achieved? Similar to the other areas we have explored, first and foremost is the awareness that people with disabilities are entitled to participate in leisure, and that they might aspire to any leisure experience to which non-disabled people aspire. Once we begin to design leisure spaces and experiences with this in mind, the whole picture changes. No longer is costly retro-fitting necessary to permit disabled people to participate. Instead, cost-effective and, more importantly, acceptable design features are incorporated from the outset.

For health, education, and social service professionals, there is the opportunity to be a part of the *deployment* of this reality. It starts with *not* thinking that leisure is a luxury — not thinking that the disabled people with whom we engage should be more concerned with self-care and productivity than with leisure. Leisure is the third leg of the three-legged stool, and it needs to be just as robust as the other two if the stool is keep from wobbling.

SECTION 4

Disability in Society

This penultimate section of the book looks at three topics related to how people with disabilities relate to society, and how society engages with them. The most basic element of society's relationship with people with disabilities is affirming the citizenship and personhood by guaranteeing their human rights. Chapter 16 looks at the origins of the notion of human rights and how Canada ensures the rights of disabled citizens at several levels. Chapter 17 looks at other policy, in addition to policy relating to human rights. Finally, Chapter 18 examines the evolving epistemology regarding disability — what we know about the condition of living with a disability, how we have acquired that knowledge, and the extent to which it is or is not responsive to the real issues faced by disabled people on a daily basis.

Chapter 16

Human rights and disability

Introduction

The dominant discourse when addressing the issues faced by people with disabilities worldwide is the human rights approach. This approach asserts what seems like it should be an obvious claim — that people with disabilities are entitled to equal consideration with others in all aspects of society. The assertion of these rights constitutes the state of full citizenship.

Canada is seen by many as "human rights heaven" (Kim, 2011) — a place where equality and access to opportunity are highly valued, and rights are not sacrificed to other public or private interests. However, every year the Human Rights Commissions in both provincial and federal jurisdictions receive more complaints based on disability than any other cause. In each of these cases, the complainant asserts that he or she has suffered discrimination because of the fact of having a disability — that his or her rights have been violated as a result of disability (Canadian Human Rights Commission, 2012, 2015). Not only do disability claims outweigh other sources of human rights complaints, they also constitute the highest proportion of successful claims, confirming that, in fact, disability discrimination continues to exist.

This chapter examines the concept of human rights — where they come from, what they include, and how we arrived at our modern conception of human rights. It also looks at related issues, like discrimination, ableism, equity, citizenship, and justice. There are three levels of rights protections in Canada, and we will examine these to discover how they work and what each covers. Finally, we will conclude with a discussion of the benefits and limitations of the human rights approach as a way of making Canada a more equitable and supportive society for people with disabilities.

Definition

According to the Canadian Human Rights Commission (www.chrc-ccdp.gc.ca):

> Everyone in the world is entitled to the same fundamental **human rights**.... They describe how we instinctively expect to be treated.... They define what we are all entitled to — a life of equality, dignity, respect and freedom from discrimination. You do not have to earn your human rights. You are born with them and they are the same for every person. No one can give them to you, but they can be taken away.

Specifically, Canada recognizes 26 rights set out in the United Nations' *Universal Declaration of Human Rights* (2015). These are spelled out in Table 16.1. The Declaration does not specifically mention disability as one of the grounds for protection of rights, but it states in its preamble that

> All human beings are born free and equal in dignity and rights. They are endowed with reason and conscience, and should act towards one another in a spirit of brotherhood.

History of the modern concept of human rights

The first known attempt at codification of human rights is believed to be the Cyrus Cylinder, a document written by King Cyrus the Great of Persia in the 6th century BC. Preserved on clay, it testified to the liberation of the people of Israel from captivity in Babylon, and represented a declaration of the king's vision of peace and order.

Ideas about human liberty and dignity have been at the root of every civilization throughout history, but it was not until the 17th century that explicit reference was made to human rights — that is, entitlements based on "natural laws", or universal principles

Table 16.1: Comparing the articles of the *Universal Declaration of Human Rights* (1948) with the UN *Convention on the Rights of Persons with Disabilities* (2006)

Universal Declaration of Human Rights	Convention on the Rights of Persons with Disabilities
3. Right to life, liberty and security of person	10. Right to life 11. Right to security in situations of risk or humanitarian emergency 14. Right to liberty and security of the person
4. Freedom from slavery or servitude	
5. Freedom from torture or cruel, inhuman or degrading treatment or punishment	15. Freedom from torture or cruel, inhuman or degrading treatment or punishment 16. Freedom from exploitation, violence or abuse 17. Protection of the integrity of the person
6. Right to recognition as a person before the law	12. Right to equal recognition before the law
7. Equality before the law and equal protection of the law	13. Access to justice
8. Right to an effective remedy for acts violating a fundamental right	
9. Freedom from arbitrary arrest, detention or exile	
10. Right to a fair and public hearing of any criminal charge against him	
11. Right to be presumed innocent until proved guilty	
12. Freedom from arbitrary interference with privacy, family, home or correspondence, or attacks upon his honour and reputation	22. Respect for privacy

continued....

Table 16.1 continued

Universal Declaration of Human Rights	Convention on the Rights of Persons with Disabilities
13. Freedom of movement and residence, including the right to leave and return to his country	18. Liberty of movement and nationality 20. Freedom of personal mobility
14. Right to seek and enjoy in other countries asylum from persecution	
15. Right to a nationality	
16. Right to marry and to found a family	19. Freedom to live independently in the community 23. Respect for home and family
17. Right to own property	
18. Right to freedom of thought, conscience and religion	
19. Right to freedom of opinion and expression	21. Freedom of expression and opinion
20. Right to freedom of peaceful assembly and association	
21. Right to take part in the government of his country	29. Right to participation in political and public life
22. Right to social security, economic, social and cultural rights indispensable for his dignity and the free development of his personality	
23. Right to work, to free choice of employment, to just and favourable conditions	27. Right to work and employment
24. Right to rest and leisure	30. Right to participate in cultural life, recreation, leisure and sport

continued....

Table 16.1 continued

Universal Declaration of Human Rights	Convention on the Rights of Persons with Disabilities
25. Right to a standard of living adequate for the health and well-being	25. Right to health 26. Right to habilitation and rehabilitation 28. Right to adequate standard of living
26. Right to education	24. Right to education
27. Right freely to participate in the cultural life of the community	30. Right to participate in cultural life, recreation, leisure and sport
28. Right to a social and international order in which the rights and freedoms set forth in this Declaration can be fully realized	

of morality and proper human conduct. These statements were mostly the result of abolitionist movements seeking an end to slavery.

Human rights as we understand them today were finally established after the horrors of the two World Wars in the 20th century. The newly formed United Nations in 1947 engaged the recently widowed Eleanor Roosevelt to chair an international panel charged with developing a global bill of rights. In 1948, the UN passed the *Universal Declaration of Human Rights*, which identified seven substantive rights:

1. The right to life — that is, not to be killed by another person;
2. Freedom from torture — including punishment, interrogation, or coercion;
3. Freedom from slavery — including any form of human trafficking;
4. Right to a fair trial — a public hearing in front of an impartial authority;
5. Freedom of speech — expression without censorship;

6. Freedom of thought, conscience, and religion; and
7. Freedom of movement — to travel, reside, or work where one wishes.

The list has subsequently been fleshed out and clarified to include the 28 articles itemized in Table 16.1.

Canada's first Bill of Rights was passed by the Diefenbaker government in 1960, and is considered one of the most significant legacies of that government. In 1977, the *Canadian Human Rights Act* was passed, and in 1982 the *Canadian Charter of Rights and Freedoms* became an amendment to the *Constitution Act of Canada*. Between 1947 (Saskatchewan) and 1975 (Quebec), each of the provinces passed human rights legislation governing areas under provincial jurisdiction. Between 2002 and 2003, the Yukon, Northwest Territories, and Nunavut enacted human rights laws.

Related concepts

Here are some key concepts that are related to human rights. It is important to be clear and precise in our language when discussing abstract ideas like these.

Equity

A key concept in discussing human rights is the idea of equity. At the root of any consideration of human rights is the desire to achieve equity — but what do we mean by equity? There are typically three ways of understanding equity:

1. **Formal equity** — Also referred to as *equality* or *horizontal equity*. This is the easiest to achieve and, arguably, it is not equity at all. As pictured in the first diagram of Figure 16.1, it simply means that everyone is treated the same. Regardless of whether one has a disability or other special requirement, all are entitled to exactly the same treatment. It is easy to see that this approach will often result in significant disadvantage for people with disabilities.

2. **Substantive equity** — The next two approaches are referred to as two types of *substantive equality*. Both of these approaches are pictured as "equity" in Figure 16.1.

Figure 16.1: Equality versus equity

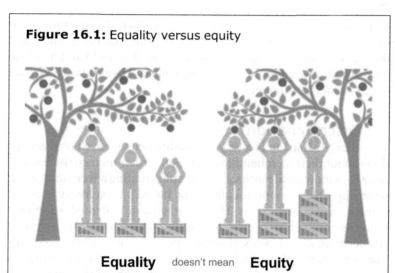

Equality   doesn't mean   **Equity**

Source: Saskatoon Health Region, *Advancing health equity in health care*, Better Health for All: Health Status Reporting Series 3 (June 14, 2014). © 2017, Saskatchewan Health Authority

- *Outcome equity* means doing whatever it takes to achieve equal outcomes for all.
- *Vertical equity* seeks to create equal opportunity for all by affording special considerations based on need. Instead of aiming to achieve the same outcomes for everyone, which may not ever be possible, this approach seeks to create an equal starting point for all, ensuring that some are not left behind right from the start.

Justice

Justice is a moral ideal that governs how people decide upon the correct course of action or thought. To act justly means to act with fairness, righteousness, and lawfulness. Justice may be construed as a situation where systemic barriers have been removed entirely, and all can participate without any special considerations for minority groups. When we talk about justice with regard to people with disabilities, it requires us to invoke principles discussed throughout this book, such as inclusive attitudes and universal design. Justice is achieved when consideration and thoughtfulness are given to the needs of *all* people, including those with disabilities, and solutions to problems are devised with a broad spectrum of users in mind.

Discrimination

Discrimination is a way of treating people based on assumptions about their membership in a group, rather than on the basis of their own individual merits. For example, treating a woman as if she were physically or emotionally weak, based on a stereotype about women, is discrimination. Thus, if a woman is denied a job that requires her to be physically strong simply because she is a woman (rather than on the basis of some legitimate test of her strength), that is discrimination. Disabled people are frequently the victims of discrimination based on misunderstandings about the complexity and variety of disabilities. To assume that a disabled person cannot do a particular job because he or she has a disability may be discrimination if the particular skill-set required for the job is not a part of the person's disability.

There are at least five different forms that discrimination may take, and over the past 40 years, they have been clarified and distinguished in case law (Ontario Human Rights Commission (OHRC), 2016).

- *Direct discrimination* occurs where people with certain characteristics, or people seen to belong to particular groups, are excluded due to negative attitudes, stereotypes, or biases toward those groups. Incredibly, there are still organizations that exclude or differentially relate to people on the basis of race or ethnicity. Direct discrimination is seldom the issue when people with disabilities experience exclusion; for the most part, Canadians are sufficiently sophisticated to know that it is wrong to systematically exclude someone because he or she has a disability.

- The Ontario Human Rights Commission includes a category in their classification that they term *subtle discrimination*. This refers to a situation where stereotypes are invoked implicitly, without ever declaring them — for example, when the disabled job applicant doesn't get called back for a second interview, despite having the best skills and experience in the applicant pool. It appears that discrimination has taken place, but the case is difficult to make on objective evidence. The only way to identify subtle discrimination is to identify an otherwise inexplicable departure from usual practice, or to note a pattern of apparent exclusion.

- *Indirect discrimination*, or *adverse-effects discrimination*, occurs where certain groups of people are systematically excluded, even though there was no overt intent to exclude them; however, neither was there any outright effort to include them (Lepofsky, 1998). This is the most common type of discrimination experienced by disabled people in Canada. It typically arises because no consideration was given to the situation of a disabled person when the law, rule, policy, building, or other structure or process was designed. Policies or processes that on the surface appear neutral may actually be discriminatory to individuals who are effectively excluded because of failure to consider their situation.

- *Systemic discrimination* refers to the situation where it is not an individual perpetrating the discriminatory behaviour but an organization, an institution, or a state. Systemic discrimination is self-perpetuating, since the exclusion of the particular group means that their voice is not represented when decisions about future policies or practices are discussed, and thus the situation is permitted to continue.

- *Harassment* is also considered a form of discrimination because it subjects individuals to unwanted comments or conduct based on their membership in a group — be it a gender group, a cultural group, or a disability group.

Nierobisz and Theroux (2008) suggest that most disability discrimination is a function of lack of awareness of obligations toward disabled citizens, either as employees or customers. However McKenna (1997) thinks the problem goes much deeper. He refers to concepts like "management rights" and "free market doctrine" as examples of the excuses proffered by businesses to avoid having to accommodate disabled employees or customers. Businesses invoke concerns for "undue hardship" or "commitment to quality" to exempt themselves from fulfilling statutory obligations toward people with disabilities. Armstrong (2003) notes that the cost of *not* including people with disabilities, either as customers or as employees, is seldom figured into the equation.

Ableism

Ableism is a particular form of discrimination that is deeply and subliminally embedded in our culture (Campbell, 2009; OHRC, 2017). Ableism results from a physical and social ideal that favours the non-disabled, that says that what is beautiful, whole, and desirable is a non-disabled brain, body, and experience. Not only that, but this way of thinking implicitly communicates that to be disabled is to be "less than" or "worse than" being non-disabled, that disability is an undesirable way to go through life. It starts from a tacit assumption of "ability", and constructs disability as something other, alien, marginal, undesirable (Chouinard, 1997).

Perhaps most distressing about ableism is the extent to which it becomes internalized by disabled people who are repeatedly exposed to this way of thinking. It becomes their default identity, to the extent that they begin to foreclose on opportunities for themselves in order not to disturb the status quo. An example in our own culture is the practice of situating disability seating at the back of an auditorium or theatre. Although a number of practical justifications can be advanced, the subliminal message is that seating for people with disabilities is not a priority, that it was an afterthought, that it is an inconvenience that will be tolerated but not embraced. Such messages can't help but contribute to a feeling of second-class status and tenuous membership.

Citizenship

What is at stake in all the forms of discrimination and marginalization described above is the issue of citizenship. **Citizenship** is the status of recognition, sovereignty, and membership in a society. It includes not only political and legal status, such as being allowed to vote and being protected by laws, but also social, cultural, and economic citizenship. It entitles one to all the benefits and privileges of membership, while at the same time imposing expectations about contribution and conformity. Political citizenship can be conferred through parentage, birthplace, marriage, or naturalization (meaning the intentional adoption of citizenship). Social and economic citizenship is typically conferred on those who participate in society in the expected ways, such as retaining employment, upholding role expectations, and looking and behaving in expected ways. Symbolic citizenship is reflected in the rhetoric and imagery of our cultural and political discussions, and the extent to which disability issues are reflected in those discussions (Prince, 2010).

Layers of human rights protection in Canada

In Canada, human rights are protected at three levels: provincial/territorial, national, and international.

Provincial/Territorial level

Most goods and services that affect the day-to-day lives of Canadians are governed by the province or territory in which they live. Issues such as housing, health care, education, shops, services, and transportation are all provincial/territorial issues. As mentioned above, every province or territory has a Human Rights Code or Act that sets out the rights of its citizens and describes a procedure for seeking redress if those rights are violated. If, for instance, an individual felt that his or her rights had been violated in a restaurant where he or she was refused seating, because customer services are under provincial jurisdiction, the Human Rights Commission or Tribunal of that province would be the appropriate place to report the violation.

Federal level

The federal government in Canada oversees a number of specific sectors, including Indigenous affairs, airline and rail travel, banks, marine navigation, and postal services, to name a few. The *Canadian Human Rights Act* (1985) outlaws discrimination in any of those sectors under federal jurisdiction, and establishes the terms of the Canadian Human Rights Commission to deal with complaints.

Another form of rights protection at the federal level is the *Canadian Charter of Rights and Freedoms* (1982; part of the *Constitution Act of Canada*). Canada was the first country to embed disability rights in its constitution (Pooran & Wilkie, 2005). Although a declaration of individual rights was initially felt by some to be antithetical to Canada's parliamentary democracy, the *Charter of Rights and Freedoms* has become a cornerstone of Canada's system of justice. It holds an iconic place in Canadian society as the primary guarantor of minority rights, alongside federal and provincial human rights codes. It is lauded as a powerful legal tool that has invigorated the struggles of people with disabilities in Canada (Armstrong, 2003).

Following the framework established by the American *Bill of Rights* and the *United Nations Universal Declaration of Human Rights*, the Charter guarantees political, legal, mobility, equality, language, and religious rights to Canadian citizens, and civil rights to all physically present in Canada. Most significantly, Section 15 ensures freedom from discrimination for five designated groups: people with disabilities, Indigenous people, women, visible minorities, and sexual/transgendered minorities. Specifically, the Charter guarantees

- equality before the law — in the administration of justice by law enforcement and the courts;
- equality under the law — in the application of the law and assignment of penalties;
- equal benefit of the law — proportionality in the conferring of benefits enshrined in law; and
- equal protection of the law — proportionality in protections to ensure human dignity is safeguarded.

As a part of the Canadian constitution, the Charter extends to all levels of government, and supersedes laws at every other level. The task of interpreting and enforcing the Charter falls to the courts, rather than to a government agency or panel. Governments and governmental bodies at all levels are accountable to the judiciary for the constitutionality of their practices and policies.

Another important piece of human rights legislation at the federal level is the *Employment Equity Act* (1986). The stated purpose of the Act is the achievement of equality in the workplace, envisioning a society where no person would be denied employment opportunities or benefits for reasons unrelated to qualifications (Department of Justice Canada, 1995). Four groups were designated for protection under employment equity law: women, visible minorities, Indigenous people, and people with disabilities. The Act is limited in its jurisdiction to industries that are federally regulated; thus, most employers — such as retailers, manufacturers, or hospitality providers — are exempt. The *Employment Equity Act* differs from the other two federal instruments (the Charter and the Human Rights Act) in that it requires employers to engage in proactive measures to improve employment opportunities for the four protected groups.

International level

In 2006, the United Nations adopted the *Convention on the Rights of Persons with Disabilities* (UNCRPD), which is an agreement among countries around the world to ensure equality and freedom from discrimination for people with disabilities. As Table 16.1 shows, the rights spelled out in the Convention are not new rights, but rather the same rights found in the *Universal Declaration of Human Rights* interpreted as they apply to people with disabilities.

By the end of 2017, 175 countries had signed and ratified the Convention (including Canada in 2010), meaning that they had agreed to uphold and enforce the terms of the Convention in their own country. It is essential to understand that the Convention does not carry the authority of law in Canada or in any other nation. Ratification is an expression of agreement in principle and intention to comply, but it is not an enforceable contract. It requires countries to report periodically about the status of their disabled citizens and the infrastructure in place to protect their rights. Canada made its first report in 2014 (http://publications.gc.ca/collections/collection_2014/pc-ch/CH37-4-19-2013-eng.pdf).

Therefore, while ratifying the Convention offers a degree of reassurance of a country's intention toward its citizens with disabilities, it does not offer specific rights protection to the citizens of any of the signatory countries. In order for the Convention to be enforceable, countries must also sign on to the Optional Protocol. To date, 92 countries have also signed the Optional Protocol, which recognizes the authority of an international complaints body, entitled the Committee on the Rights of Persons with Disabilities, with the power to investigate and make recommendations to member governments. The Government of Canada tabled the Optional Protocol in the House of Commons in November 2017, according to a commitment from the current government.

Is it enough?

Canadian human rights laws, and the Charter in particular, have achieved a number of important legal milestones (Lepofsky, 1998; Armstrong, 2003; Peters, 2004; Porter, 2005; Arthurs & Arnold, 2005). For example, the Andrews case (1989) clarified that discrimination includes unintentional (as well as intentional) effects — that is, failure to take account of the circumstances of a designated group. The Meiorin case (British Columbia, 1999) validated that the burden of proof in discrimination lies not with the complainant but with the alleged discriminator. *Eaton* (1997) and *Eldridge* (1997) affirmed the use in law of the social model of disability, accounting for context in the definition of disability. Eaton (1997) reinforced the presumption of the value of integration vs. segregation in providing services to people with disabilities. *Granovsky* (2000), *Martin/Laseur* (2003), and a number of other cases further refined the definition of disability to include pain, mental illness, HIV, and temporary and episodic disabilities.

While the Charter has afforded a significant degree of discrimination protection in specific cases, some commentators suggest that it has made little difference in the day-to-day lives of people with disabilities. They look back over achievements during the 30+ years that the Charter has been in force with disappointment, noting that its impact is considered by some more symbolic than substantive (Peters, 2004; Arthurs & Arnold, 2005; Porter, 2005). They claim that the Charter has not achieved the far-reaching social change that was initially expected, and designated groups have not made the progress anticipated in mitigating disadvantage (Porter, 2005).

Instead of leading to systemic change, Charter cases have typically resulted in individual compensation (Lepofsky, 1998). While Charter-based jurisprudence has consolidated the primacy of the social model of disability (specifically, the necessity of removing barriers and the duty to accommodate), it has had only modest effects on the legal infrastructure of Canada (Vanhala, 2011). In many instances, it has merely codified judicial practices already in place (Arthurs & Arnold, 2005). Furthermore, there is still no consistently applied "disability lens" in the policy environment, while other enumerated groups enjoy considerations like a ministry devoted to their issues (Stienstra, 2012).

Inherently, human rights are bestowed on individuals and discrimination is pursued by individuals (Prince, 2009a). The process is individualized and complaint-based — a corrective form of rights protection, rather than a proactive one (Bickenbach, 2006; Kelly, 2005). The process is onerous and costly, and the burden is borne almost entirely by the aggrieved individual. It usually involves a lawyer to interpret the law and specify the violation that has occurred. In addition, there are many other real and hidden costs associated with court appearances and representation. The cost to individuals can be great — both financially and personally — and often beyond the means of individuals already struggling for their fair share. Financial assistance was formerly available to assist with costs in some jurisdictions, but this has largely been eliminated in recent years.

Do people with disabilities then need further explicit rights protections in Canada, specifically in the form of national anti-discrimination laws, such as those of the United States, United Kingdom, and Australia? According to Prince (2010), there are three camps of responses to the idea of a national disability rights law:

1. Some believe that the current legislative framework provides all the safeguards and provisions necessary. They believe that explicit disability rights legislation would be nothing more than window-dressing and would distract the attention of policy-makers from the persistent and pressing problems of disabled people in Canadian society, such as poverty and unemployment. They oppose further disability discrimination legislation, believing that the effects would at best be negligible and at worst detrimental.

2. A second group expresses ambivalence toward the idea of disability discrimination legislation. They acknowledge the possibility of benefits, but they also point out the possible pitfalls of an overarching legislative response to the multi-dimensional, multi-sectoral problems experienced by the heterogeneous community of disabled people in Canada. They advocate for a highly consultative process to ensure appropriate considerations and representation.

3. Finally, there are those who support the proposal wholeheartedly, and who feel that it is long overdue. This group tends to believe that for both real and symbolic reasons, the enactment of federal disability anti-discrimination legislation would provide the impetus needed for the disability community to gather steam and correct some of the slippage in disability programs and services in recent years (Boyce et al., 2001; McColl & Jongbloed, 2006).

Conclusion

In this chapter, we have taken both a historical and contemporary look at human rights as they pertain to people with disabilities. We have *discovered* definitions and related concepts, and we have examined three layers of legal protection of human rights available to disabled people in Canada — provincial/territorial, federal, and international. But human rights law is not the only way to promote equity and opportunities for disabled people.

A robust system of human rights protection is essential to ensure against the grievous injustices of the past, including restrictive immigration, involuntary sterilization, institutionalization, restraint, labour exploitation, and even eugenics (OHRC, 2016; Withers, 2012). It is clear that a corrective system of justice is needed to act as a watchdog against wrong-doing and to ensure that individuals are compensated when violations occur. This type of corrective justice approach is a reflection of a neo-liberal ideology that sees disability as a private issue, and justice as an individual matter (Prince, 2009a; Bickenbach, 2006; Begley, Lairson, Morgan, Rowan, & Balkrishnan, 2013). It focuses on preventing exclusion rather than on promoting inclusion. But is a corrective approach to justice alone enough?

Rather than further rights protections, perhaps what Canada needs is a more positive, proactive form of legislative assurance of inclusion — a system that puts resources in place to make society more accessible, that is more attentive to disability issues, and that is more receptive to the gifts that disabled people contribute when given the opportunity. A number of authors advocate for a distributive justice approach — one that emphasizes collective responsibilities as well as individual rights (Bickenbach, 2006; Prince, 2009a). Distributive justice flows out of a social welfare political ideology, rather than a free-market ideology. The free-market approach has historically failed to serve not only people with disabilities but minorities in general, who typically don't represent a significant market force with their numbers or purchasing power.

The social welfare ideology instead emphasizes the common good, social solidarity, and humanitarian ideals. It accepts a degree of government intervention in order to achieve the type of society we seek; it acknowledges that leaving political decisions entirely to market forces will not benefit the disenfranchised. It sees disability issues as a public matter rather than a private matter. The welfare of disabled Canadians concerns us all, not only the 15% who experience disability first-hand. When we *dream* about the kind of society we seek in Canada vis-à-vis disabled people, I suspect it embraces not only the human rights of people with disabilities but also the collective responsibility of society to promote equity.

How do we *design* such a society? The subsequent chapter on policy will address some of approaches that have been advanced in Canada and elsewhere, and will offer tools to evaluate the relative success or failure of these approaches. As we conclude this chapter, let us reflect on the importance of rigorous human rights protections for people with disabilities, and also let us *deploy* our voices to seek positive assurances that disability issues appear front and centre on the political agenda, and that we continue to move toward a society that recognizes and *appreciates* the contributions of disabled citizens.

Chapter 17

Disability policy

Once upon a time not so very long ago, on a lake not far from here, an old man, a little girl, and a man using a wheelchair decided to go fishing. Just as they were going ahead and making their plans, it occurred to the man in the wheelchair that they might need a fishing licence. He phoned the local authority to inquire and was advised that if you were over 65 years of age, under 12, or a legitimate holder of a disability parking permit, you were entitled to fish without a licence. So off they went ... but silently, the man in the wheelchair was puzzled. What did it mean?

Introduction

This is just a silly story and a trivial example in the whole scheme of disability policy, but it provides us with a good opportunity to take a deeper look at how government and society think about their relationship to people with disabilities.

- Does it mean that we think people with disabilities are like elderly people? Or like children?

- Does it mean that we think disabled people are unlikely to want to or to be able to fish?

- Or does it mean that they are unlikely to be fishing independently — that is, unaccompanied by a licensed fisherman?

- Does it mean that we think people with disabilities are poor and can't afford the modest investment of a fishing licence?

- Or perhaps we think they are already on social assistance, so it doesn't make sense for government to give them money with one hand and take it away with the other?

- Or is it simply an attempt to give people with disabilities a break — a sort of recognition of the struggles they face, and a small attempt to compensate them for their circumstances? And, if so, why fishing and not skiing, or going to the movies, or any number of other non-subsidized leisure pursuits?

None of these options provides a very satisfactory explanation for why someone with a disability would be exempt from requiring a fishing licence. So, let's look more deeply at what policy is and why we have it. In this chapter, we explore more specifically what disability policy is and where it came from, and we look in more detail at some key disability policies. Finally, we explore the ultimate expression of citizenship — the ability to vote and participate in the democratic process.

Definition

Policy can be defined as a course of action (or inaction) chosen by public authorities to address problems experienced in society (Pal, 1992; Boyce et al., 2001). Policy is the way governments express what they intend to do in response to the issues they deem to be most pressing. Torjman (2005, p. 18) sums up the role of government as "making good decisions for the public good". Governments express the actions they intend to take and the directions they intend to pursue through various kinds of policy (Barton & Armstrong, 2001).

In democracies like Canada, we elect governments to raise funds (usually through trade and taxes) and to use those funds to create the kind of society we aspire to: fair, peaceful, caring, prosperous. Governments have at their disposal a number of options for achieving their goals:

- *Legislation and regulations:* Governments can pass laws that commit both government and citizens to act in certain ways.

- *Official statements and published documents* (such as the Throne speech, public reports, Web-based resources, and media releases): These documents express the beliefs, culture and goals of government, and contribute to public awareness.

- *Programs:* By creating funded programs with specific eligibility criteria, governments attempt to meet the needs and desires of particular groups of Canadians, such as people with disabilities.

- *Standards development:* Governments can require organizations to live up to certain expectations or standards in order to qualify for funding.

- *Bilateral agreements:* Governments can enter into agreements with other levels of government (such as the provinces and territories) to meet certain requirements on cost-shared programs.

- *Procurement and contracting policies:* Finally, government has considerable purchasing power, and it can require private sector companies from which it procures goods or services to operate in ways that are consistent with government's goals and aspirations.

Policy-making involves choices — choices among issues, choices between groups, choices among policy options. The first choice is which issues the government is going to address. As an electorate, we have many expectations for the kind of society our government will create. In a country like Canada, we expect environmental responsibility, good health, low poverty, minimal crime, high literacy, full employment, commercial prosperity, international recognition, and social cohesion, to name just a few issues. None of these things happens without a policy framework that supports, funds, monitors, and ensures it.

Secondly, government is charged with choosing whose interests they will serve — the interests of the population as a whole or the interests of subsets of the population. There are literally hundreds, perhaps thousands, of groups within the population who believe they have a special claim on the government's attention and resources by virtue of their circumstances. People with disabilities and, even more specifically, people with certain types of disabilities are included among these groups. They seek to attract the attention of government through politicians (meaning elected officials), or through members of public service (those non-partisan professionals and administrative personnel who do the day-to-day business of government). In Canada, some of the interest groups that command the government's attention at the moment are Indigenous people, especially women and girls; refugees and new Canadians; unemployed people; and business and commerce.

Finally, government has the choice about the best way to address a particular problem. The policy instruments that they have at their disposal (outlined above) exist on a continuum from formal to informal, with the most formal type of policy being legislation (and regulations associated with legislation). Legislation refers to laws passed through Parliament. It is the strongest and most durable expression of the government's intentions. The passage of a new law, or even the amendment of an existing law, may take years from inception to assent. Legislation commits not only the current government but also future governments to a particular course of action.

What is disability policy?

We use the term *disability policy* as if it refers to an entity that is a unified whole, with coordinated and consistent approaches and philosophies. The reality, however, is quite different (Boyce et al., 2001; Prince, 2016a). Policy of interest to people with disabilities is a complex web of legislation, regulations, and programs that ranges across jurisdictions, across sectors within government, and across programs within ministries.

Disability policy exists to fulfil the role of government toward people with disabilities. It is distinguished in that it refers explicitly to the situation of people with disabilities, and exists to acknowledge the special circumstances faced by people with disabilities. Disability policy may be seeking to compensate for the fact that people with disabilities:

- have extraordinary expenses associated with daily living, such as drugs, supplies, and equipment;
- have fewer options for transportation, housing, recreation, and many other aspects of life;
- may need assistance, supervision, or attendant care;
- may experience "double jeopardy" associated with multiple vulnerabilities;
- may have fluctuating abilities to participate, depending on their underlying health condition;
- may have uncertainty about future ability;
- are statistically more likely than their non-disabled contemporaries to be disadvantaged in terms of education, employment, and income; and
- may have less future earning potential.

How does disability policy come about?

Governments create disability policy specifically in order to achieve three goals (Bickenbach, 2006; Crocker, 2009):

1. *Equity:* To ensure that disabled citizens are not discriminated against, either wilfully or inadvertently;
2. *Access:* To ensure that disabled citizens are able to participate in all aspects of society; and
3. *Support:* To ensure that disabled citizens are able to acquire the goods and services necessary to meet their needs.

In order to achieve these three goals, different policy instruments are typically used to meet different aims or objectives (Scanlon, 2013):

1. Equity is typically addressed with human rights and non-discrimination legislation, and with the support of advocacy organizations and citizen groups.

2. Access is typically addressed with specifications and standards, such as building codes, operating/training policies, and funding or incentives to enhance accessibility.

3. Support is usually addressed with programs providing financial resources, goods, and services, including
    *   pensions, compensation, income replacement;
    *   taxation measures, credits, and relief; and
    *   programs providing funding for specific assistance, such as drug benefits, adaptive equipment, or attendant care.

Disability policy sometimes arises through a top–down approach, meaning the government initiates it and puts it on the agenda (Priestley, 2007). The government identifies it as a priority to commit human and financial resources to making something happen. The recently tabled draft legislation governing access and inclusion in Canada — Bill C-81: *An Act to Ensure a Barrier-Free Canada* — is an example of such a process. It emanated from the Prime Minister's Office, charging a particular minister (Sport and People with Disabilities) to make it happen.

Other times, disability policy arises through a bottom–up approach. Members of the community create awareness of the need for change. They use a variety of strategies to get the attention of both policy-makers and the public, and to convince them of the legitimacy of their issue and the urgency of their need. This process typically involves organizations whose mandate reflects either the people or the issue at stake. The process can be collaborative or confrontational, but either way, it requires considerable political sophistication, committed resources, and experienced leadership in order to be successful (Boyce et al., 2001; Prince, 2009a).

Political activism is more likely to be successful — that is, to result in the outcomes sought — in the following circumstances (Boyce et al., 2001):

*   if it is not likely to generate strong opposition from any particular sector;
*   if it is pursued in an incremental rather than a radical way;
*   if it focuses on one particular, specific policy objective;
*   if it is based on a political rationale that is compatible with that of the government;
*   if it is based on empirical or scientific findings;
*   if it is consistent with the government's agenda and timelines;

- if it depends on knowledge and technology that already exist; or
- if it requires relatively little coordination among sectors, ministries, and/or departments within government.

It is often a struggle for organizations in the community — with under-staffing, changing leadership, and limited resources — to sustain a grassroots effort that can realistically effect change. One common tactic for enhancing the success of citizen participation in the political arena is coalitions (Prince, 2009a). Coalitions refer to either durable or ad hoc collaborations between organizations to achieve an agreed-upon goal with regard to policy. Coalitions are challenging to negotiate and maintain, often due to underlying issues that participating groups can't agree on. From the perspective of government, as long as community interest groups continue squabbling among themselves, government doesn't have to do anything (Boyce et al., 2001).

History of disability policy in Canada

The beginning of a deliberate focus on disability policy came at the end of the Second World War, during the expansion of the welfare state that took place in many Western liberal democracies. In Canada, the zeal of victory and the re-dedication to social values resulted in expanded government programs and generous social spending. The gratitude toward wounded veterans made disability a natural focus for some of this goodwill.

Since 1981, the governments of Canada and the provinces expressed the goal of improving inclusion and equity for people with disabilities. The following chronology illustrates the sustained attention that disability policy has received in Canada between 1981 and the present. It also, however, shows the variable progress that has been made in this policy area over the past 35 years (Boyce et al., 2001; Driedger, 1989; McColl & Jongbloed, 2006). Canadian disability policy has evolved over four periods: international pull (1980–1995), provincial push (1996–2005), federal monitoring (2006–2014), and federal leadership (2015–present).

International Pull (1980–1995)

Canada's impetus for developing disability policy came largely from an international consensus that the needs of people with disabilities required more attention (Prince, 2010). In 1981, the United Nations declared the International Year of Disabled Persons (1981), and Canada responded with the highly influential *Obstacles* report (1981), which recommended rights-based omnibus legislation and a full array of enhancements to government programs and services. This was the first official mention of the idea of a national disability act, aimed at ensuring full citizenship.

In 1982, disability policy achieved a major milestone when disabled people were designated as one of five groups whose rights were specifically guaranteed in Section 15 of the *Canadian Charter of Rights and Freedoms* (1982). At the same time, the UN's Decade of Disabled Persons (1983–1992) prompted the development of rights-based disability legislation in other English-speaking countries — the *Americans with Disabilities Act* in 1990, Australia's *Disability Discrimination Act* in 1992, and the United Kingdom's *Disability Discrimination Act* in 1995. In Canada, rights protections were already guaranteed by the *Canadian Human Rights Act* (1977), the provincial/territorial human rights acts, the *Charter of Rights and Freedoms* (1982), *and the Employment Equity Act* (1986). This period culminated in the five-year *National Strategy for the Integration of Persons with Disabilities* (1991–1996).

Provincial Push (1996–2005)

The second time period is characterized by growing provincial leadership in disability policy. It began in 1996 with the delivery of the report of the *National Strategy for the Integration of Persons with Disabilities*, known as the Scott Report (Federal Task Force on Disability Issues, 1996). The Scott Report recommended a larger role for the federal government in disability policy, and again recommended a national disability act for Canada.

At the same time that the 1996 Scott Report was calling for less talk and more action on disability issues, provinces were facing significant fiscal challenges because of unprecedented cuts to federal transfers. In response to growing national debt, developments were stalled on many policy fronts. Provinces banded together under the Federal/Provincial/Territorial (FPT) Council on Social Policy and advocated for the recovery of millions of dollars in lost transfers for health and social services. Disability issues were high on the first ministers' agenda, with emphasis on the Scott Report.

In 1998, the Federal/Provincial/Territorial (FPT) Working Group on Disability Issues was created, and several more landmark reports were produced: *In Unison* (1998), *Future Directions* (Government of Canada, 1999), and *In Unison 2000* (2000). These documents outlined the federal government's goals for the policy area, including a number of lasting initiatives, such as the Opportunities Fund and the Social Development Partnerships Program. In 2001, the Office of Disability Issues was created by consolidating a small hub of people in the federal public service to coordinate disability issues and report annually on their progress.

The federal government also implemented the *Multilateral Framework for Labour Market Agreements for Persons with Disabilities* in 2003 (ESDC, 2018), resulting in a series of bilateral agreements with provinces aimed at promoting employment for people with disabilities. While many of the initiatives launched during this period failed to produce all of the results that were intended, this time period saw important building blocks put in place. The last real challenge from the provinces on disability was issued in December 2004, when the FTP Working Group released its report, continuing to apply pressure for enhanced supports and services for adults and children with disabilities.

Federal Monitoring (2006–2014)

The third period of development of disability policy had an auspicious beginning. The Harper Conservatives came to power with a promise of national legislation protecting disability rights (Prince, 2006a). That promise was subsequently reiterated through 2008. However, there was little decisive action on the disability file in the next few years, despite the outspoken support of Finance Minster Jim Flaherty. Prince (2006a) described the Harper government's response to people with disabilities as "delivering, dithering and declining". The federal government "delivered" by introducing a number of financial measures, such as the Registered Disability Savings Plan, the Accessibility Fund, the Tax-Free Disability Savings Account, the Canada Student Grants for Students with Permanent Disabilities, and caregiver grants and expenses. The focus in this period was on economic self-sufficiency rather than citizenship and inclusion. Responses to disability issues mirrored the government's larger concerns — specifically, economic growth, financial self-sufficiency, and labour market diversification and participation (Torjman, 2014).

In 2007, the federal government signed the UN *Convention of the Rights of Persons with Disabilities* (2006), and in 2010 ratified the agreement (Council of Canadians with Disabilities [CCD], 2010; UN, 2010). They then adopted a "wait and see" stance on any legislative agenda, and instead continued to monitor disability concerns. They declined to sign the Optional Protocol to the Convention — an instrument that recognizes the authority of an international body to oversee compliance with the Convention.

Federal Leadership (2015–present)

The election of the Trudeau Liberals in 2015 brought about the latest period in the development of disability policy in Canada. After a decade of unfulfilled promises, the new federal government took aggressive steps toward proposing federal disability legislation. The government demonstrated its commitment to the disability agenda by naming a Minister of Sport and Persons with Disabilities, with a mandate to examine barriers experienced by people with disabilities and to establish new law to promote accessibility and inclusion. The minister immediately initiated community-based consultations to seek input from Canadians living with disabilities. At the time of writing this book, draft legislation has been tabled to identify, remove, and prevent barriers to participation for disabled Canadians (Government of Canada: House of Commons [2018]). In addition, a commitment has been made to sign the Optional Protocol to the UN *Convention on the Rights of People with Disabilities* within the year. Needless to say, it is an exciting time to be involved with disability policy, and a period of hopeful anticipation.

Jurisdiction in Canada

There are 38 federal statutes explicitly pertaining to disability, as well as many more that have implications for people with disabilities (even if those are not specifically stated). Additionally, legislation relating to disability exists in each of the 13 provincial and territorial jurisdictions, and municipalities also play a role in administering disability programs and standards, such as building codes and welfare services. There are a number of key areas where policy is needed to ensure that the goals stated earlier (equity, access, and support) are achieved with regard to people with disabilities, such as human rights and citizenship, income, access, taxation, employment, education, housing, and health. In this section, we will take a brief look at how the three main levels of government deal with these issues. (For more detailed information about legislation explicitly pertaining to disability issues in the 14 federal and provincial/territorial jurisdictions in Canada, please consult the Canadian Disability Policy Alliance's [2017] *A Review of Disability Policy in Canada*; http://www.disabilitypolicyalliance.ca/wp-content/uploads/2018/01/A-Review-of-Disability-Policy-in-Canada-3rd-edition-Final-1-1.pdf.)

Federal government

The role of the federal government in Canada is spelled out in the *British North America Act* of 1867 — the Act of the British parliament that gave Canada its sovereignty. The federal government is responsible to maintain "peace, order and good government", and to undertake such duties as not explicitly assigned to the provinces. It uses its fiscal power to "bring innovative programs and responses to issues with strong clear national characteristics" (Department of Finance Canada, 2006). Figure 17.1 summarizes the functions that are central to the role of the federal government in Canada.

Unlike several other Western democracies, such as the United States, Britain, and Australia, there is no explicit national disability legislation in Canada. Some researchers argue that the situation is no worse off for that (Cameron & Valentine, 2001). They state that the combined effects of our human rights protections, our *Charter of Rights and Freedoms*, and our universal health care system amount to an equally accessible environment for people with disabilities. Boyce, Krough, and Boyce (2006) disagree — they identify a pattern of erosion of disability programs in recent years, at least in part due to the lack of a national standard for disability supports and services.

There are four landmark pieces of legislation that create the policy infrastructure for the federal government's relationship with people with disabilities: the *Pension Act* (1965), the *Canadian Human Rights Act* (1977), the *Charter of Rights and Freedoms* (1982), and the *Employment Equity Act* (1986).

Included under the *Pension Act* (1965) is the Canada Pension Plan Disability program (CPP-D). The plan was intended to provide financial support to workers who had paid into it over their working life and who became unable to work because of a disability. In order to qualify, the disability must be "severe and prolonged", and must completely prevent the person from working. The amount of the pension is unrelated to financial need, but rather is based on the sal-

Figure 17.1: The role of the federal government in Canada

Census & Statistics

Corrections & Penitentiaries

Criminal Law

Defense

Federal Civil Service

Fisheries

Foreign Affairs

Immigration & Citizenship

Indigenous Peoples

Inter-provincial Matters

Marriage & Divorce

Money & Banks

Navigation & Shipping

Patents & Copyrights

Postal Services

Taxation

Telecommunications & Broadcasting

Trade & Commerce

Transportation: Rail, Air, Ferries

Unemployment Insurance

Weight & Measures

The role of the Federal Government is to maintain "peace, order, and good government" (*BNA Act. 1867*) and to undertake such duties as not explicitly assigned to the provinces or municipalities.

Source: McColl, Jaiswal, & Roberts (2017)

ary level and contributions made at the time of the onset of disability (Human Resources and Skills Development Canada [HRSDC], 2007). Discussions have arisen about the adequacy of the CPP-D and its relationship with provincial disability support plans (OECD, 2010b). Some policy analysts suggest that disabled citizens would be better served by a harmonized disability benefit system that transcends current federal–provincial–territorial barriers.

The *Canadian Human Rights Act* (1977) was passed to protect citizens against discrimination by the federal government, Crown corporations, chartered banks, airlines, television and radio, inter-provincial communications and telephone companies, interprovincial buses and railways, First Nations, and other federally regulated industries (Canadian Human Rights Commission, 2009). The Act created the Canadian Human Rights Commission and Tribunal, which investigate claims of discrimination, and pronounce judgment on cases (Canadian Human Rights Tribunal, 2007). The Act recognizes that mere rights protection is a necessary but not sufficient condition for full social inclusion.

The *Canadian Charter of Rights and Freedoms* (1985) was also discussed in the previous chapter. It warrants mention here as an essential part of the suite of legislative measures that underpins the federal government's role in relation to people with disabilities. The Charter guarantees political, legal, mobility, equality, language, and religious rights to Canadian citizens and civil rights to all physically present in Canada. Section 15 ensures "equal protection and equal benefit of the law" for five designated groups, including people with disabilities, alongside women, visible minorities, Indigenous people, and gay/lesbian/transgendered groups. Because it is part of the Canadian constitution, the Charter extends to all levels of government, and the task of interpreting and enforcing the Charter falls to the courts.

The *Employment Equity Act* (1986) grew out of a report authored by Judge Rosalie Abella, who coined the term *employment equity* (Abella, 1984). The Act exists to create equality in the workplace, ensuring that no person is denied employment opportunities or benefits for reasons unrelated to qualifications (Department of Justice Canada [DOJC], 1995). Four groups were designated for protection under employment equity: women, visible minorities, Indigenous people, and people with disabilities (DOJC, 1995). The *Employment Equity Act* requires employers to engage in proactive measures to improve the employment opportunities of the four protected groups. The Canadian Human Rights Commission is designated as the enforcement agency for this legislation.

As mentioned previously, at the time of writing this book, draft legislation has been tabled governing access and inclusion for people with disabilities in Canada — *Bill C-81: An Act to Ensure a Barrier-Free Canada.*

Provincial governments

The Canadian constitution explicitly assigns jurisdiction to the provinces for many of the issues that significantly affect day-to-day life for ordinary Canadians. Issues like education, health care, property rights, policing, marriage and divorce, and highways and vehicles all fall under provincial legislation. Each province and territory also has human rights or anti-discrimination legislation pertaining to institutions under their authority (HRSDC, 2008). The provinces and territories have authority to collect taxes to pay for their operations.

Provinces and territories also have authority over municipalities, and delegate many of their responsibilities to municipal governments in order to permit responsiveness to local needs. Issues like the collection of property taxes, the administration of welfare and social assistance, the enforcement of the building code, the governance of local schools, and the monitoring and enforcement of traffic and parking regulations are just a few of the functions under provincial/territorial authority that are actually operated at the municipal level.

Similar to the federal level, the provinces and territories each have a number of statutes with explicit provisions for people with disabilities that address the province's responsibility toward disabled citizens. These 13 jurisdictions (10 provinces and 3 territories) also have many other pieces of legislation that affect people with disabilities, for better or worse, without explicitly stating how they relate to disability. Inevitably, some jurisdictions do a better job than others at creating programs to serve people with disabilities. A good example is the variation in coverage for assistive devices across the country. This is clearly an issue that is provincially governed, but a comprehensive scan shows significant differences from one jurisdiction to the next in what is covered, for whom, and to what extent (Smith et al., 2017).

Another example of differences at this level is the three provinces who since 2001 have passed overarching accessibility legislation: Ontario (*Accessibility for Ontarians with Disabilities Act*, 2005), Manitoba (*Accessibility for Manitobans Act*, 2013), and Nova Scotia (*Accessibility Act*, 2017). Quebec has also had a long-standing Act offering additional rights protection explicitly to its citizens with disabilities (*Loi assurant l'exercice des droits des personnes handicapées en vue de leur integration scolaire, professionelle et sociale*, 1978; 2004). British Columbia has laid out a plan to increase accessibility by 2024 but, generally, the other provinces and territories seem to be waiting to see what is going to happen at the federal level before actively pursuing the accessibility agenda.

Evaluating disability policy

Since 1981, governments in Canada have systematically enacted policy aimed at bringing people with disabilities into the mainstream of Canadian life and ensuring them the same opportunities as non-disabled citizens (McColl & Schaub, 2013). Data, however, show that disabled persons remain unemployed or under-employed at significantly greater levels than their non-disabled contemporaries. They are well below the national average in educational achievement and well above the national average in poverty. Human rights tribunals across the country report that by far the highest number of complaints they receive come from disabled people — almost half of all complaints.

Disability policy in Canada has been described as conflicting, fragmented, incoherent, not user-friendly, and a hit-or-miss affair (Boyce et al., 2001; Prince, 2004; Cameron & Valentine 2001). It is a patchwork that requires considerable probing to reveal and considerable patience to understand (McColl & Jongbloed, 2006). According to Lande (1998), disability policy has been the victim of vague statutory definitions and capricious judicial opinions leading to flawed case law. It is perceived by people with disabilities as being impenetrable and unnecessarily complex, with little in the way of a coherent underlying ideology or policy framework.

Disability is such a complex construct that it is exceedingly challenging to formulate a policy response that benefits all. According to Ville, Crost, and Ravaud (2003), only 56% of disabled people in Canada even believe that there is such a thing as a "disability community" — that is, a group with a unifying experience the binds them together and transcends their differences. Of those, only 34% admit that they are a member of that community. That does not mean that the remaining 66% do not want any special considerations for their needs; it simply means that they would not affiliate with the label of disability, nor would they necessarily cast their votes or exert their influence in favour of disability issues.

Another challenge for disability policy-makers is the lack of a sound evidence base upon which to build disability policy. Difficult questions and significant ideological tensions persist about how disability policy should be framed (Prince, 2004). These issues have made it difficult for policy-makers to relate to the disability community and to achieve consensus on the needs of people with disabilities (Joiner, 2006; Prince, 2006b). Furthermore, the debate is typically highly polarized and inflamed by the rhetoric of rights (Bickenbach, 2006). A number of areas exist where there are strong disagreements about how disabled citizens should be viewed, what they need, and how they can be best served by governments in Canada (McColl & Jongbloed, 2006). Any fractiousness within the community permits the government to do nothing until a clear policy direction emerges with some support and momentum.

In 2010, the Organisation for Economic Co-operation and Development (OECD, 2010a) evaluated the disability policy environments of its 28 member nations (particularly as they relate to provisions for disabled workers). Using 2007 data, it rated countries on the generosity of benefits they pay out to disabled citizens (compensation), and on how actively they promoted integration.

- On the compensation scale, Canada was third from the bottom (just above the United States and Korea).
- On the integration scale, Canada scored just below the median (comparable with Belgium and Luxembourg).

These ratings placed Canada in the lowest cluster, characterized by stringent eligibility criteria, low benefit levels, and underdeveloped rehabilitation systems. Other countries in this cluster included the United Kingdom, Japan, Australia, and New Zealand.

Another indicator of the robustness of disability policy is the amount of public spending on disability, compared with other similarly prosperous countries. The OECD (2017) offers such a comparison. Using 2014 data, it showed that Canada spends less than 1% of its gross domestic product (GDP: the value of all goods and services produced by a country in a given year, expressed in US dollars) on benefits to people with disabilities — comparable with Korea and Chile — while countries like Australia, Israel, and New

Table 17.1: The AIMS framework

		Are the group's needs recognized and met within the society?	
		Yes	No
Is the group valued and included in society?	Yes	INTEGRATION	ASSIMILATION
	No	SEGREGATION	MARGINALIZATION

Source: Minnes, Buell, Feldman, McColl, & McCreary, 2002

Zealand spend more than 2.5%. The GDP in 2014 in Canada was $1.8 trillion, while in Australia it was only $1.5 trillion.

In order to effectively evaluate disability policy, we need a clear specification of what we are trying to achieve. Minnes, Buell, Feldman, McColl, and McCreary (2002) offer the AIMS (assimilation, integration, marginalization, segregation) framework to assess the effectiveness of disability policy, based on Berry's Acculturation Framework. They identify four conditions that are more or less desirable as a way of addressing minority needs within a population (see Table 17.1):

- *Marginalization* occurs when a society does not recognize or support the needs of a minority group, such as people with disabilities, nor does it encourage their participation.

- *Segregation* occurs when the society does recognize and supply the needs of the group, but makes no attempt to include them in the mainstream.

- *Assimilation* occurs when the group is actively encouraged to participate in mainstream society, but no special consideration is given for its particular needs.

- *Integration* reflects a situation where the group's needs are recognized and met, and its participation in society is facilitated. This is similar to what Ravaud and Stiker (2001) call *differentiation*, where groups are treated as overtly equal, with a recognition that some may require special resources in order to participate equally.

Obviously, the condition of integration is the preferred response to disabled people within the population, and it is clearly the one that is sought in Canada (Ville, Crost, & Ravaud, 2003).

But how do we judge how effectively we achieve integration? Prince (2009a) states that we need a macro-level social index that shows how effectively people with disabilities are integrated. Such an index would operate at the population level and would reflect the participation of all disabled people regardless of the many variations in their needs and circumstances. Wilson, McColl, Zhang, and McKinnon (2017) proposed such an index. They began with an assumption that if disabled people are becoming increasingly integrated in Canadian society, then the way they spend their time should be looking more and more like the way non-disabled people spend theirs. In other words, if disability policy is working to create a more equitable, accessible, and inclusive society, we would expect the daily activities of disabled and non-disabled people to be increasingly similar over time.

Using data from the 1992 and the 2010 Time Use Surveys (Statistics Canada, 1992, 2010) and using a disability screening question that was included in both surveys, we were able to create a Dissimilarity Index that summed all the individual dissimilarities between disabled and non-disabled populations over 18 activity categories (Wilson et al., 2017). Here are some observations:

- From 1992 to 2010, the Dissimilarity Index within the disabled population was 5.2%. In other words, disabled people spent about 5.2% of their time differently in 2010 than they did in 1992. For non-disabled people, the change was 3.7% over the same period. Thus, activity patterns changed more for disabled than non-disabled people.

- In 1992, the dissimilarity between disabled and non-disabled people was 10.1%, meaning disabled and non-disabled people spent 10% of their time differently. In 2010, the dissimilarity between disabled and non-disabled was 8.9%. Thus, disabled people looked *more* like non-disabled in their time use over an 18-year period.

- These differences held for both men and women. Disabled men went from being 10.7% dissimilar to non-disabled men in 1992 to 9.8% dissimilar in 2010; disabled women went from 8.9% dissimilar in 1992 to 8.0% in 2010.

- In 2010, the Dissimilarity Index between disabled men and disabled women was 8.3%, a considerable reduction from 9.9% in 1992. Even within the disabled population, disabled men and women are looking more alike in their time use as time goes along.

These findings suggest that in fact disabled people are experiencing more equitable activity profiles with their non-disabled counterparts in Canadian society. If the stated assumption holds, then we can assert that disability policy is succeeding in creating a more equitable society.

Electoral participation

> Contemporary struggles by people with special needs to participate fully in the electoral process are a useful reminder of how significant voting is for formal citizenship, exercising individual capacity and self-expression, and experiencing a sense of civic belonging. (Prince, 2007, p. 41)

Perhaps the most direct and tangible expression of citizenship is the ability to participate in democracy by voting and engaging in elections (Prince, 2009a). And yet, research has shown that people with disabilities are 15% to 20% less likely to vote than those without disabilities (Prince, 2012; Matsubayashi & Ueda, 2014; McColl & Jongbloed, 2006; Schur et al., 2017). This leads to disabled individuals becoming what Prince (2007) refers to as "absent citizens" — individuals who are "missing" from civic engagement and political participation.

As idyllic as the Canadian democratic system may appear (Kim, 2011), Stienstra and D'Aubin (2006, p. 210) observe that

> Canada is portrayed both within its border and across the world as a leader in electoral democracy. We say our citizens enjoy full democratic rights, including the right to participate in the electoral process. Yet this picture fails to capture the situation of people with disabilities in Canada, for whom enjoyment of full citizenship rights is still emerging and opportunities that exist to participate have been hard-fought struggles.

The *United Nations Convention on the Rights of Persons with Disabilities* acknowledges that disabled persons must participate in the political process. The Convention — in particular articles 9

[Accessibility], 19 [Living independently], and 29 [Participation in Political and Public life] — guarantees accessibility in the political sphere.

Prince (2012) identifies five types of barriers that interfere with voting and political participation for people with disabilities:

1. *Physical barriers:* Architectural obstacles to electoral involvement for people with disabilities include inaccessible polling sites/stations, meeting venues,campaign offices, and constituency offices (Shannon, Giancarlo, & McColl, 2015; Prince, 2004, 2009a).

2. *Attitudinal barriers:* Social and psychological barriers also exist, in the form of erroneous assumptions about the desire and ability to vote (Prince, 2012; Schur, Shields, Kruse, & Schriner, 2002). These not only have direct effects on the accessibility of the electoral process, they also have indirect effects on the extent to which disabled people view their vote as valued and important.

3. *Informational barriers:* Communications about candidates, issues, and election procedures also sometimes contribute to the exclusion of people with disabilities from the democratic process.

4. *Procedural barriers:* Administrative processes observed at election or campaign facilities can also serve to exclude people with disabilities; for example, having to produce certain forms of identification, like a driver's licence or piece of mail, may effectively exclude some otherwise eligible voters.

5. *Socio-economic barriers:* Finally, it has been shown that voting is associated with social class, and that poorer, less educated, or unemployed people are less likely to vote. These three conditions describe many people with disabilities, who are over-represented among the non-voting population (Miller & Powell, 2016).

Merely extending the franchise to underrepresented groups does not necessarily promote participation. Specific policies and measures must be instituted to ensure that people with disabilities can overcome barriers to participation in the democratic process (Prince, 2009a). Below are some of the options available to improve access:

- physical modifications to polling stations and meeting venues, including level access, adequate seating, accessible washrooms, sufficient manoeuvring room, and assistive devices;

- service considerations, such as the availability of attendant care, sign-language interpreters on request, the ability to bring a friend or assistant;

- informational services, such as telephone services for those with hearing impairments, accessible web-based information, documents designed for people with different disabilities, sign-language and captioning;

- staff training on accessibility, sensitivity toward people with disabilities, and customer service;

- procedural changes to make voting more accessible, such as a voting template, large-print list of candidates, transfer certificates to allow voting at a level-access station, mobile polling stations, voting at home, voting by telephone, absentee or mailed ballots; and

- outreach services, including accompaniment and transportation to encourage voting. In some jurisdictions, this role has been taken on by disability organizations in the community.

It is worth noting that Canada offers one of the broadest ranges of electoral options to its citizens in the world. It is also noteworthy that Canada is one of very few countries in the world that do not have a competency requirement for voting (Prince, 2012). There is no minimum level of mental capacity required in order to be eligible to vote in this country. Consistent with the UN Convention, all citizens are eligible to vote.

Conclusion

In summary, this chapter has defined policy as the actions (or deliberate inaction) of government in response to priority problems in the population. In particular, we have discussed disability policy, or policy that influences daily life for people with disabilities. In addition to *appreciating* what disability policy means for disabled people, we have also tried to be realistic about the ability of government to enact broad-based solutions that benefit not only all people with disabilities but all Canadians.

We have *discovered* the range of disability policy in Canada — with 3 policy aims, 14 jurisdictions, and numerous policy options — and we have explored how we got to the place we are today. But is it enough? Using time use data, we have *discovered* that the situation for people with disabilities appears to be improving, and perhaps even converging with the situation of all Canadians. However, there are still significant margins between disabled and non-disabled Canadians in the key indicators of prosperity: income, education, and employment.

It can be said that the policy environment is perfectly *designed* to produce the problems that disabled people experience! Stated another way, virtually any problem can be tracked back to a location in the policy environment, where policy is either flawed, inadequate, or missing altogether. As mentioned earlier, a long-held *dream* about disability policy appears to be closer to coming true than ever before. The federal government has recently tabled draft legislation to ensure access and inclusion for disabled Canadians.

If you were the federal Minister of Sport and Disabled Persons, which of many policy options at your disposal would you choose?

- Would you increase pensions and guaranteed incomes, putting more money in the hands of people with disabilities? Of course, you would either have to raise taxes or take money away from someone else in order to do that.

- Would you target employment strategies that favoured disabled job-seekers? And how would such a move play out among youth, who are also experiencing significant challenges to entering and maintaining a place in the job market?

- Would you sponsor public awareness campaigns that try to draw the attention of all Canadians to the issues of people with disabilities? Research has shown that while people sympathize with the plight of others, they seldom change their practices or behaviour in response to information campaigns.

One thing is for certain: the policy-making process needs to be more sensitive to the issues of people with disabilities. In Chapter 16, we acknowledged that most discrimination in Canada is unintentional. While this does not excuse discrimination, it does change the way we approach the problem. In the same way that policy-makers have learned to take into account the issues of women, Indigenous people, and cultural minorities, they must also learn to consider the impact of policy on disabled people. In order to do that, they must *deploy* a disability lens, such as the one proposed in Figure 17.2. It does not explicitly evaluate policy from a disability perspective, but it does ask a number of key questions that must be confronted in attempting to create equity, access, and support through policy.

Figure 17.2: The Disability Policy Lens (version 2.0)

The Disability Policy Lens was developed to assist scholars, policy-makers, and advocates to analyze policy affecting people with disabilities in Canada. The seven questions take readers through a process of considering the implications of specific policies for people with disabilities. The Lens is unique in that it is *brief*, and *non-prescriptive*. There are no correct or incorrect answers to the questions, but each question has important implications that should be carefully considered when creating or amending policy.

1. Does the policy specifically mention people with disabilities? Has explicit consideration been afforded to the consequences for people with disabilities?

2. If so, how is *disability* defined? Who is considered "disabled" according to the policy? Does the policy refer specifically to people with:
   - physical, cognitive, sensory, or mental illness-related disabilities?
   - permanent, long-standing, temporary, or episodic disabilities?
   - severe, moderate, or mild disabilities?

   Who is considered eligible for consideration under the policy? Who is included/excluded, and who decides who qualifies as disabled?

3. Which of the following three aims does the policy seek to achieve?
   - *Access:* Ability to participate
   - *Support:* Resources to address special needs
   - *Equity:* Freedom from discrimination

continued....

Figure 17.2 continued

If the goal is *equity,* how does the policy define equity?
- *Outcome equity:* Whatever it takes to achieve *equal outcomes* with non-disabled.
- *Vertical equity:* Special considerations to create *equal opportunity* for disabled people.
- *Horizontal equity: Equal treatment* for disabled people; that is, the same as everyone else.

4. Does the policy view disabled people as members of a minority group with special needs, or as one of the many citizen groups whose issues must be considered in establishing policy? As individual rights holders, or as members of the collective responsible for the good of the whole population?

5. How does the policy relate to other policies:
- within the jurisdiction — in the same ministry, in other ministries (including both disability-specific and non-disability–specific policy)?
- in other jurisdictions — national, provincial, regional, municipal?

(For a survey of legislation, regulations, programs related to disability in Canada, see www.disability policyalliance.ca/wp-content/uploads/2013/10/Disability-Policy-Scan-2013.pdf)

6. How is the allocation of scarce resources affected by this policy? Who wins and who loses when this policy is implemented? What would be the impact on other disability groups? The business/private sector? Other minority groups? Other citizens? Taxpayers?

7. How did this policy come into effect? What is the history associated with it? Who were the champions/detractors? Where might one anticipate support/opposition?

Source: An earlier version appears in McColl & Jongbloed, 2006, pp. 414–415.

Chapter 18

Disability and research

Introduction

What is disability research, and what are some of the issues associated with conducting research that contributes to a better understanding of disability? This chapter focuses on defining the scope of disability research, examining how it has evolved over time, and some of the unique methodological and ethical issues faced by disability researchers.

Defining *disability research*

Disability research is defined as the creation of new knowledge about disability in two areas (Priestley, Waddington, & Bessozi, 2010):

1. the barriers that inhibit full participation and equality of disabled people in society, and
2. the strategies and solutions that remove barriers.

Disability studies, meaning the academic enterprise associated with teaching and research on disability, is an emerging field. While perhaps not yet acknowledged as a separate discipline, it is an inter-disciplinary field with a defined body of knowledge that has developed primarily over the past 40 years. Disability studies may sit within faculties of arts, humanities, law and policy, or even health sciences. It is essential, however, to distinguish disability studies from two other fields — medical research on impairment and rehabilitation research.

Medical research on impairment aims to understand the epidemiology, pathology, diagnosis, and treatment of underlying health conditions that may be associated with disability. It functions primarily at the cell, organ, or system level, but also at the population level in terms of understanding the prevalence, distribution, and determinants of impairment.

Understanding impairment is important work, duly valued by most people with disabilities (McDermott & Turk, 2011). For example, if it is possible to prevent the progression of a deteriorating condition, people with that condition want to know and want that research to be funded and conducted. They want to know the risk factors that might alert someone to the potential for impairment, so that early intervention might optimize ability. They also want to better understand what happens in their brains or bodies to cause the impairment that, to a greater or lesser degree, is responsible for their disability. Finally, they want to sharpen the tools available to health professionals, so that when they become a patient at different stages in their lives, the knowledge and expertise is there to maximize the effectiveness of treatment.

Rehabilitation research focuses on function and aims to understand the effectiveness of interventions undertaken by rehab professionals to promote independence and optimal function. These professionals might include occupational and physical therapists, speech therapists, rehab psychologists, physiatrists or medical rehabilitation specialists, recreation therapists, vocational counsellors, special educators, rehab nurses, and others.

Rehab research functions at the level of the person and is a clinical research enterprise dedicated to promoting the effectiveness of rehabilitation. To understand rehabilitation research, we need to acknowledge that most people with disabilities undergo some form of rehabilitation at some stage in their lives — often at the onset of a disability, or at intervals when function changes. Rehabilitation may happen in the hospital, in the community, in the workplace, or in the home, and it is time-limited and goal-oriented. It depends on active involvement of the client in partnership with a therapist or other professional.

Most people with disabilities also value rehabilitation research. They want to know that rigorous, diligent research is being done to contribute evidence about what works and what doesn't work in rehabilitation. For example, someone who has had a stroke wants to know that once the acute effects of the stroke resolve, someone is equipped with sound, scientifically derived knowledge about how to optimize their recovery and give them back as much of their life as possible. Someone with a brain injury wants his or her counsellors to be able to precisely assess strengths and weaknesses, and to help to set realistic goals for work, housing, and support needs.

While both medical research on impairment and rehabilitation research are important knowledge enterprises, neither one is "disability research". According to Priestley and colleagues (2010), while 100% of the disabled persons' organizations they surveyed agreed with the need to support academic medical and rehab research, two-thirds (67%) felt that the real needs of people with disabilities were not well understood by academic researchers.

Disability research, by contrast, attempts to address the real needs associated with living in society with a disability. It operates at the level of society and culture, and its relationship to disabled people. It does not ask questions about how we can change disabled people to optimize their participation; rather, it asks how society interacts with disabled people to produce disability. It acknowledges that disability is a socially constructed phenomenon, and that social values themselves must be studied, not ruled out in an attempt to achieve neutrality or objectivity (Mmatli, 2009).

While it is possible to see these three fields as entirely complementary to one another, in practice disability studies tends to be in conflict with medical and rehabilitation research. That conflict arises for a number of reasons, not least of which is *economic*. As Barnes (2008) puts it, academic orthodoxies reinforce the existing hierarchical power structure that controls the material relations of research production. In other words, funding agencies, peer-review processes, academic structures, and professional allegiances all contribute to a distinct hierarchy, where the bulk of available resources go to medical research, with a considerably smaller proportion going to rehabilitation research, and only a tiny portion to disability studies (Flicker & Nixon, 2018). Some disability researchers believe that medical and rehabilitation researchers are part of the problem rather than the solution — that their research is used to perpetuate segregation, discrimination, oppression, and inequality (Stone & Priestley, 1996).

There are also *ideological* tensions that place disability research at odds with medical and rehabilitation research. There is inherent skepticism among disability researchers about the theory that underpins medical and rehabilitation research, most of which was developed within a medical model by the very academic orthodoxies referred to above (Goodley, 2017). Conventional theory informing medical and rehabilitation research situates the cause of disability in the person, and thus the target for intervention as well. It fails to take account of social and cultural contributions to the creation of disability, or to see the self-perpetuating nature of this approach for maintaining the status quo.

Methodologically, disability research is also somewhat resistant to the standards that govern medical and rehabilitation research (Johnston et al., 2009). For example, most health conditions associated with disability are relatively rare conditions (compared to common medical conditions like hypertension or diabetes). It is challenging to generate large samples, normal distributions, precise estimates, or significance levels that are the hallmarks of scientific research. Further, the heterogeneity and complexity of disability means that it is difficult to standardize therapeutic approaches and uphold a high degree of fidelity when evaluating interventions. Blinding, randomization, and other controls for bias are often either ethically or practically prohibitive. These factors together lead to marginalization of disability research by the traditional scientific community.

Perhaps the largest gulf between disability studies and medical/rehabilitation research is the *perspective* of researchers toward people with disabilities. In medical and rehabilitation research, people with disabilities are seen as a minority with a problem — a problem that needs to be fixed, cured, treated, resolved. That problem lies within them, and represents a challenge to be faithfully and benevolently addressed. There is no question in my mind that medical and rehabilitation researchers are working toward what they believe to be a better reality for people with disabilities, despite being perceived as oppressors by some radical commentators (Stone & Priestley, 1996).

What medical and rehabilitation researchers sometimes don't realize is that "vulnerability" is an imposed category that sets up a duality between privileged and oppressed (Thomas, 2007). By treating disability as a vulnerability, researchers situate themselves in the dominant majority and disabled people in the disenfranchised minority. This dualism upholds the very structures that disadvantage people with disabilities — the status quo, where education, heredity, birth-right, and social class maintain a power differential (Mmatli, 2009). Their privilege invests researchers with a kind of "unintentional blindness" that prevents them from seeing the world through any lens but their own (Nixon, 2017). Thus, they perpetually approach disability issues from a perspective of "How can we help disabled people?" rather than "How can we alter the status quo to achieve equity, citizenship, and inclusion for people with disabilities?" (Beauchamp-Pryon, 2011). Lilla Watson, an Indigenous activist from Australia, expresses it best in the following quote:

> If you have come here to help me, you are wasting your time. But if you have come because your liberation is bound up with mine, then let us work together. (www.en.wikipedia.org/wiki/Lilla_ Watson; accessed 29.10.18)

The research agenda for disability studies

What questions, then, are legitimate for disability researchers to ask? What do we want to know about disability? Who sets the agenda and the priorities for disability studies?

Disability studies potentially covers the range of human experience — from the most pedestrian to the most esoteric — and it does so from the perspective of how people and environments interact to either hinder or enable participation, freedom, and flourishing. It is carried out in equitable partnerships between academic researchers and disabled people, and it features the authentic voices of people with disabilities. Several recent surveys have asked disabled people and organizations representing disability issues for their priorities for disability research (Priestley et al., 2010; Nierse & Abma, 2011; Mmatli, 2009; van Kraayenoord, 2010; Shakespeare, 2015). The priorities appear to be the following:

- education, especially post-secondary education, given its power to create opportunities;
- attitudes, stigma, and non-discrimination;
- policy and political infrastructure;
- work, particularly paid work, and the barriers and facilitators to employment;
- poverty, income sources, and the real costs of disability;
- adequate housing, home modifications, and adaptations;
- friendships, social relationships, and social exclusion;
- transportation and travel;

- leisure, sport, and accessibility of community facilities; and
- health care and community supports and services.

In each instance, the questions of interest range from the needs and preferences of people with disabilities to the barriers experienced and accommodations required and the social machinery that facilitates or enables ability. The emphasis is on a structural or macro-level analysis of the institutions and factors that impinge on the lives of people with disabilities, from the family to the society (Bynder & New, 1976).

Methods for disability research

What research methods are available to disability studies researchers, and which are most conducive to the task at hand? We will explore three areas of research methodology to address this question: design, sample, and data collection. (Discussion of data analysis is beyond the scope of this book, and has relatively few implications that are peculiar to disability research.)

Design

Design refers to the overall organization of the research so as to produce the most complete, accurate, and truthful picture of the phenomenon of interest. The design of a study is the plan or blueprint that ensures that it produces a response to the research questions, and that there are strategies in place to control noise, error, and extraneous factors (Gitlin, Winter, Dennis, & Hauck, 2007). Table 18.1 gives examples of the most common research designs and their applications.

Research by definition seeks relationships among variables. All research, regardless of its philosophical or methodological origins, seeks to understand the world in terms of how things are related to one another. Thus, any research question should be reducible ultimately to the form

Is _____ related to _____?

Of course, most research questions look a lot more complicated than this, but this basic formula should be at their root. If it is not, I am a bit suspicious as to whether the researcher really knows what

Table 18.1: Major categories of disability research design

Basic science	Experimental	Operates at the cell, organ, or system level to discover basic biological, psychological, or social processes.
Theory development	Qualitative	Subjective, context-dependent processes to discover real-world manifestations of phenomena of interest.
Epidemiology / Demographics	Observational	Quantitative research at the population level to discover occurrence, risk factors, and distribution of outcomes of interest.
Needs survey	Survey	Sample research to discover how a problem is expressed in a population and what the resource requirements are of addressing the problem.
Pilot study	Quasi-experimental	Non-controlled trial of a novel intervention or approach to ascertain preliminary outcomes and needs of a more definitive study.
Clinical trial	Experimental	Controlled trial of an intervention to contribute to a definitive assessment of its effectiveness and efficiency.
Review & meta-analysis	Synthesis	Qualitative and quantitative methods to synthesize existing literature to identify convergence of evidence, themes, and gaps.
Knowledge translation	Dissemination	Research to discover the most effective ways to reach desired audiences with specific messages.

he or she is looking for. An effective research design permits the researcher to offer original, innovative intelligence to further our understanding of that relationship.

There are a number of different ways to classify research designs in order to consider their merits and demerits for disability research. The first is proposed by Goodley (2017). Research can be non-participatory, participatory, or emancipatory.

Non-participatory research

Non-participatory research refers to that initiated and carried out by academic researchers without explicit partnership with people with disabilities or disability organizations. In this scenario, academic researchers develop research questions out of their knowledge of the published literature, their own clinical experience, and the traditions of their academic discipline. Disabled people serve as subjects of the research, providing data as requested by the researchers. The creativity or ingenuity of the research is a product of the researcher's own depth and understanding of the field. The aim is to produce an original, novel contribution to our knowledge — something no one has ever published or discovered before. It is a highly competitive enterprise in which credentials and track record are important considerations. It is not a field in which novice researchers can be successful, unless allied with successful, experienced researchers. This has been the standard scientific approach to producing new knowledge.

Participatory research

Participatory research refers to research where consumer partners are invited by academic researchers to play a central role in the research. The emphasis is on responding to questions that are salient to consumers, that have real-world implications, and that offer opportunities for skill and capacity development. Participation is expected at three junctures:

- problem identification and research question definition;
- study design and execution; and
- messaging, outreach, and knowledge translation.

Participatory models (in particular, participatory action research [PAR]) emerged in the late 1970s and early 1980s, when the disability movement began to insist on "nothing about us without us", and to establish explicit terms for participation in research. They would no longer simply serve as subjects in the research, but instead wanted to express their agency at all stages of the research enterprise. One of the challenges that plagued this approach was the differential in qualifications and experience between researchers and disabled participants. This typically meant that researchers remained in control of the resources and the ultimate outcome of the research, and that equality of participation was seldom achieved.

Emancipatory research

Emancipatory research was a further development of participatory research emerging in the 1990s. This approach expressed an explicit agenda not only to contribute new knowledge, but to engage politically with the dominant structures in society to confront social oppression and remove disabling barriers (Barnes, 2003; Oliver, 1997). A number of manifestos outline the requirements for emancipatory research, but perhaps the most direct is a much-quoted article by Stone and Priestley (1996) that identifies six principles that govern emancipatory research:

1. Researchers must adopt the social model of disability.
2. Researchers must surrender any claim to scientific neutrality, acknowledging that the study of disability is essentially value-laden and socially constructed.
3. Researchers must focus only on research that supports political action to remove barriers for people with disabilities.
4. Researchers must devolve control of the means of production, and render themselves accountable to people with disabilities.
5. Researchers must give voice to the personal experiences of people with disabilities.
6. Once all the above criteria are met, a plurality of methodological approaches are embraced.

Of course, such a strident approach has attracted critique. One criticism is the scarcity of methodological detail or attention to scientific rigour in emancipatory research (Hammersley, 1995; Barnes, 2008; Danieli & Woodhams, 2005).

The emancipatory approach has also been criticized for polarizing the research community into "insiders" and "outsiders" (Macbeth, 2010). One is rendered an insider by virtue of having first-hand experience with disability; all others, regardless of their connections, qualifications, or commitment, are considered outsiders. According to the emancipatory approach, only insiders are qualified to make decisions and control resources. The research process must be accountable to insiders, despite any lack of research qualifications or track record in successfully executing research.

How, then, does one judge who is suitable to be considered an insider, the arbiter of all questions methodological, ideological, theoretical, or political? Barnes (2008) points out that the singular personal experience of disability offers little assurance that the insider has a good grasp of the heterogeneous and often subtle issues that inform disability studies. Being an insider to a particular type of disability does not necessarily render one an expert in other areas of disability research (Shakespeare, 1996). Furthermore, the "us and them" approach does little to build successful research teams that can procure funding in a highly competitive arena and successfully execute and disseminate research. Rather, an oppressive dualism divides the research effort, instead of galvanizing it to make meaningful contributions to change (Goodley & Moore, 2000; Macbeth, 2010; Shakespeare, 1996).

A third critique of the emancipatory approach is the need to forgo the illusion of objectivity, and with it any attempt at impartiality or the pursuit of a broader truth. Instead, research is preferred that is candid about its biases, and highly utilitarian in its service to a particular political goal. Emancipatory research is usually characterized by the testimonials of individual voices and narratives. While individual voices have inherent authenticity, they can appear anecdotal or even sentimental in the eyes of policy-makers faced with many compelling priorities (Barnes, 2003). Transparent self-interest is typically viewed as highly suspect by decision-makers. Policy-makers seek macro-level analysis that persuades not only about the presence of a problem, but also about the scope and magnitude, consequences, and implications of the problem (Carden, 2009; Prince, 2009a). They seek evidence that can assist them in allocating scarce resources to the most compelling problems. If research is to make a difference in the structures that disable, then it must be taken seriously by decision-makers, which means that it must uphold standards of evidence applied in other research communities. All these caveats led Barnes (2008) to conclude that emancipatory research is an "impossible dream".

One model of emancipatory research that upholds a high standard of evidence and policy relevance is the Learning Collaborative (McColl, Adair, Davey, & Kates, 2013). The Learning Collaborative is a process aimed at producing accelerated change toward structural improvements. It was originally developed to assist in the redesign of health systems (Institute for Healthcare Improvement, 2003) and has been used with some success to promote effective disability policy (McColl et al., 2013).

Learning Collaboratives consist of high-functioning teams made up of three types of partners:

- *Academic partners*, who use their research skill to formulate questions and conduct research in consultation with partners; undertake reviews of literature to identify best practices; seek external funding if needed to supplement resources; conduct policy analysis; prepare policy briefs to assemble policy-relevant research.

- *Community partners*, who use their experience and membership to identify important issues that respond to priority needs of consumers; identify and recruit research participants; reach out to policy-makers on behalf of their membership; get information out to their distribution networks.

- *Policy partners*, who function in an advisory capacity to assist in understanding the policy environment of particular issues; assist in identifying appropriate contact persons in government; assist in framing messages to take government priorities, sensitive issues, and program developments into consideration; assist in understanding timelines of particular policy issues and opportunities for citizen engagement.

All three partners work together, combining their expertise to identify research questions that are of practical, policy, and theoretical importance. With a commitment to change, strong leadership, and open communication, the process unfolds in the four steps shown in Table 18.2, taking best advantage of the skill sets of each of the partners.

Whalley Hammell (2006) suggests principles to govern collaborative research approaches in disability studies, drawing on postcolonial and feminist perspectives. Research must be all of the following:

- collaborative;
- inclusive of an action component;
- based on priorities of the disability community;
- focused on the person–environment interaction;

Table 18.2: The four-step process of the Learning Collaborative

PLAN	Assemble evidence in brief and compelling fashion, with recommendations for best practices.	Academic partners
DO	Mobilize consumers and use networks to disseminate research findings to policy partners.	Community & Policy
STUDY	Study effectiveness of "Do" phase; gather new information from policy partners on what worked and what didn't; furnish additional information as needed.	Academic partners
ACT	Reach out to a broader group of stakeholders, using best advice from all partners.	Community & Policy

- sensitive to intersectoral issues associated with disability (e.g., gender, age, ethnicity);
- reflexive and critical in its philosophical stance;
- contributing to a solid evidence base; and
- subject to evaluation by consumers/participants.

Another important decision to be made about research design is whether the problem is better addressed using qualitative or quantitative methods. This decision mostly comes down to how one sees the world and the role of research with that world. Challenge for readers #7 is a quiz to help you situate yourself on a continuum based on your preference for qualitative versus quantitative approaches to knowledge.

Among the three groups identifed by the quiz, I am concerned, particularly as a researcher and educator, when I encounter people in either of the first two categories — confirmed positivist and confirmed relativist — in disability research. I fear that they are more aligned with their scientific paradigm than they are with disability studies. They are willing to sacrifice the best answer to a particular research question (and therefore the best interests of those disabled people with whom they work) in favour of their particular ontological worldview.

Challenge for readers #7

Check one of the two options under each question:

1. What is the purpose of scientific inquiry?
    ☐ To explain the world around us in terms of a consistent set of principles.
    ☐ To understand the world relative to time, place, and person.

2. How can we come to know more about the world?
    ☐ By standing apart from it and observing it dispassionately.
    ☐ By interacting with it and developing a relationship with it.

3. What is the nature of "reality"?
    ☐ There is a single objective reality, and we are consistently approaching a better understanding of it.
    ☐ There is no "reality" — there are multiple realities that reflect our perceptions and social construction of the world.

4. How do we access what is real and what isn't?
    ☐ By finding evidence for or against our hypotheses — deductively.
    ☐ By observing and reconciling our observations — inductively.

5. How do we judge the merit of research?
    ☐ By evaluating the extent to which the factors of interest have been isolated in the design.
    ☐ By evaluating the extent to which all aspects of context, experience, and meaning are accounted for in the design.

6. What is the role of social values in research?
    ☐ Every attempt should be made to ensure that the values of researchers and subjects do not influence the outcome of the study.
    ☐ Values of researchers and subjects should be explicitly stated and used to understand observations.

continued....

Challenge for readers #7 continued

7. What do we believe about natural phenomena?
   ☐ They are governed by laws or principles, and behave rationally and consistently.
   ☐ They are dependent on context and cannot be considered independently of their environment.

For every time you chose the first of the two responses offered, give yourself one point. For every time you chose the second, give yourself two points.

Is your preference for qualitative or quantitative ways of knowing?

- If you scored 7 or 8, you are a *confirmed positivist.* You see the world in terms of a set of interacting laws and principles that are eventually, ultimately possible to understand. The way to understand them is to patiently and rigorously observe and document, to be as neutral and dispassionate as possible, to strip away any possible confounders from the environment, and to create a value-free opportunity to witness those principles in action.
- If you scored 13 or 14, you are a *confirmed relativist.* You see the world as a socially constructed reality that must be understood through the lens of the observer. You resist the idea that there is a single underlying truth that we can eventually know. Instead, you see truth as dependent on history, geography, culture, gender, and the many other lenses through which individuals see their world.
- If you scored in between 9 and 12, you are amenable to mixed methods or to both approaches to research design in different situations. This is where I hope most disability researchers find themselves — understanding that both traditions have much to offer to our understanding of the world that people with disabilities navigate.

Sample

Sampling refers to the selection of people who can provide information about the variables or phenomena of interest. Who are the people best positioned to offer data, observations, and intelligence on the factors that we are interested in studying? How many people do we need to engage with in order to feel that we have covered the scope of the phenomenon we are interested in? Where will we find these people, and how will we contact them without violating their privacy? How long will it take to accrue as many participants to our research as needed? These are the kinds of questions we need to address in order to begin sampling.

A sample is usually defined in terms of inclusion and exclusion criteria:

- *Inclusion criteria:* What qualities does a person need to possess in order to be eligible to participate in our study?

- *Exclusion criteria:* Once identified as a potential participant (i.e., meeting the inclusion criteria), what does a person need to do to render himself or herself ineligible and be excluded from the study?

Note that inclusion and exclusion criteria are not simply the opposite of each other, but rather represent a two-phase process of sampling.

There are a number of issues in sampling that are particularly salient to disability research. For example, an inevitable inclusion criterion in disability research tends to be having a particular type of disability. We have talked throughout this book about sensitivities with regard to labelling and classifying disability, and yet that is precisely what researchers need to do in order to attract the most appropriate participants.

Often inclusion criteria are framed in terms of diagnosis rather than disability: "We are looking for people with spinal cord injuries ... a history of depression ... a recent stroke...." In so doing, we acknowledge the broad range of disabilities that might be associated with each of these diagnoses. However, the consumer organizations, clinical settings, and community groups that often serve as the source of potential participants are usually organized along the lines of underlying health conditions. Therefore, in order to attract their members/clients, researchers may be forced to identify them according to their diagnosis, rather than their disability.

If, on the other hand, we wish to attract people on the basis of their disability, what language and tactics do we use to find them? The only real way to identify someone with a disability is to ask them — do they experience limitations in fulfilling their daily roles, as a result of a health condition (see Chapter 2; WHO, 2001)? Take for example the challenge of doing a national population survey of people with disabilities — an invaluable statistical tool for understanding the scope and breadth of issues facing people with disabilities. This sort of survey is often attached to the national census. On the basis of one or more questions, it identifies people with disabilities for follow-up with a more detailed survey about disability issues. For example, the Canadian Survey on Disability uses two questions to define disability (Grondin, 2016):

1. Impairment, including hearing, seeing, walking, climbing stairs, reaching, grasping, bending, communicating, or dealing with psychological conditions; and
2. Activity limitations, including restrictions at home, at work, or at other places.

The responses to these questions are inevitably self-reported, and some researchers are skeptical about the reliability of self-report (McDermott & Turk, 2011). But there is really no other option when defining disability. There is no definitive biological marker for disability. It is a personal experience of a socially constructed phenomenon. Thus, the only qualified reporter is the individual himself or herself. There is no alternative source of this information, not even a family member or health professional, that is more definitive than the person himself or herself.

Some kinds of disability may make it difficult for disabled individuals to participate in research — to provide data, to answer questions, to attend a focus group, or to undertake the necessary manoeuvres to be tested or observed. In those instances, the researcher must consider the possibility of obtaining the information needed from a proxy source. The use of proxy respondents lacks the authenticity of gathering data from people themselves, but it sometimes makes a particular avenue of inquiry possible — for example, with people who are non-verbal or unable to give informed consent.

Where do we find the people from whom we wish to gather data? Our consumer partners are best positioned to inform and direct the sampling process. Through their knowledge of the issues at hand, they help to define who are the most suitable reporters on the issue, and where and how to enlist their support of the research. They are often also the best people to reach out to prospective participants, and their endorsement of the research can be the stamp of approval that encourages people with disabilities to engage with this research and with these researchers.

As mentioned previously, it can be a challenge to undertake disability research that requires a large sample. Disability is such a complex and heterogeneous category that it may be difficult to find many people who share the same issue. Furthermore, because most conditions associated with disability are somewhat rare or uncommon, it may take a considerable time period to attract enough people to do a credible study. If a control group is involved, or if multiple levels or groups need to be observed, this can add to the challenge of attracting participants in a timely fashion.

Data collection
Data collection addresses a number of questions:

- *What* factors, variables, or phenomena do we want to know about?
- *How* will we obtain that information from our participants?
- *Who* is the best person to elicit the information?
- *When* and where can we achieve the optimal conditions for high-quality data?

Qualitative researchers will resist the idea of collecting data on variables; however, we do need to be absolutely clear and specific about what data we are seeking to obtain. Then we need to communicate that effectively to the people from whom we seek data, so that they can do their best to give us what we are seeking. We must be able to provide precise substantive definitions of the constructs the research is addressing, even if they are abstract or emerging constructs. Unless we can tell our participants exactly what we want from them, we place them at a significant disadvantage, where they are left guessing what we are looking for and how they can help us. Variables simply refer to constructs that can take on different values — for example, 1 to 100; poor, fair, good, excellent; different religious affiliations; experiences or meanings attributed to events. We must be able to offer a "dictionary definition" of the underlying construct of interest.

The next challenge is to discern the best way to hear from participants about their experience. In order to do that, we need to offer participants a way to tell us about their experience — to anticipate the full range of experiences the construct can assume in our population and ask participants to situate their experience within that range. Sometimes researchers refer to this as the *operational definition* of the variables of interest. How does the variable operate in reality, and how can we capture the variance or range of possible values it takes on in our sample?

In disability studies, a key consideration is the best way to structure the data collection experience so as to maximize the possibility of receiving high-quality information from the people we seek to better understand. Standardized questionnaires, while the lingua franca of many research activities, may simply fail to capture the experiences of disabled people. Like so many things that we have discussed throughout this book, they were often designed with people *without* disabilities in mind, and they simply don't ask the right questions for disability research.

Finally, who is the best person to collect data, and under what circumstances of time and place will the highest quality of data be achieved? Will you get better information by interviewing someone alone rather than in a group? At home versus in a clinic or office? By a disabled peer or by a graduate student? Morning, afternoon, or evening? Weekday or weekend? Face-to-face, on the phone, or by computer? These questions are too often answered to accommodate the convenience and efficiency of the researcher, rather than the participants. What's at stake in these decisions is the quality of the data upon which you will rely for your findings and conclusions. If you are not prepared to commit the resources needed to obtaining high-quality data, then why should volunteer participants commit their valuable time to your studies?

Ethics in disability research

Research ethics refers to norms of behaviour in research that uphold basic ethical principles (autonomy, non-maleficence, beneficence, and justice) in relationships between researchers and the people they study. These include the duties to

- minimize the risk of harm;
- obtain informed consent;

- protect anonymity and confidentiality;
- avoid deceptive practices; and
- provide the right to withdraw.

Ethical issues have particularly been a topic of discussion in the literature on research with people with intellectual disabilities, mental illnesses, and cognitive impairments (Gupta, 2017; McDonald & Kidney, 2012; Thompson, Roberts, & Bittles, 2014). Past abuses have sharpened the focus on the need for special provisions to ensure ethical treatment of research participants with disabilities. While anyone is vulnerable to ethical violations when participating in research, investigators must be especially vigilant in circumstances that might prevent participants from effectively advocating on their own behalf.

Knowledge translation

Shakespeare (1996) makes an important distinction when he observes that research is nothing more than an intellectual activity resulting in knowledge products. It does not necessarily result in practical change in and of itself. In order for change to happen, advocates and activists need to have access to research, and to use it strategically to bring about change. As Macbeth (2010) puts it, it is not enough to simply hope that the right people with find the results of your research, and respond to your findings with appropriate action. Barton (1992) observes that decades of employing this approach in disability research have led to a lack of any real improvement in the quality of lives of disabled people.

Knowledge translation is the process by which research finds its way into the hands of people who can use it to bring about change. It has become a significant focus in disability research in recent years (Beauchamp-Pryon & Symeonidou, 2013; Johnston et al., 2009). Barnes (2008) identifies broad, accessible knowledge translation as an additional standard for ethical conduct in disability research.

Knowledge translation consists of three decisions:

1. *Audience:* Who are the people you seek to reach with the results of your research?

2. *Media:* What is the best vehicle for getting information to those people? How do they typically seek and find informa-

tion? What media are most compatible with how they work? Who is best suited to carry the message in terms of credibility, authenticity, and access?

3. *Message:* What specifically tailored message do your wish to transmit to each audience of interest?

Audiences for disability research typically include policymakers, employers, educators, health professionals, and the general public, as well as traditional academic audiences (other researchers and students). Each has its preferences for receiving information and each is more likely to receive messages that are carefully conceived and situated to conform to their usual practices for information consumption.

With regard to medium, most disability organizations have well-developed networks for dissemination of pertinent information. These networks may be composed of a variety of stakeholders, and have usually been carefully cultivated and tended over many years. The newsletters, websites, and publications of consumer organizations often reach the very people with whom we are seeking to share our research. Not only that, but consider the authenticity and authority of the message when carried by a disability organization versus an academic researcher.

The final element in knowledge translation is the message. In order to be effective, the message needs to be definitive and declarative; it can't be cautious, rambling, or full of qualifying phrases. It needs to be brief and to the point. It needs to be tailored to address the perspective of the particular audience. And it needs to offer a solution to a clear problem that consumers would recognize as important.

Many of these features of a strong message are anathema to academic researchers, who tend to focus on theory, literature, methodology, limitations, and caveats. Academic researchers have been socialized to be cautious about coming right out and saying something. And yet, effective knowledge translation depends on being able to figure out what you have to say — what you can realistically claim based on your data, and what you are prepared to stake your reputation on. Unless you have a clear message, you are just adding to the noise on the airwaves.

The matrix in Table 18.3 offers a useful way to conceptualize the aspirations and intentions for knowledge translation on a particular project.

Table 18.3: Conceptualizing aspirations and intentions for knowledge translation

	MEDIA			
AUDIENCES	*Partner newsletter*	*Op-ed in national paper*	*Policy brief*	*Peer-reviewed publication*
Policy-makers			message	
Consumer organizations	message			
General population		message		

Roles in research

Roles and relationships in research are difficult at the best of times, but over the years they have been particularly fraught between researchers and people with disabilities or organizations representing disability. People with disabilities have felt that researchers have an agenda that is at odds with the disability agenda, and that academic research has exacerbated, rather than assisted in, their struggles for human rights, citizenship, and equality. Outspoken critics have called researchers "parasites", and disabled research participants "pawns", to illustrate how polarized this relationship can be (Stone & Priestley, 1996).

Roles and relationships can be a significant source of tension if not negotiated at the outset and treated with candor and trust. To this end, we offer the following guidelines for research roles, authorship, intellectual property, and ownership:

- The principal investigator is the person who holds ultimate responsibility for the project funds and operations. He or she is legally and/or contractually responsible to the granting agency for delivery of the final report and all interim reports on time and on budget. He or she is also responsible to his or her respective organization or university for the sound and ethical management of the project.

- An investigator is a member of a research team who is involved in grant writing and development. He or she typically makes an original intellectual, theoretical, methodological, or practical contribution to the development of the project. He or she contributes a CV to the grant package and is a signatory on the grant. All investigators have financial and instrumental responsibility for the completion and execution of the project. All investigators may expect to have involvement in decision-making throughout a project.

- Community partners are involved in the project at every stage, from inception through execution and knowledge translation. They typically represent a constituency in the community, and bring applied experience to the project team.

- An author is someone involved in an instrumental way in writing — a book, a manuscript, an article, a poster or presentation, a knowledge product. The first author is typically the person who prepares the first draft of a written product. Decisions about authorship are made on the basis of original intellectual contribution to each paper or presentation. It should be understood that being an investigator does not necessarily entitle one to authorship without any meaningful contribution to the actual manuscript or presentation. The minimum requirement for authorship is to read and provide comments on the manuscript. More substantive contributions, such as writing a paragraph or section, may be requested by the first author. The order of authors on any publication or presentation is at the discretion of the first author.
  The principal investigator is typically afforded the opportunity to author the first manuscript from a particular project. If he or she does not act on this within one year, any of the other investigators may avail themselves of the opportunity to author a paper. As a courtesy, we typically invite all investigators to be authors on publications. We usually also invite the project coordinator to be an author on all publications, if he or she has made an original contribution to the project.

- Ownership of the data belongs to all investigators on a project. They may expect to receive a copy of the final dataset upon completion of the study. Once the first manuscript has been accepted for publication, all investigators will have the opportunity to develop future research directions and research products from the data.

- Access to the data by students or others may be offered on the consent of the investigators, and should be governed by a written agreement. Non-investigators should understand that they are not owners of the data. They are not entitled to keep a copy of the dataset or to use it beyond the purposes covered in the agreement.

In an effort to create a culture of trust and transparency, deliberate measures can be implemented in disability research (Flicker & Nixon, 2018). Based on the successful experience of the Canadian Disability Policy Alliance (see Appendix 18.1), a number of guiding principles are offered at the end of this chapter as a starting place for cultivating collegiality in research relationships.

Conclusion

In this chapter, we have discussed the complexity and intricacy of conducting research in the area of disability studies. We have attempted to *appreciate* the importance of research as a way of contributing to the knowledge base about disability, and to the real-world implications of that knowledge. We have *discovered* a range of methodological possibilities and have attempted to situate them in terms of how they might contribute to advancing the disability agenda.

We have examined a number of important considerations that must be *designed* into research in order to ensure that it represents a step forward for people with disabilities and not a step backwards, or even sideways for that matter. Goodley (2017) suggests the following questions for researcher to ask themselves to ensure equitable and appropriate collaboration:

- Are people with disabilities *included* in meaningful roles in the study?
- To whom is the research *accountable*, and how is that accountability overseen?
- Has *praxis*, or real-world implication of the research, been duly considered and ensured?
- Whose *knowledge or ontology* counts in the study, and how is this demonstrated?

- Is the research *impairment or disability* focused?
- Who are the *stakeholders*, and are entrenched interests transparent?
- What is the *level of analysis* — individual, organization, society?

Oliver (1992), one of the earliest proponents of emancipatory research, expresses his *dream* for disability research in the following quote:

> Do researchers wish to join with disabled people and use their expertise and skills in the struggles against oppression? Or do they wish to continue to use these skills and this expertise in ways which disabled people find oppressive? (p. 102)

Perhaps, like me, you find this quote reminiscent of the quote from Lilla Watson cited earlier in the chapter. Despite what might sometimes be perceived as alienating rhetoric against academic researchers, this quote is clearly an invitation to *deploy* the talents, ingenuity, and resourcefulness of disabled people alongside that of researchers to create a world that is more inclusive and attentive to issues faced by people with disabilities in our society.

APPENDIX 18.1
Guiding principles for research conducted under the auspices of the Canadian Disability Policy Alliance

1. **Representation:** The Alliance is composed of three types of partners: researchers, community partners and policy partners. Every project, group or body within the Alliance needs to ensure an appropriate level of representation of these three. We likewise seek to ensure appropriate representation of consumers and different disability groups (physical, sensory and cognitive disabilities). Finally, being a national coalition, we are aware of other types of representation that we would like to achieve, such as by gender, region, and age.

   Each individual in the Alliance has been invited to participate due to his or her recognized expertise in disability policy (investigators, community partners and policy partners). It should be acknowledged that at some times, individuals speak on behalf of their organization, and at other times, they speak from their own experience and expertise. We must be sensitive to the "political" context of all of our members, and seek to clarify when they are expressing a personal viewpoint versus their organization's official position.

2. **Communication:** We commit to and urge open, honest and direct communication. We encourage members to make intentional use of the many modalities available for communication, as some are more appropriate than others to particular types of discussions. We seek to maintain a high degree of trust among the partners. We seek to streamline communications, and to avoid overwhelming already busy people.

3. **Meetings:** We are committed to face-to-face meetings, as a way of building trust, collegiality and understanding. We acknowledge that there is significant cost associated with this, but without these relationships, the research is doomed to fail.

   We also commit to full accessibility of all aspects of our meetings, and to helping one another to achieve this goal.

To this end, we have developed accessibility guidelines for hotels and meeting rooms. For all meetings, we will endeavour to circulate agendas one week in advance, and minutes one week after the meeting, with action items clearly indicated.

4. **Decision-Making:** Wherever possible we seek to make decisions by consensus. This does not mean that everyone has to agree with every decision, but rather that everyone feels heard, not voted down, and can live with the outcome of a decision. We understand that decision-making is assisted by clear goals and objectives. We endeavour to be clear and precise about what we are trying to achieve; specifically, about what knowledge we are seeking to discover and disseminate, and what we expect to be the impact of it.

5. **Language:** We are aware that there is considerable sensitivity around language referring to disability. Our guiding principle is "inclusivity". We seek to use language that invites others into the dialogue, and that welcomes a variety of perspectives. We refer to federal guidelines for non-discriminatory language. We are guided by our community partners and the preferences of their members.

6. **Position Statements:** The Secretariat has been empowered by the partners to make public statements on behalf of the CDPA [Canadian Disability Policy Alliance]. All media communications will be coordinated through the Secretariat. In the case of issues that are known to be controversial, the Secretariat employs the following guidelines:
   - If it is known that the disability community generally holds divergent viewpoints on an issue, this will be acknowledged in the statement.
   - Wherever possible, partners will not openly contradict the official positions of other partners.
   - If a partner feels it is inevitable to publicly contradict the position of another partner they will attempt to contact them by phone first to let them know their reasons for doing so.

7. **Conflict of Interest:** The opportunity for conflict of interest arises
   - when a partner uses his or her membership in the Alliance to derive personal financial benefit; or
   - when alliance duties come into conflict with partners' other duties to their affiliated organization.

- We respectfully request that partners advise the Secretariat if they are in a conflict of interest.

8. **Conflict Resolution:** In all instances, we attempt to function in a collaborative manner, and to avoid confrontation; however, we understand that some conflict is constructive and produces positive outcomes. If decision-making is being held up, or if conflict is becoming destructive to the partnership, a process will be undertaken to overcome conflict.

9. **Training/Knowledge Translation:** We are committed to enhancing opportunities for learning wherever possible. We offer specific learning opportunities to all of our partners at our meetings. We involve students in the work of the Alliance at every possible opportunity. We speak broadly whenever the opportunity arises about the work of the Alliance, so that others become more aware of our activities and impact.

Source: Canadian Disability Policy Alliance, "Guiding Principles", http://www.disabilitypolicyalliance.ca/about-cdpa/guiding-principles (accessed January 20, 2019).

SECTION 5

Themes in Appreciative Disability Studies

In this concluding section, I hope to bring together for readers some of the key messages that have been discussed in this book. My task is to draw out themes and extract messages from the foregoing chapters.

- What have we learned about how we think about and talk about disability?
- How many people are we talking about anyway, and who are those people?
- How did we get to where we are today in our relationships with disabled people?
- What are the most important barriers that people with disabilities encounter as, like all of us, they attempt to carve out a life filled with meaning, connection, and prosperity?
- How do we each play a part in moving toward a world where that is possible?

Introduction

As I reflect on what we have learned about disability, I am guided by our initial aims:

- to appreciate the condition of living with a disability;
- to understand the struggles disabled people face;
- to appreciate the resourcefulness they marshal in confronting those struggles;
- to notice the world they encounter — particularly the barriers — and to understand that we are all complicit in preserving these barriers;
- to recognize where inequities and injustices persist based on disability; and
- to consolidate our roles in relation to people with disabilities — as health, social service, or education professionals; as citizens of a prosperous democracy; and as fellow human beings.

This has been my starting point and my ending point in this book — an attempt to understand, to see, to appreciate. In this final chapter, I will try to bring together the personal and the professional, and to reflect on what it means to devote one's career to some aspect of the field of disability studies.

Definitions and language

We have given considerable focus in this book to how we talk about disability and the impact of language — its effect on how disabled people are perceived and how they internalize those perceptions in the formation of identity. Language is vitally important in conveying meaning and attitudes.

And yet, there is no clear consensus about the right language to use. There is no formula that we can offer to ensure that language does not offend; no fail-safe "correct" language. Even the most basic tenet of people-first language is resisted by some.

There are, however, a number of themes that have emerged from the discussion to guide us in the use of language. The first, and perhaps most universally agreed upon, is that *disability is not diagnosis*. To say that someone has cerebral palsy, for example, is to convey a diagnosis. It does not help us to understand the individual's disability or experience of that condition. It may suggest a constellation of disabilities that often accompany the diagnosis of cerebral palsy, but it does not give us specific information about the difficulties a particular person has in navigating his or her world. When we hear the diagnosis of cerebral palsy, we may conjure an image of someone who walks with a scissoring gait, who speaks with difficulty, who struggles to hold a pencil or a fork. These are all disabilities that may or may not be associated with cerebral palsy. In order to understand the disability of a particular individual with cerebral palsy, we need to engage in a discussion of the activities he or she needs or wants to do, and the ease or difficulty with which those activities can be achieved in his or her environment. Disability exists in the space between the person, his or her desired activities, and the extent to which those can be accomplished in a particular context.

Neither are symptoms disabilities. Pain, for example, is not a disability; neither is ataxia, paralysis, or low self-esteem. These are symptoms that may be associated with disability, but they are not synonymous. These are the manifestations of a diagnosis or health condition, but they too are not disabilities.

To be clear, *disabilities refer to activities* that are restricted, limited, or otherwise impeded by encounters with an environment that does not provide the necessary supports, accommodations, or configuration to permit a person to do what he or she wishes to do. Disability is all about *doing* — or not doing — partially because of a health condition, but also because of living in a world that was designed without consideration for the full breadth of humanity. Instead, our society was designed for the *usual* way that humans operate, rather than for all the ways that humans can operate. It was designed for "normal", whatever that may mean.

Another challenge in talking about disability is to find language that is suitable for the broad spectrum of different types of disabilities, that is, for the *heterogeneity of disability*. In this book, we have talked about disabilities that are primarily physical, cognitive, or sensory in origin. This is one dimension of disability — the type of health condition that is associated with it. Another is the severity of disability, from mild to severe. Another is the course of disability — it can be congenital or acquired, static or progressive, permanent or temporary, steady or episodic. Is it realistic to think that one formulation of language can encompass all of these experiences? Probably not.

Furthermore, disability does not exist in a vacuum. Rather, it exists alongside the other qualities and characteristics of a person. It is as multi-dimensional as human beings are. The experience of disability differs depending on whether the person is male or female, young or old, single or married. Disability intersects with race, ethnicity, sexual orientation, social class, literacy, poverty, and any number of other social identities. In many instances, this intersectionality results in double jeopardy — a situation where multiple identities cause layered disadvantages that are not simply additive, but rather that compound one another multiplicatively or exponentially.

What does all this mean for how we talk about and think about disability? First it means that it is very difficult — perhaps even impossible — to talk about disability in general. It means that when we talk about disability, we can't assume that the person to whom we are talking is making the same set of assumptions that we are. We need to be specific about what we mean by disability. We need to begin by defining our terms and stating our assumptions.

It may also be advisable to simply assume that we cannot make broad statements about disability. The condition of disability is simply too varied and multi-dimensional to be amenable to sweeping generalizations. Let's ask ourselves some questions when we are tempted to make pronouncements about disability:

- Does what we are about to say pertain to all types of disabilities — those originating from conditions that are physical, cognitive, and sensory?

- Does it hold true for disabled people of all ages, genders, and living situations?

- Is it equally meaningful for people who have been disabled from birth versus those with the prior experience of no disability? Those whose disability is bound to become more demanding versus those whose disability will improve or disappear? Those who experience disability all day every day versus those who have good days and bad?

- Would disability even exist if the environment were structured to take it into account?

Demographics of disability

Throughout this book, we have used statistics about disability from a variety of sources as a way of understanding the scope and magnitude of disability issues. Statistics can be helpful, but they can also be deceptive, in that they summarize complex situations and some-times sacrifice specificity in favour of generalizability. However, if we understand the assumptions underlying statistics, they can help to bring clarity and focus to issues of concern. With that caveat in mind, here are a few of the statistics that have emerged from our discussions that are worthy of reiterating in this final chapter:

- It is estimated that 15% of the world's population live with a disability, or about 1 billion people. About 3% live with a moderate to severe disability, or one that significantly influences how they go about their daily life, and how they encounter the world.

- Disability looks very different in high-income countries than it does in developing countries. Economic conditions, cultural factors, access to services, specific health risks, and geo-political conditions all affect the profile of disability in a population and result in differences internationally.

- Statistics comparing disabled and non-disabled subsets of the population reveal inequalities in education, income, and employment. These three key indicators of prosperity and opportunity suggest that the quality of life differs significantly for disabled versus non-disabled people.

- The way people use their time is an important indicator of access to resources and opportunities. Data from time use surveys show that people with disabilities use their time in significantly different ways from non-disabled people, particularly in activities like work, screen time, education, and household duties.

History of disability

We have referred a number of times to a historical trajectory in how we think about and relate to the issue of disability. The history of disability is neither majestic nor auspicious. Prior to the late 20th century, it is checkered with horrors and injustices that are incomprehensible to our modern sensibilities. And yet they are undeniable. Even if they do not persist today, practices like involuntary sterilization, imposed segregation, and deliberate discrimination enter the psyches of disabled people and leave scars that can't easily be healed.

Like other civil rights movements, the disability movement coalesced in the late 20th century, and employed radical tactics to say "Enough!" Marches, rallies, slogans, and manifestos were the hallmarks of disability identity politics. These tactics, along with a new field of dedicated disability scholarship, moved disability issues from the personal to the political, from private concerns of individuals and families to matters for public debate and civic concern. Since the United Nations International Year of Disabled Persons in 1981, disability has become politicized, and significant strides have been achieved in creating equality and citizenship.

Where do we go from here? How is the momentum maintained to continue to address systematic inequalities in income, education, employment, and opportunity? How do we keep attention on disability issues in societies like Canada and the United States, where there are legislated protections against discrimination and yet where discrimination continues to exist, as evidenced by objective inequalities? How do we deal with discrimination that is much more subtle and difficult to expose?

Barriers

In many chapters in this book, the discussion has focused on **barriers** — impediments encountered in society that prevent disabled people from accessing and participating in the life they seek. We have repeatedly employed a taxonomy of barriers consisting of

- *Physical barriers:* Obstacles in the built environment that exclude or impede access;

- *Attitudinal barriers:* Ideas about disability that result in differential treatment and unfair practices;

- *Informational barriers:* Lack of knowledge about disability itself, or about how to engage with someone with a disability in a constructive way; and

- *Systemic barriers:* Policies, processes, and customs that systematically work against people with disabilities. These are often unintentional, but they are nonetheless discriminatory.

Identifying barriers is the first step in removing barriers. By examining barriers, we are propelled along a trajectory that ensures that the responsibility for change lies not exclusively with the disabled person, but equally with the environment that erects barriers. Focusing on barriers involves a systemic approach to change, not simply a personal approach. It takes us outside of the traditional biomedical way of thinking about disability, where the person with a disability is expected to adapt, adjust, and be rehabilitated. Instead, focusing on barriers leads us toward a socio-political way of thinking about change, where society accepts the responsibility to remove barriers, thus making the world a more equitable and just place.

What are we going to do about it?

Here are some suggestions to start you thinking:

Models of service

As we said at the beginning, this book is aimed primarily at students in the health, education, and social services fields. Its aim is to help them to understand disabled people, and to configure a role in their chosen profession in relation to people with disabilities. Therefore, one of the goals of this book must surely be to offer guidance to future professionals in terms of relating to their clients or students with disabilities.

Perhaps the AIMS matrix from Chapter 17 helps us to think about this. The AIMS matrix is constructed from two questions:

1. Are disabled individuals valued in the environment?
2. Are resources devoted to meeting their needs?

Depending on a positive or negative response to these two questions, the model of service can be assimilation (Yes/No), integration (Yes/Yes), segregation (No/Yes), or marginalization (No/No). Hopefully we don't have to consider the situation of marginalization.

Surely integration is the approach we seek. Integrated services are provided in the same venue for disabled and non-disabled clients alike, *and* they include provision for the special needs of disabled clients. We have discussed several approaches within this book to providing integrated services under the rubric of universal design. Universal design involves thinking differently about how services are offered. Rather than seeing disabled clients as a minority group to whom we must devote special attention, universal design considers disabled individuals as part of the whole, many of whom have preferences and particularities in their ability to benefit from services. Universal design embraces diversity and seeks to ensure that all aspects of the environment and the services offered are characterized by choice, variety, and accessibility.

While integration is clearly the preferred form of service delivery, there is no consensus that segregation is all bad. Segregation is often how services to disabled people are configured. Segregation occurs when resources are devoted to meet the needs of disabled people, but where those services are offered in a different space or facility from those offered to the population at large. In other words, participation by disabled people is not sufficiently valued to ensure that they can be served in the same environment as non-disabled people.

This often happens when the needs of people with disabilities are assumed to be so specific that they can only be met by a targeted service offered in a specialized environment. Many people claim that the needs of disabled people are best served in highly specialized environments that are perfectly designed to address disability issues. Highly trained expert personnel, specially designed equipment, organizational culture that favours disability, and optimal accessibility — all these are the features of specialized environments where segregated disability services are offered. Compare the gymnasium at a rehabilitation centre with a community fitness facility, and you will see clearly the immediate benefits of a specially equipped segregated facility.

Some degree of segregation is accepted as the norm. For example, it is not expected that every dentist's office will have the expertise, tools, or equipment to provide services to people with disabilities. Instead, in a community one or two dentists will be identified who can provide accessible services to disabled patients. Another example is when disabled children are removed from their classroom to be seen individually for special tuition. The class as a whole is not expected to be made accessible to disabled children, but necessary services are offered in a separate environment.

The segregated environment also provides opportunities for a number of important processes that happen among people with disabilities:

1. *Peer support:* People with disabilities learn from each other, and they derive support and companionship from their interactions with others who have faced similar challenges.

2. *Solidarity:* A sense of belonging and membership, shared identity, and normality about disability. Shared assumptions, common vocabulary, inside jokes, and the absence of the need to explain things to others who don't share your experience all contribute to a sense of solidarity and belonging.

3. *Social comparison:* Comparing your own situation to that of others, recognizing that there are those both worse off and better off than yourself, and seeing your own experience along a continuum.

These three important processes often happen during rehabilitation, and are part of the development of what we have referred to in several places as the "disability community".

The disadvantage of segregation, however, is that disability remains a minority concern, and the world doesn't become even incrementally more accessible or more enlightened about disability. Furthermore, there is the psychological disadvantage of being relegated to the margins and having your issues dealt with outside of the mainstream of society.

Assimilation is another model of service where disabled people are offered service with no special consideration for their particular needs. This is often the case in the health care system, where the assumption is made that the services are already accessible, because they are designed for people who are ill. Additional resources are not expected to be needed to serve people with disabilities.

An example is the primary care office that doesn't offer an examining table that can be adjusted to wheelchair height, an accessible washroom, education and prevention materials in alternate formats, or assistance with dressing and undressing or other personal care activities. Instead, disabled people are expected to assimilate with non-disabled patients, and not place any additional demands on the time or resources of the practice.

Another example is the hospital ward or other health care facility that has no portable lift or other equipment to help transfer patients to bed, stretcher, X-ray table, or other diagnostic equipment. The needs of disabled patients are not distinguished from those of all other patients, and no consideration is given to providing service in a special or tailored way.

Rights versus Responsibilities?

How do we ensure that things get better? There are primarily two approaches to making the world a better place for people with disabilities. The first and most prominent in contemporary discourse on disability is the human rights approach — an individually oriented approach that seeks to draw attention to discrimination and provide redress wherever and whenever discrimination occurs. This approach asserts a slate of rights to equal treatment of people with disabilities in all spheres of society. It outlines the penalties that may be exacted when those rights are violated. As we have discussed, rights protections are well entrenched in Canadian law and policy, with legislation and bureaucracy at all levels of jurisdiction. And yet the rights of people with disabilities continue to be violated at higher rates than any other designated group in Canada, according to human rights statistics at all levels.

The other approach to making society a more equitable place for people with disabilities focuses not on individual rights, but rather on collective responsibilities. What are governments, organizations, corporations, and institutions within society responsible for in terms of ensuring equity and access for all people? What are we entitled to expect when we interact with institutions in society, and how do we hold them accountable for upholding those responsibilities? This approach has only begun to be considered in jurisdictions where policy exists that sets standards for access and equity, and where those standards are enforceable and robust. Instead of placing the burden of making society more accessible at the doorstep of individuals with disabilities, the collective approach puts it squarely in the camp of those with the power and resources to make it happen.

The problem, however, in our society increasingly characterized by individualism, is that the enforcement of such collective responsibilities can appear to entail government interference, restrictions on freedom, and constraints on free enterprise and profitability. These are powerful criticisms in a capitalist economy. They often mean that good ideas are non-starters because of the entrenched opposition of influential forces.

Information and evidence

Another arrow in the quiver of making the world a better place for people with disabilities is research. Research in disability studies brings the promise of better information and evidence upon which to base decisions about service delivery, about policy formation, and about resource deployment. In order to make a meaningful contribution, however, that research needs to meet a number of important criteria:

- It needs to be developed in authentic partnerships between disability organizations and experienced academic researchers.

- It needs to focus on barrier removal and opportunity creation in the areas of life that are of greatest concern to people with disabilities.

- It needs to be clearly distinguished from medical and rehabilitation research, and it needs to receive its fair share of the funding envelope.

- It needs to be methodologically robust, and to uphold the highest standards of scientific rigour.

- It needs to be communicated effectively to a variety of different audiences, all of whom have a role to play in promoting access and opportunity, such as disability advocacy organizations, policy-makers, the general population.

Attitudes toward disability

Finally, we have devoted a fair bit of time talking about attitudes toward disability, and some of the difficult beliefs people hold about disability. Here are some of the most persistent and troubling attitudes that prevent us from moving forward to improve access and opportunity:

- Disability is inherently a bad thing, a loss, a tragedy.
- Disability is abnormal and only *other* people experience it.
- Disability is a minority concern that we don't need to be worried about unless we are directly affected.
- Things are already pretty good for people with disabilities, and we don't need to do any more.
- A person's disability is his or her most dominant and important feature.
- People with disabilities may be nice, but they are not competent.

Attitudes are a shortcut that our brains take to evaluate people, places, or objects without having to process all the particular data about that person, place, or thing. They are made up of both a thought or idea and a feeling, and they are often so deeply held that we are not even aware of them.

Chapter 5 discussed a number of strategies that have been shown to be effective in helping to change attitudes. These strategies all have the following in common:

- They address both the cognitive and emotional aspects of the attitude.

- They force us to go beyond our conscious responses to people and objects, and to become aware of how our behaviour is coloured by underlying attitudes.

- They target the people who are most amenable to changing their attitudes, and don't expend precious energy and resources on people with entrenched attitudes that are unlikely to change and who are resistant to intervention.

Strategies like co-participation, rewards or incentive programs, and discrepancy awareness have been shown to be effective in all these areas. Furthermore, the research suggests an emphasis on children and youth, health professionals, and older people who share some of the issues of disabled people.

How do we know if it's enough?

When I think about how we would know if we were making progress toward a world that is more equitable, I think the best indicator would be a sense among people with disabilities that they belong, and that they are understood and valued. Perhaps the best way for me to explain this is through a personal story — the one I know best after my own — that of my husband, W. Kirby Rowe.

Kirby was born in London, Ontario, in 1948. He excelled at school, both academically and athletically. At 18, he went to university in the United States on a full scholarship to study economics and to play hockey. He graduated, went to work for one of the big banks in Toronto, got married, and continued to enjoy an active lifestyle. He was on a path to a successful and somewhat predictable middle-class life when, at age 28, he was injured in a small-plane crash in Northern Ontario. He had gone to Pickle Lake for the weekend to be best man at his brother Tom's wedding, and wound up staying several months after an early morning recreational flight left Kirby with a spinal cord injury and Tom with multiple fractures.

Gifted with a competitive spirit and a hearty work ethic, he excelled in rehabilitation, and went on to work for the Canadian Paraplegic Association, initially as a rehab counsellor and, before long, as executive director. He got back in an airplane less than two years after his accident, and earned the first licence issued in Canada to a disabled pilot flying with hand controls. Based on a successful career as a disability advocate, he was awarded Ontario's Bicentennial Medal for his contributions to the lives of disabled people in Ontario (1984), and the Canadian Paraplegic Association's Ken Langford Award for Lifetime Achievement (2015). He also served as Coordinator of Rehabilitation Services for the province of Ontario from 1990 to his retirement in 2005, a role that permitted him to bring his experience in disability advocacy to the policy arena.

And yet, despite all these achievements and successes, his experience of life was tainted by a profound sense of alienation. The overarching meta-narrative was one of being underestimated and overlooked or, perhaps more accurately, not seen. If that was true of Kirby, who had so many of the good things in life — enough money, a successful career, a strong support system — how much more is this sense of alienation the bedrock of the disability experience for those with fewer resources? Surely the alleviation of this sense of alienation must be the guiding force in all our efforts on behalf of people with disabilities.

We'll know it's enough only when disabled people no longer feel outside of the mainstream, misunderstood, overlooked, a special case. We'll know we've done enough when we automatically and reflexively consider how every aspect of our social world — our services, buildings, policies, communications — affect people with all different sorts of disabilities.

In conclusion, I hope this book has achieved the goals of *Appreciative Disability Studies*:

- to *discover* what is and what is not working well in the lives of people with disabilities;
- to *dream* of what could be and how the world would look if our individual and collective relationships with people with disabilities were optimized;

- to *design* a plan for how to get there from here, including practical first steps; and
- to *deploy* our talents and our voices to make the world more equitable and accessible for people with disabilities.

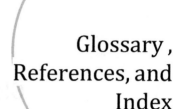

Glossary , References, and Index

Glossary

ableism (Chapter 5)   The systematic disadvantaging of people with disabilities, because of the fact of disability, and because of a constellation of beliefs that accompany the idea of "disability".

accommodation (Chapter 12)   Considerations afforded to ensure that no discrimination takes place on the basis of disability.

activities of daily living (ADLs) (Chapter 7)   Self-care activities, including bathing, dressing, eating, toileting, grooming, and functional mobility in the home.

activity limitations (Chapter 3)   Difficulties in executing activities.

adaptive equipment / assistive devices (Chapter 7)   A n external tool, machine, or device designed to enable someone with a disability to perform a specific function.

affirmation model (Chapter 2)   A model of disability that focuses on the advantages experienced by people with disabilities, including eschewing class distinctions, freedom from society's expectations and requirements, and empathy for other oppressed minorities.

appreciative disability studies (Chapter 1)   An approach to disability studies that combines critical disability studies with appreciative inquiry.

appreciative inquiry (Chapter 1)   An approach to knowing that asks not "What is wrong with the world?" but rather "What does the world look like when it is at its very best, and how can we imagine moving toward that?"

asset poverty (Chapter 14)   An economic situation that occurs when a family's total assets minus total debts are not sufficient to meet their basic needs for three months.

assets (Chapter 14)   Economic resources that include real property (home and land), business assets, savings, and securities.

attendant care (Chapter 7)   Service provided to people with disabilities, including light housekeeping, meal preparation, and personal and intimate care, such as bathing, toileting, and dressing. Workers are referred to as personal support workers, attendants, home support workers.

attitude (Chapter 5)   A learned idea that grows out of socialization and experience.

attribution, over- (Chapter 5)   Refers to situations where every detail of a person's story is seen through the lens of his or her disability; where the disability is the most important quality the person possesses — one that affects everything else in his or her life.

attribution, under- (Chapter 5)   Inadequate consideration for disability. The person is described or characterized as though the disability did not exist.

autonomy (Chapter 8)   The capacity to be self-governing; to make informed decisions without the involvement of another person or organization.

barriers (Section 5)   Impediments encountered in society that prevent disabled people from accessing and participating in the life they seek.

biomedical model (Chapter 2)   A way of thinking about disability that locates disability entirely within the person — in an impairment, a fault, a flaw in the person. There is an assumption that if the impairment can be corrected, then the person could be restored to health, happiness, and function.

biopsychosocial model (Chapter 2)   An attempt to reconcile the biomedical and social models of disability by situating disability at the interface of a person with an impairment and a society that fails to adequately adapt for that impairment.

capabilities approach (Chapter 2) A model of disability focusing on 10 human functions and the freedom to pursue them.

capacity (Chapter 8) The ability of individuals to make decisions for themselves.

capital (Chapter 14) A way of thinking about economic prosperity and usually considered from four perspectives:

> **Human capital** — the education, skills, health, and other personal resources of the individual; his or her personal ability to participate in the economy;
>
> **Physical capital** — the tangible assets that the individual possesses that enhance his or her productivity, such as housing, transportation, or business assets;
>
> **Social capital** — the networks, connections, and personal relationships that contribute to the welfare of the individual; and
>
> **Financial capital** — the actual income and liquid assets the individual has at his or her disposal.

charitable model (Chapter 2) A model of disability defined by religious authorities, who identified a sense of mission toward people they saw as the victims of misfortune and objects of pity.

choice (Chapter 8) A process of identifying options and selecting among them.

citizenship (Chapter 16) The status of recognition, sovereignty, and membership in a society.

client (Chapter 3) The recipient of services from a professional, where there is an expectation that choice is retained about how the process will unfold.

consumer (Chapter 3) An agent in a commercial relationship who typically either pays directly for service or authorizes payment from a third party.

critical disability studies (Chapter 1) An academic discipline that seeks to uncover the sources of power that affect how people with disabilities experience participation and citizenship.

dignity of risk (Chapter 8) The right to be self-determining with regard to potentially risky behaviour.

disability arts (Chapter 15) Cultural and media representations of disability issues.

disability pride (Chapter 15)   An awareness movement that emphasizes pride and solidarity among disabled people.

disability studies (Chapter 1)   The academic enterprise associated with teaching and research on disability; an emerging field.

discrimination (Chapter 16)   A practice that systematically disadvantages a category of people on the basis of possession of a particular characteristic, e.g., disability; can arise intentionally or unintentionally — by failing to consider how people with disabilities will interact with the physical, social, and legal environment.

economic model (Chapter 2)   A definition of disability arising in the labour market, specifically among employers and businesses, based on the ability or inability to work, to be economically self-sufficient, and to represent an economic force in society.

employment (Chapter 12)   Work or productivity undertaken for compensation; typically a competitive environment in terms of acquiring and maintaining employment.

environmental factors (Chapter 3)   Environment = the space outside of the person; includes the following factors: products and technology; natural and human-made structures; support and relationships; attitudes; services, systems, and policies.

equity, formal (Chapter 16)   Everyone is treated the same.

equity, substantive (Chapter 16)   Doing whatever it takes to achieve equal outcomes for all; or creating equal opportunity for all by affording special considerations based on need.

free will (Chapter 8)   The ability to choose one's own destiny, to act in ways that are compatible with our beliefs, requirements and values.

handicap (Chapter 3)   A situation where a person experienced a significant social disadvantage in social relationships because of a disability.

health (Chapter 9)   A major resource for social, economic, and personal development and an important dimension of quality of life.

human rights (Chapter 16)   Those expectations that we are entitled to as human beings — a life of equality, dignity, respect, and freedom from discrimination. These rights are outlined in the United Nations *Universal Declaration of Human Rights*.

human rights model (Chapter 2)   A model of disability that focuses on the potential for an insensitive society to discriminate against people with disabilities by virtue of society's failure to account for the needs of disabled people when establishing structures and programs within society.

impairments, body function (Chapter 3)   Mental functions; sensory functions and pain; voice and speech functions; functions of the cardiovascular, hematological, immunological, and respiratory systems; functions of the digestive, metabolic, and endocrine systems; genitourinary and reproductive functions; neuromusculoskeletal and movement-related functions; functions of the skin and related structures.

impairments, body structure (Chapter 3)   Nervous system; eye, ear, and related structures; structures involved in voice and speech; structure of the cardiovascular, immunological, and respiratory systems; structures related to the digestive, metabolic, and endocrine systems; structure related to genitourinary and reproductive systems; structure related to movement; skin and related structures.

inclusive education (Chapter 13)   Attempts to remove barriers to participation in education by offering alternatives in the learning environment and by practising inclusion; a system-focused vs. individually focused approach.

independence (Chapter 8)   A state of being able to perform functions without assistance.

independent living model (Chapter 2)   A model of disability where disabled people are considered *consumers* (rather than patients or clients), that is, rational decision-makers in control of the resources that shape their lives.

instrumental activities of daily living (IADLs) (Chapter 7) A broader span of self-care activities, including interactions with the community, light and heavy housework, meal preparation, errands/ appointments, finances/bill payments, care for children or others, and minor health care procedures.

justice (Chapter 16)   A moral ideal that governs how people decide on the correct course of action or thought.

knowledge translation (Chapter 18) The process by which research finds its way into the hands of people who can use it to bring about change.

leisure (Chapter 15) Activities that one engages in when one is freed of the obligation to be productive.

locus of control (Chapter 8) A personality characteristic that governs whether one believes that destiny lies in one's own hands vs. in the hands of fate, chance, or powerful others.

low-income cut-off (Chapter 14) The threshold beyond which more than 63% of after-tax revenues are spent on necessities, e.g., food, shelter, clothing, and personal needs, leaving only 37% to cover health, education, transportation, recreation, and all other expenses.

participation restrictions (Chapter 3) Limitations on the ability to engage in nine areas of life: learning and applying knowledge; general tasks and demands; communication; mobility; self-care; domestic life; interpersonal interactions and relationships; major life areas; and community, social and civic life.

patient (Chapter 3) Refers to someone who is ill and who has surrendered his or her care to a medical professional.

pension (Chapter 14) A fund into which one makes regular contributions, usually through employment, in order to ensure an income stream when one ceases working, typically due to retirement.

policy (Chapter 17) A course of action or inaction chosen by public authorities to address problems experienced in society; specifically, the way governments express their intentions relative to problems they deem priorities.

productivity (Section 3, Introduction) Those activities that fill the main portion of a person's day, that afford one a livelihood, entail an obligation, represent a contribution, or include achievement.

risk (Chapter 8) A behaviour deemed to carry a high probability of danger or exposure.

self (Chapter 6) A constructed entity that represents the individuality and identity of each person.

self-care (Chapter 6)   All activities that one undertakes that provide maintenance and support to self, including physical, emotional, intellectual, and spiritual self:

> **Physical** — the basic personal functions that we do every day, or otherwise routinely and regularly.

> **Emotional** — the skills and aptitudes that individuals possess for understanding their feelings, coping with them, and seeking resolution of stressful or troublesome feelings.

> **Intellectual** — engagement in activities that maintain one's interest, offer stimulation or challenge, and provide reassurance of a competent level of cognitive functioning.

> **Spiritual** — an abstract set of abilities that allows individuals to preserve faith, connection, belief, and trust, and to achieve some measure of peace with the shape their lives have taken and with their place in the world.

self-determination (Chapter 8)   The degree to which an individual's behaviour is self-motivated, i.e., guided by three innate, universal needs: competence, autonomy, and relatedness.

service animal (Chapter 7)   Animals trained to perform specific tasks to assist a disabled person. They are usually dogs, but can also be horses, monkeys, or even birds.

sexuality (Chapter 11)   The human capacity for sexual feelings, sexual orientation, and activity.

sick role (Chapter 9)   A social construction that describes the freedoms and responsibilities that society confers on those it deems to be sick or ill.

social assistance (Chapter 14)   Government programs aimed at ensuring a minimum level of income and access to necessary resources.

social comparison (Chapter 6)   The process of understanding one's own situation on a social continuum; recognizing that there are those both better off and worse off than oneself.

social model (Chapter 2)   A definition of disability where disability is entirely socially constructed by a society oriented toward the average or norm of performance.

sociological model (Chapter 2) A definition of disability whereby individuals with disabilities are seen as being outside of the mainstream of society, at the margins — a minority group.

special education (Chapter 13) An educational approach for disabled students characterized by specialized teachers, facilities, equipment, and resource materials.

spirit (Chapter 10) The force that animates living things.

spirituality (Chapter 10) Sensitivity to or desire for the presence of spirit; a sense of connection with the self, the world and a higher power.

stereotype (Chapter 5) A preconceived notion whereby a constellation of qualities are attributed to an individual or group based on assumptions that are typically oversimplified and fixed in people's minds.

universal design for learning (UDL) (Chapter 13) An educational framework that uses insights from neuroscience to permit learners to perceive, comprehend, organize, express, and engage in education in multiple ways.

wealth (Chapter 14) The presence of income, but also the ownership of assets.

References

Aaberg, V. (2012). A path to greater inclusivity through understanding implicit attitudes toward disability. *Journal of Nursing Education, 51*(9), 505–510.
doi:10.3928/01484834-20120706-02

Abele, A.E., Cuddy, A.J.C., Judd, C.M., & Yzerbyt, V. (2008). Fundamental dimensions of social judgment. *European Journal of Social Psychology, 38,* 1063–1065.
doi:10.1002lejsp

Abella, R. (1984). *Equality in employment: A royal commission report.* Retrieved from http://crrf-fcrr.com/images/stories/Equality_in _Employment.pdf

Access Economics. (2010). *The economic value of informal care in 2010.* Retrieved from http://carersaustralia.com.au/storage/Economic-Value-Informal-Care-Oct-2010.pdf

Accessibility for Manitobans Act, C.C.S.M., 2013, c. A1.7.

Accessibility for Ontarians with Disabilities Act, 2005, S.O. 2005, c. 11.

Accessibility Act, S.N.S. 2017, c. 2.

Allport, G.W. (1954). *The nature of prejudice.* Cambridge, Mass: Addison-Wesley.

Altuntug, K., Ege, E., Akin, B., Kal, H.E., & Salli, A. (2014). An investigation of sexual/reproductive health issues in women with a physical disability. *Sexuality and Disability, 32*(2), 221–229.
doi:10.1007/s11195-014-9342-z

Andrews v. Law Society of British Columbia, [1989] 1 S.C.R. 143.

Angus Reid Institute (2015a). *Disability and Accessibility: Canadians see significant room for improvement in communities where they live.* Retrieved from http://angusreid.org/rhf-accessibility/

Angus Reid Institute. (2015b). *Disability in Canada: Does closing the accessibility gap literally start from the ground up?* Retrieved from http://angusreid.org/disability-in-canada/

Antonak, R.F., & Livneh, H. (2000). Measurement of attitudes towards persons with disabilities. *Disability and Rehabilitation, 22*(5), 211–224.

Arim, R. (2015). *Canadian Survey on Disability, 2012: A profile of persons with disabilities among Canadians aged 15 years or older, 2012.* Statistics Canada.

Armstrong, M., Morris, C., Abraham, C., Ukoumunne, O., & Tarrant, M. (2016). Children's contact with people with disabilities and their attitudes towards disability: A cross-sectional study. *Disability and Rehabilitation, 38*(9), 879–888.
doi:10.3109/09638288.2015.1074727

Armstrong, S. (2003). Disability advocacy in the Charter era. *University of Toronto Journal of Law & Equality, 2*(1), 34–90.

Arthurs, H., & Arnold, B. (2005). Does the Charter matter? Review of constitutional studies. *Canadian Journal of Disability Studies, 11*(1), 37–118.

Azzopardi-Lane, C. & Callus, A.M. (2014). Constructing sexual identities: People with intellectual disability talking about sexuality. *British Journal of Learning Disabilities, 43*, 32–37.
doi:10.1111/bld.12083

Bahm, A., & Forchuk, C. (2009). Interlocking oppressions: The effect of a comorbid physical disability on perceived stigma and discrimination among mental health consumers in Canada. *Health & Social Care in the Community, 17*(1), 63–70.
doi:10.1111/j.1365-2524.2008.00799.x

Barg, C.J., Armstrong, B.D., Hetz, S.P., & Latimer, A.E. (2010). Physical disability, stigma, and physical activity in children. *International Journal of Disability, Development and Education, 57*(4), 371–382.
doi:10.1080/1034912X.2010.524417

Barnard, D. (1995). Chronic illness and the dynamics of hoping. In S.K. Toombs, D. Barnard, & R.A. Carson (Eds.), *Chronic illness: From experience to policy.* Bloomington, IN: Indiana University Press.

Barnes, C. (2003). What a difference a decade makes: Reflections on doing "emancipatory" disability research. *Disability & Society, 18*(1), 3–17.

Barnes, C. (2008). An ethical agenda in disability research: Rhetoric or reality? In D.M. Mertens & P.E. Ginsburg (Eds.), *The handbook of social research ethics* (pp. 458–473). London, UK: Sage.

Barnes, C., & Mercer, G. (2001). Disability cultures: Assimilation or inclusion? In G. Albrecht, K. Seelman, & M. Bury (Eds.), *Handbook of disability studies* (pp. 515–534). London, UK: Sage Publications.

Barros, P.P. (2003). Cream-skimming, incentives for efficiency and payment system. *Journal of Health Economics, 22*(3), 419–443.
doi:10.1016/S0167-6296(02)00119-4

Barton, L. (1992). *Disability and the necessity for a socio-political perspective.* World Rehabilitation Fund, Inc., New York, NY; New Hampshire Univ., Durham. Inst. on Disability.

Barton, L., & Armstrong, F. (2001). Disability, education, and inclusion: Cross-cultural issues and dilemmas. In G. Albrecht, K. Seelman, & M. Bury (Eds.), *Handbook of disability studies* (pp. 693–710). London: Sage.

Baylies, C. (2002). Disability and the notion of human development: Questions of rights and capabilities. *Disability & Society, 17*(7), 725–739. doi:10.1080/0968759022000039037

Beacom, A., & Brittain, I. (2016). Public diplomacy and the international Paralympic committee: Reconciling the roles of disability advocate and sports regulator. *Diplomacy & Statecraft, 27*(2), 273–294.

Beauchamp-Pryon, K. (2011). Impairment, cure and identity: "Where do I fit in?" *Disability & Society, 26*(1), 5–17.

Beauchamp-Pryon, K., & Symeonidou, S. (2013). *Purpose, process and future direction of disability research.* London, UK: Sense Publishers.

Begley, C., Lairson, D., Morgan, R., Rowan, P., & Balkrishnan, R. (2013). *Evaluating the healthcare system: Effectiveness, efficiency, and equity* (4th ed.). Foundation of the American College of Healthcare Executive.

Behnia, B., & Duclos, E. (2003). *Children with disabilities and their families: Participation and activity limitation survey.* Statistics Canada: Housing, Family and Social Statistics Division.

Bickenbach, J.E. (2006). Canadian Charter v. American ADA: Individual Rights or Collective Responsibilities. In M. McColl and L. Jongbloed (Eds.), *Disability and Social Policy in Canada* (pp. 77–86). Concord, ON: Captus Press.

Bickenbach, J., Cieza, A., & Sabariego, C. (2016). Disability and public health. *International Journal of Environmental Research and Public Health, 13*(123), 1–3.

Booth, S., & Kendall, M. (2007). Benefits and challenges of providing transitional rehabilitation services to people with spinal cord injury from regional, rural and remote locations. *Australian Journal of Rural Health, 15*(3), 172–178.

Boshara, R., Cramer, R., & Sherraden, M. (2006). *The politics of aspiration: Creating inclusive asset-building policies in the U.S. Wealth and wellbeing, ownership and opportunity.* Canada Social and Enterprise Development Innovations (SEDI) Canada. Retrieved from http://www.sedi.org/html/resources/publications.asp

Bowers, B., Esmond, S., Lutz, B., & Jacobson, N. (2003). Improving primary care for persons with disabilities: The nature of expertise. *Disability & Society, 18*(4), 443–455.

Boyce, W., Krough, K., & Boyce, E. (2006). Policy shifts and challenges: Coping strategies of disability organizations. In M.A. McColl & L. Jongbloed (Eds.), *Disability and social policy in Canada* (2nd ed., pp. 254–266). Concord, ON: Captus Press.

Boyce, W., Tremblay, M., McColl, M.A., Bickenbach, J., Crichton, A., Andrews, S., ... D'Aubin, A. (2001). *A seat at the table: Persons with disabilities and policy making*. Montreal, QC: McGill-Queen's University Press.

Brain Injury Institute. (2012). *Living with brain injury: Costs of care*. Retrieved from https://www.braininjuryinstitute.org/living-with-brain-injury/costs-of-care

British Columbia (Public Service Employee Relations Commission) v. BCGSEU, [1999] 3 S.C.R. 3 (Meiorin)

British North America Act, 1867, 30 Victoria, c. 3.

Brown, C. (1954). *My left foot*. London, UK: Minerva Paperbacks.

Bu, P., Veloski, J.J., & Ankam, N.S. (2016). Effects of a brief curricular intervention on medical students' attitude toward people with disability in healthcare settings. *American Journal of Physical Medicine & Rehabilitation, 95*, 939–945.

Buckland, J. (2010). Are low-income Canadians financially literate? Placing financial literacy in the context of personal and structural constraints. *Adult Education Quarterly, 60*(4), 357–376.

Bundy, A.C. (2005). Measuring play performance. In M. Law, C. Baum, & W. Dunn (Eds.), *Measuring occupational performance: Supporting best practice in occupational therapy* (2nd ed.). Thorofare, NJ: SLACK Incorporated.

Burchardt, T. (2004). Capabilities and disability: The capabilities framework and the social model of disability. *Disability & Society, 19*(7), 735–751. doi:10.1080/0968759042000284213

Bureau of Labor Statistics. (2017). *American Time Use Survey*. Retrieved from https://www.bls.gov/tus/

Burge, P., Ouelette-Kuntz, H., Issacs, B., & Lunsky, Y. (2008). Medical students' views on training in intellectual disabilities. *Canadian Family Physician, 54*, 568–569.

Burlock, A. (2017). *Women with disabilities*. Statistics Canada. Retrieved from https://www150.statcan.gc.ca/n1/en/pub/89-503-x/2015001/article/14695-eng.pdf?st=Tax8o_4e

Burton, P., & Phipps, S. (2009). Economic costs of caring for children with disabilities in Canada. *Canadian Public Policy, 35*(3), 269–290. Toronto, ON: University of Toronto Press.

Bynder, H., & New, P. (1976). Time for a change: From micro-to-macro-sociological concepts in disability research. *Journal of Health and Social Behavior, 17*(1), 45–52.

Byron, M., & Dieppe, P. (2000). Educating health professionals about disability: "Attitudes, attitudes, attitudes". *Journal of Royal Society of Medicine, 93*(8), 397–398.

Cameron, D., & Valentine, F. (2001). *Disability and federalism: Comparing different approaches to full participation*. Montreal/Kingston: McGill-Queen's University Press.

Campbell, F. (2009). *Contours of ableism: The production of disability and abledness.* London, UK: Macmillian Publishers.

Campbell, J., Gilmore, L., & Cuskelly, M. (2003). Changing student teachers' attitudes towards disability and inclusion. *Journal of Intellectual and Developmental Disability, 28*(4), 369–379. doi:10.1080/13668250310001616407

Canadian Charter of Rights and Freedoms, Part I of the *Constitution Act, 1982,* being Schedule B to the *Canada Act 1982* (UK), 1982, c. 11.

Canadian Disability Policy Alliance. (2017). *A review of disability policy in Canada.* Retrieved from http://www.disabilitypolicyalliance .ca/wp-content/uploads/2018/01/A-Review-of-Disability-Policy-in-Canada-3rd-edition-Final-1-1.pdf

Canadian Human Rights Act, S.C. 1976-77, c. 33, s. 1 (1977).

Canadian Human Rights Commission. (1986). *Canadian Human Rights Act, 1985.* Retrieved from http://www.chrc-ccdp.gc.ca/eng/content /human-rights-in-canada

Canadian Human Rights Commission. (2009). *Canadian human rights commission, 2009–2010: Report on plans and priorities.* Ottawa, ON: Canada Treasury Board.

Canadian Human Rights Commission. (2012). *Report on equality rights of people with disabilities.* Minister of Public Works and Government Services. Retrieved from https://www.chrc-ccdp.gc.ca/sites/ default/files/rerpd_rdepad-eng.pdf

Canadian Human Rights Commission. (2015). *2014 Annual report to parliament.* Minister of Public Works and Government Services. Retrieved from http://www.chrc-ccdp.gc.ca/sites/default/files/pdf/chrc-annual-report-2014.pdf

Canadian Human Rights Tribunal. (2007). *Canadian human rights tribunal, 2006–2007 estimates: Part III: Report on plans and priorities.* Ottawa: Minister of Justice and Attorney General of Canada.

Canadian Medical Association. (2004). *CMA Code of Ethics* (Updated 2004). Retrieved from https://www.cma.ca/En/Pages/code-of-ethics.aspx

Carden, F. (2009). *Knowledge to policy.* Los Angeles: Sage.

Carr, J. (2016). *A Conceptual and Legal Framework for Inclusive Education.* ARCH — Disability Law Centre.

Center for Applied Special Technology. (2011). *Universal design for learning guidelines, version 2.0.* CAST.

Centers for Disease Control. (2004). *Health, United State, 2004: With chartbook on trends in the health of Americans.* Maryland: National Center for Health Statistics.

Chisholm, D., & Stewart, A. (1998). Economics and ethics in mental health care: Traditions and trade-offs. *Journal of Mental Health Policy Economies, 1*(2), 55–62.

Chouinard, V. (1997). Making space for disabling difference: Challenges ableist geographies. *Environment and Planning D: Society and Space, 15,* 379–387.

Christiansen, C.H., Baum, C., & Bass-Haugen, J. (2005). *Occupational therapy: Performance, participation and well-being* (3rd ed.). Thorofare, NJ: SLACK.

Christiansen, C.H., & Townsend, E.A. (2004). *Introduction to occupation: The art and science of living.* Upper Saddle River, NJ: Prentice Hall.

Claxton, A. (1994). Teaching medical students about disability. *British Medical Journal, 308*(6932), 805.

Conger, K.J., Rueter, M.A., & Rand, D. (2000). The role of economic pressure in the lives of parents and their adolescents: The family stress model. In L. Crockett & R.K. Silbereis (Eds.), *Negotiating adolescence in times of social change* (pp. 201–223). New York, NY: Cambridge University Press.

The Constitution Act, 1982, Schedule B to the *Canada Act, 1982* (UK), 1982, c. 11.

Cook, J., Mulkern, V., Grey, D., Burke-Miller, J., Blyler, C., Raxxano, L., ... Steigman, P. (2006). Effects of local unemployment rate on vocational outcomes in a randomized trial of supported employment for individuals with psychiatric disabilities. *Journal of Vocational Rehabilitation, 25*(2), 71–84.

Cooperrider, D.L., Whitney, D., & Stavros, J.M. (2008). *Appreciative inquiry handbook* (2nd ed.). Brunswick, OH: Crown Custom Publishing.

Corson-Rikert, J., & Christmas, W.A. (2009). The medical excuse game revisited. *Journal of American College Health, 57*(5), 561–563.

Council of Canadian with Disabilities. (2010). *Canada's involvement in developing the UN convention.* Retrieved from http://www.ccdonline.ca/en/international/un/canada/crpd-pressrelease

Crocker, C. (2009). Disability policy — A Canadian perspective: A human rights approach to providing supports and services. In C. Marshall, E. Kendal, M. Banks, & R. Gover (Eds.), *Disability: Insights from across fields and around the world* (pp. 226–243). Westport, CT: Greenwood Publishing Group.

Cuddy, A., Fiske, S., Kwan, V., Glick, P., Demoulin, S., Leyens, J., ... Ziegler, R. (2009). Stereotype content model across cultures: Towards universal similarities and some differences. *British Journal of Social Psychology, 48*(1), 1–33. doi:10.1348/014466608X314935

Cullinan, J., Gannon, B., & Lyons, S. (2011). Estimating the extra cost of living for people with disabilities. *Health Economics, 20*(5), 582–599.

Cunningham, A.J. (2000). *The healing journey: Overcoming the crisis of cancer.* Toronto, ON: Key Porter.

Curlin, F. (2008). A case for studying the relationship between religion and the practice of medicine. *Academic Medicine, 83*(12), 1118–1120.

Dana, E.R., Lalwani, N., & Duval, T.S. (1997). Objective self-awareness and focus of attention following awareness of self-standard discrepancies: Changing self or changing standards of correctness. *Journal of Social and Clinical Psychology, 16,* 359–380.

Danieli, A., & Woodhams, C. (2005). Emancipatory research methodology and disability: A critique. *International Journal of Social Research Methodology, 8*, 281–296.

Darcy, S., Lock, D., & Taylor, T. (2017). Enabling inclusive sport participation: Effects of disability and support needs on constraints to sport participation. *Leisure Sciences, 39*(1), 20–41.

Daruwalla, P., & Darcy, S. (2005). Personal and societal attitudes to disability. *Annals of Tourism Research, 32*(3), 549–570. doi:10.1016/j.annals.2004.10.008.

Day, H. (1979). Why people play? *Loisir et Société/Society and Leisure, 2*(1), 129–147.

Deci, E.L., & Ryan, R.M. (1985). The general causality orientations scale: Self-determination in personality. *Journal of Research in Personality, 19*(2), 109–134. doi:10.1016/0092-6566(85)90023-6

Deci, E.L., & Ryan, R.M. (1995). Human autonomy: The basis for true self-esteem. In M. Kernis (Ed.), *Efficacy, agency, and self-esteem*. New York, NY: Plenum.

Deegan, P. (1988). The lived experience of rehabilitation. *Psychosocial Rehabilitation Journal, 11*, 11–19.

Dejong, G. Independent living: From social movement to analytic paradigm. *Archives of Physical Medicine and Rehabilitation, 60*(10), 435–446.

Dejong, G., Palsbo, S.E., Beatty, P.W., Jones, G.C., Kroll, T., & Neri, M.T. (2002). The organization and financing of health services for persons with disabilities. *Milbank Quarterly, 80*(2), 261–301. doi:10.1111/1468-0009.t01-1-00004

DeLamater, J., & Friedrich, W.N. (2002). Human sexual development. *Journal of Sex Research, 39*(1), 10–14. doi:10.1080/00224490209552113

Deloitte & Touche. (2010). *Review of school health support services: Final report.* Retrieved from https://www.osla.on.ca/uploads/deloitte_shss_review_report.pdf

Department of Finance Canada. (2006). *A new beginning. The report of the Minister of Finance's expert panel and financial security for children with severe disabilities.* Retrieved from https://www.fin.gc.ca/activty/pubs/disability_e.pdf

DePoy, E., & Gilson S. (2011). *Studying disability: Multiple theories and responses.* Thousand Oaks, CA: Sage.

Disability Pride Parade. (2013). *Why disability pride?* Retrieved from https://web.archive.org/web/20130209165451/http://www.disabilityprideparade.com/whypride.php

Disability Statistics. (2015). *Disability Status Report United States.* Retrieved from http://www.disabilitystatistics.org/StatusReports/2015-PDF/2015-StatusReport_US.pdf?CFID=3491212&CFTOKEN=87616a2aa4897a2f-84ED38D7-E2CA-2503-CD8D8B4FA22E9FDF

Dolmage, J. (2018). *Disabled upon arrival*. Columbus, Ohio: The Ohio State University Press.

Donchin, A. (2000). Autonomy, interdependence, and assisted suicide: Respecting boundaries/crossing lines. *Bioethics, 14*(3), 187–204. doi:10.1111/1467-8519.00190

Donnelly, C., McColl, M., Charlifue, S., Glass, C., O'Brien, P., Savic, G., & Smith, K. (2007). Utilization, access and satisfaction with primary care among people with spinal cord injuries: A comparison of three countries. *Spinal Cord, 45*(1), 25–36. doi:10.1038/sj.sc.3101933

Doubt, L., & McColl, M.A. (1997). A secondary guy: Physically disabled teenagers in secondary schools. *Canadian Journal of Occupational Therapy, 70*(3), 139–151.

Dow, B., & Meyer, C. (2010). Caring and retirement: Crossroads and consequences. *International Journal of Health Services, 40*(4), 645–665. doi:10.2190/HS.40.4.e

Dowler, D., & Walls, R. (2014). A review of supported employment services for people with disabilities: Competitive employment, earnings, and service costs. *Journal of Rehabilitation, 80*(1), 11–21.

Draper, W., Hawley, C., McMahon, B., & Reid, C. (2012). Workplace discrimination and the record of disability. *Journal of Vocational Rehabilitation, 36*, 199–226. doi:1052-2263/12/$27.50

Driedger, D. (1989). *The last civil rights movement: Disabled people's international*. New York, NY: C. Hurst & Co.

Dufflo, E., Gale, W., Liebman, J., Orszag, P., & Saez, E. (2007). Savings incentives for low and moderate income families in the United States: Why is the saver's credit not more effective? *Journal of the European Economic Association, 5*(2/3), 647–661.

Duquette, M., Carbonneau, H., & Jourdan-Ionescu, C. (2016). Young people with disabilities: The influence of leisure experiences on family dynamics. *Annals of Leisure Research, 19*(4), 405–423.

Eaton v. Brant County Board of Education, [1997] 1 S.C.R. 241.

Edwards, B., Higgins, D., Gray, M., Zmijewski, N., & Kingston, M. (2008). The nature and impact of caring for family members with a disability in Australia. *Australian Institute of Family Studies*. Retrieved from http://www.aifs.gov.au/institute/pubs/resreport16/report16pdf/rr16.pdf

Eiesland, N.L. (1994). *The disabled god: Toward a liberatory theology of disability*. Nashville, TN: Abingdon Press.

Eldridge v. British Columbia (Attorney General), [1997] 3 S.C.R. 624.

Elections Canada. (1997). *Canada Elections Survey 1997: Report of the Chief Electoral Officer of Canada on the 36th General Election*. Retrieved from http://www.elections.ca/content.aspx?section=res&document=index&dir=rep/off/ceo&lang=e

Elliott, S., & McBride, K. (2014). *Spinal cord injury rehabilitation evidence.* Retrieved from http://scireproject.com/wp-content/uploads/sexual_health-1.pdf

Emerson, E., & Hatton, C. (2009). Socioeconomic position, poverty, and family research. *International Review of Research in Mental Retardation, 37,* 97–129.

Emerson, E., Shahtahmasebi, S., Lancaster, G., & Berridge, D. (2010). Poverty transitions among families supporting a child with intellectual disability. *Journal of Intellectual & Developmental Disability, 35*(4), 224–234.

Employment and Social Development Canada (2018). *Labour Market Agreements for Persons with Disabilities.* Retrieved from https://www.canada.ca/en/employment-social-development/programs/training-agreements/lma-disabilities.html

Employment Equity Act, S.C. 1995, c. 44.

Employment Equity Act, 1986, S.C. 1986, c. 35.

Escorpizo, R., Miller, W., Trenaman, L., & Smith, E. (2014). *Work and employment following spinal cord injury.* Spinal Cord Injury Rehabilitation Evidence (SCIRE).

Escorpizo, R., Reneman, M.F., Ekholm, J., Fritz, J., Krupa, T., Marnetoft, S., ... Chan, C. (2011). A conceptual definition of vocational rehabilitation based on the ICF: Building a shared global model. *Journal of Occupational Rehabilitation, 21*(2), 126–133. doi:10.1007/s10926-011-9292-6

Escorpizo, R., Stucki, G., Cieza, A., Strumbo, T., & Riddle, D. (2010). Creating an interface between the international classification of functioning, disability and health and physical therapist practice. *Physical Therapy, 90*(7), 1053–1063. doi:10.2522/ptj.200090326

Eurostat. (2015). *Disability statistics — prevalence and demographics.* Retrieved from http://epp.eurostat.ec.europa.eu/statisticsexplained/

E (Mrs) v Eve, [1986] 2 S.C.R. 388.

Every Canadian Counts. (2017). *Moving forward: Building the framework for an inclusive future for people with disabilities and their families in Canada.* National Disability Strategy Formation Report.

Fann, J.R., Bombardier, C.H., Richards, J.S., Tate, D.G., Wilson, C.S., & Temkin, N. (2011). Depression after spinal cord injury: Comorbidities, mental health service use, and adequacy of treatment. *Archives of Physical Medicine & Rehabilitation, 92*(3), 352–360.

Farah, J., & McColl, M.A. (2011). Guidelines for direct spiritual intervention. In McColl, M.A. (Ed.). *Spirituality and Occupational Therapy.* Ottawa, ON: CAOT Publications ACE.

Federal/Provincial/Territorial Ministers Responsible for Social Services. (1998). *In unison: A Canadian approach to disability issues.* Retrieved from https://www.crwdp.ca/sites/default/files/Research%20and%20Publications/Enviornmental%20Scan/5.%20In%20

Unison/1.%20In%20Unison%20-%20A%20Canadian%20 Approach%20to%20Disability%20Issues%20-%20 Compressed.pdf

Federal/Provincial/Territorial Ministers Responsible for Social Services. (2000). *In unison 2000: Persons with disabilities in Canada.* Retrieved from https://www.crwdp.ca/sites/default/files/Research%20and %20Publications/Enviornmental%20Scan/5.%20In%20Unison/ 2.%20In%20Unison%202000%20-%20Persons%20with%20 Disabilities%20in%20Canada.pdf

Federal Task Force on Disability Issues. (1996). *Scott report: Equal citizenship for Canadians with disabilities: The will to act, 1996 (MP80-2/9-1996E).* Retrieved from http://publications.gc.ca/site/eng/64264 /publication.html

Findley, P., Banerjea, R., & Sambamoorthi, U. (2011). Excess mortality associated with mental illness and substance use disorders among veteran clinic users with spinal cord injury. *Disability and Rehabilitation, 33,* 1608–1614.

Fiske, S., Cuddy, A., Glick, P., & Xu, J. (2002). A model of (often mixed) stereotype content: Competence and warmth respectively follow from perceived status and competition. *Journal of Personality and Social Psychology, 82*(6), 878–902. doi:10.1037//0022-3514.82.6.878

Flicker, S., & Nixon, S. (2018). Writing peer-reviewed articles with diverse teams: Considerations for novice scholars conducting community-engaged research. *Health Promotion International, 20*(33), 152–161.

Flower, A., Burns, M.K., & Bottsford-Miller, N.A. (2007). Meta-analysis of disability simulation research. *Remedial and Special Education, 28*(2), 72–79. doi:10.1177/07419325070280020601

Forster, D., McColl, M.A., & Fardella, J.A. (2007). Spiritual transformations in clinical relationships between social workers and individuals living with disabilities. *Journal of Religion & Spirituality in Social Work: Social Thought, 26*(1), 35–51. doi:10.1300/J377v26n01_03

Forster, D., McColl, M., Paterson, M., & Ouellette-Kuntz, H. (2009). Jean Vanier and the transformational model of rehabilitation. *Mental Health Review Journal, 14*(4), 36–45. doi:10.1108/13619322200900025

Fournier-Savard, P., Mongeon, C., & Crompton, S. (2010). Living with disability series: Help with activities of daily living for people with a disability. *Canadian Social Trends, 90,* 92.

Frawley, P., & Bigby, C. (2014). "I'm in their shoes": Experiences of peer educators in sexuality and relationship education. *Journal of Intellectual & Developmental Disability, 39*(2), 167–176. doi:10.3109/13668250.2014.890701

Frazee, C. (2006). Exile from the china shop: Cultural injunction and disability policy. In M.A. McColl & L. Jongbloed (Eds.), *Disability and Social Policy in Canada* (2nd ed, pp. 357–369). Concord, ON: Captus Press.

Fujiura, G.T. (2010). Aging families and the demographics of family financial support of adults with disabilities. *Journal of Disability Policy Studies, 20*(4), 241–250.
doi:10.1177/1044207309350560

Gainforth, H.L., O'Malley, D., Mountenay, T., & Latimer-Cheung, A. (2013). Independence and physical activity status moderate stereotypes toward people with a physical disability. *International Journal of Sport and Exercise Psychology, 11*(3), 244–257.
doi:10.1080/1612197X.2013.749001

Galli, G., & Pazzaglia, M. (2016). Novel perspectives on health professionals' attitudes to disability. *Medical Education, 50*(8), 804–806.
doi:10.1111/medu.13111

Ganz, M.L. (2007). The lifetime distribution of the incremental societal costs of autism. *Archives of Paediatrics and Adolescent Medicine, 161*(4), 343–349.

Gerber, P.J., Price, L.A., Mulligan, R., & Shessel, I. (2004). Beyond transition: A comparison of the employment experiences of American and Canadian adults with LD. *Journal of Learning Disabilities, 37*(4), 283–291.
doi:10.1177/00222194040370040101

Gewurtz, R., Langan, S., & Shand, D. (2016). Hiring people with disabilities: A scoping review. *Work: A Journal of Prevention Assessment & Rehabilitation, 54*(1), 135–148.
doi:10.3233/WOR-162265

Gibson, O. (2010, May 4). Sainsbury's announces sponsorship of 2012 Paralympics. *The Guardian*, London, UK. Retrieved from https://www.theguardian.com/uk/2010/may/04/sainsburys-sponsors-paralympic-games

Gignac, M.A.M., & Cott, C. (1998). A conceptual model of independence and dependence for adults with chronic physical illness and disability. *Social Science & Medicine, 47*(6), 739–753.
doi:10.1016/S0277-9536(98)00149-X

Gitlin, L.N., Winter, L., Dennis, M.P., & Hauck., W.W. (2007). A non-pharmacological intervention to manage behavioural and psychological symptoms of dementia and reduce caregiver distress. Design and methods of project ACT. *Clinical Intervention in Aging, 2*(4), 695–703.

Godfrey, C.M., Harrison, M.B., Lysaght, R., Lamb, M., Graham, I.D., & Oakley, P. (2011). Care of self — care by other — care of other: The meaning of self-care from research, practice, policy and industry perspectives. *International Journal of Evidence-Based Healthcare, 9*(1), 3–24.
doi:10.1111/j.1744-1609.2010.00196.x

Goodley, D. (2017). *Disability studies: An interdisciplinary introduction* (2nd ed.). London, UK: Sage.

Goodley, D., & Moore, M. (2000). Doing disability research: Activist lives and the academy. *Disability & Society, 15*(6), 861–882.

Government of Canada: House of Commons. (1981). *Obstacles: Report of the special committee on the disabled and the handicapped.* Minister of Supply and Services Canada.

Government of Canada: House of Commons. (2018). *Bill C-81: An Act to ensure a barrier-free Canada.* Retrieved from http://www.parl.ca/DocumentViewer/en/42-1/bill/C-81/first-reading.

Government of Canada. (1991). *Future directions to address disability issues for the government of Canada: Working together for full citizenship.* Retrieved from http://publications.gc.ca/collections/Collection/MP80-2-11-1999E.pdf

Government of Canada. (1996). *National strategy for the integration of persons with disabilities, 1991–96.* Retrieved from http://publications.gc.ca/site/eng/9.658445/publication.html

Government of Canada. (2011). *The well-being of Canada's young children: Government of Canada report 2011.* Government of Canada.

Government of Canada. (2014). *Convention on the rights of persons with disabilities: First report of Canada.* Retrieved from http://publications.gc.ca/collections/collection_2014/pc-ch/CH37-4-19-2013-eng.pdf

Government of Ontario. (2017). *Ontario's Education Equity Action Plan.* Service Ontario.

Granovsky v. Canada (Minister of Employment and Immigration), 2000 SCC 28, [2000] 1 S.C.R. 703.

Grant, T. (2015, February 28). The disability edge. *The Globe and Mail.*

Gray, P. (2008). The value of play I: The definition of play gives insights. *Psychology Today.* Retrieved from https://www.psychologytoday.com/us/blog/freedom-learn/200811/the-value-play-i-the-definition-play-gives-insights

Grondin, C. (2016). *A new survey measure of disability: The disability screening questions (DSQ).* Ottawa, ON: Statistics Canada.

Gruhl, K. (2012). Transitions to work for persons with serious mental illness in northeastern Ontario, Canada: Examining barriers to employment. *Work — A Journal of Prevention Assessment & Rehabilitation, 41*(4), 379–389. doi:10.3233/WOR-2012-1315

Guilcher, S.J.T., Craven, B.C., Lemieux-Charles, L., Casciaro, T., McColl, M.A., & Jaglal, S.B. (2013). Secondary health conditions and spinal cord injury: An uphill battle in the journey of care. *Disability and Rehabilitation, 35*(11), 894–906. doi:10.3109/09638288.2012.721048

Gupta, S., McColl, M.A., Guilcher, S., & Smith, K. (2018). Cost-related nonadherence to prescription medications in Canada: A scoping review. *Dovepress, 12,* 1699–1715. https://www.ncbi.nlm.nih.gov/pubmed/30233150

Hammell, K. (2016). Empowerment and occupation: A new perspective. *Canadian Journal of Occupational Therapy-Revue Canadienne d Ergotherapie, 83*(5), 281–287. doi:10.1177/0008417416652910

Hammersley, M. (1995). *The politics of social research.* London, UK: Sage.

Handicap International. (2012). *Disability and development.* Retrieved from http://www.hiproweb.org/fileadmin/cdroms/Handicap_Developpement/www/index_en.html

Haveman, R., & Wolff, E. (2005). Who are the asset poor: Levels, trends and composition, 1983–1998. In M. Sherraden (Ed.), *Inclusion in the American dream: Assets, poverty, and public policy* (pp. 61–86). New York, NY: Oxford University Press.

Hawkins, B., Peng, J., Hsieh, C., & Eklund, S. (1999). Leisure constraints: A replication and extension of construct development. *Leisure Sciences, 21*, 170–192.

Healy, E., McGuire, B., Evans, D., & Carley, S. (2009). Sexuality and personal relationships for people with an intellectual disability. Part I: Service-user perspectives. *Journal of Intellectual Disability Research, 53*(11), 905–912. doi:10.1111/j.1365-2788.2009.01203.x

Henry, A., Petkaukos, K., Stanislawzyk, J., & Vogt, J. (2014). Employer-recommended strategies to increase opportunities for people with disabilities. *Journal of Vocational Rehabilitation, 41*, 237–248. doi:1052-2263/14/$27.50

Hoekstra, F., Roberts, L., van Lindert, C., Martin Ginis, K., van der Woude, L., & McColl, M.A. (2018). National approaches to promote sports and physical activity in adults with disabilities: Examples from the Netherlands and Canada. *Disability and Rehabilitation, 15*, 1–10. doi:10.1080/09638288.2017.1423402

Hosking, D. (2008, September). *Critical disability theory.* Paper presented at the 4th Biennial Disability Conference at Lancaster University, United Kingdom.

Hughes, B. (2007). Being disabled: Towards a critical social ontology for disability studies. *Disability & Society, 22*(7), 673–684. doi:10.1080/09687590701659527

Human Resources and Skills Development Canada. (2006). A way with words and images. Retrieved from https://www.canada.ca/content/dam/esdc-edsc/migration/documents/eng/disability/arc/way_with_words.pdf

Human Resources and Skills Development Canada. (2007). *Physician's guide: Canada pension plan disability benefits.* Retrieved from http://www.hrsdc.gc.ca/eng/isp/pub/cpp/physguide/benefits.shtml

Human Resources and Skills Development Canada. (2008). *Federally regulated businesses and industries.* Retrieved from http://www.hrsdc.gc.ca/eng/labour/employment_standards/regulated.shtml

Iezzoni, L.I. (2002). Using administrative data to study persons with disabilities. *Milbank Q., 80*(2), 347–379. Retrieved from https://www.ncbi.nlm.nih.gov/pmc/articles/PMC2690114/

Iezzoni, L.I., Davis, R.B., Soukup, J., & O'Day, B. (2003). Quality dimensions that most concern people with physical and sensory disabilities. *Archives of Internal Medicine, 163*(17), 2085–2092. doi:10.1001/archinte.163.17.2085

Imrie, R. (1997). Rethinking the relationship between disability, rehabilitation, and society. *Disability and Rehabilitation, 19*(7), 263–271.

Institute for Healthcare Improvement. (2003). *The breakthrough series: Institute for healthcare improvement's collaborative model for achieving breakthrough improvement.* Retrieved from IHI Innovation Series White Paper: http://www.ihi.org/IHI/Results/WhitePapers

International Olympic Committee. (2010). *Olympic Charter.* Lausanne, Switzerland: International Olympic Committee.

International Paralympic Committee. (2003). *Paralympic vison and mission.* Retrieved from https://www.paralympic.org/sites/default/files/document/141113141204499_2014_10_01%2BSec%2Bi%2B chapter%2B1_1_Paralympic%2BVision%2Band%2BMission.pdf

Isler, A., Beytut, D., Tas, F., & Conk, Z. (2009). A study on sexuality with the parents of adolescents with intellectual disability. *Sexuality and Disability, 27*(4), 229–237. doi:10.1007/s11195-009-9130-3

Iwasaki, Y., & Mactavish, J.B. (2005). Ubiquitous yet unique: Perspectives of people with disabilities on stress. *Rehabilitation Counseling Bulletin, 48*(4), 194–208. doi:10.1177/00343552050480040101

Jamieson, M., Hutchinson, N., Taylor, J., Westlake, K., Berg, D., & Boyce, W. (2009). Friendships of adolescents with physical disabilities attending inclusive high schools. *Canadian Journal of Occupational Therapy, 76*(5), 368–376.

Johnston, M., Vanderheiden, G., Farkas, M., Rogers, E., Summers, J.A., & Westbrook, J. (2009). *The challenge of evidence in disability and rehabilitations research and practice: A position paper.* National Centre for the Dissemination of Disability Research. Retrieved from www.ncddr.org/kd/products/tfpapers/tfse_challenge/

Joiner, I. (2006). Perhaps not yet: Policy making through citizen engagement. In M.A. McColl & L. Jongbloed (Eds.), *Disability and social policy in Canada* (2nd ed., pp. 254–266). Concord, ON: Captus Press.

Jones, K., & Tamari, I. (1997). Making our offices universally accessible: Guidelines for physicians. *Canadian Medical Association Journal, 156*(5), 647–656.

Jorgensen, M. (2005). A disability paradox. *Canadian Family Physician, 51*, 1474–1476.

Kahneman, D. (2011). *Thinking, fast and slow*. New York, NY: Farrar, Straus and Giroux.

Kasperski, J., & Ontario College of Family Physicians. (2005). *Family physicians and public policy: The light at the end of the tunnel*. Ontario: Ontario College of Family Physicians.

Kauffmann, J., Anastasiou, D., Badar, J., Travers, J., & Wiley, A. (2016). Inclusive education moving forward: General and special education inclusion in an age of change: Roles of professionals involved. *Advances in Special Education, 32*, 153–178. doi:10.1108/S0270-401320160000032010

Kelly, J.B. (2005). *Governing with the Charter: Legislative and judicial activism and framers intent*. Vancouver, BC: UBC Press.

Kerzner, L. (2006). Mental capacity through a disability law lens. In M.A. McColl & L. Johngloed (Eds.), *Disability and social policy in Canada* (2nd ed.). (pp. 336–356). Concord, ON: Captus Press.

Kielhofner, G. (1988). Model of human occupation. In S. Robertson (Ed.), *Mental health focus*. Rockville, MD: American Occupational Therapy Association.

Kim, E. (2011). "Heaven for disabled people": Nationalism and international human rights imagery. *Disability & Society, 26*(11), 93–106.

Kim, J., Heinemann, A., Bode, R., Sliva, J., & King, R. (2000). Spirituality, quality of life, and functional recovery after medical rehabilitation. *Rehabilitation Psychology, 45*(4), 365–385.

King, G., Petrenchik, T., Law, M., & Hurley, P. (2009). The enjoyment of formal and informal recreation and leisure activities: A comparison on school-aged children with and without physical disabilities. *International Journal of Disability, Development and Education, 56*(2), 109–130.

Kingsley, E.P. (1987). *Welcome to Holland*. Retrieved from https://natanshai.com/trip-to-holland-poem

Kittson, K., Gainforth, H., Edwards, J., Bolkowy, R., & Latimer-Cheung, A. (2013). The effect of video observation on warmth and competence ratings of individuals with a disability. *Psychology of Sport and Exercise, 14*(6), 847–851. doi:10.1016/j.psychsport.2013.07.003

Klein, B.S. (1998). *Slow dance: A story of stroke, love and disability*. Berkley, CA: Page Mill Press.

Knapp, M., Romeo, R., & Beecham, J. (2009). Economic cost of autism in the UK. *Autism, 13*(3), 317–336.

Knott, T.C. (2013). *Home-based rehabilitation and its impact on hospital utilization*. (Doctoral dissertation, Queen's University, Kingston, Canada).

Kober, R., & Eggleton, I.R.C. (2005). The effect of different types of employment on quality of life. *Journal of Intellectual Disability Research, 49*(10), 756–760. doi:10.1111/j.1365-2788.2005.00746.x

Kohen, D., Uppal, S., Guevremont, A., & Cartwright, F. (2001). *Children with disabilities and the educational system: A provincial perspective.* Statistics Canada.

Korzinski, D. (2016). *Disability in Canada: Does closing the accessibility gap literally start from the ground up?* Retrieved from http://angusreid.org/disability-in-canada/

Kruger, H., & Associates. (2011). *Spinal cord injury: Progress in care & outcomes in the last 25 years.* Rick Hansen Institute. Retrieved from http://rickhanseninstitute.org/images/stories/Article_PDFs/Report_on_SCI_Prog ress.pdf

Krupa, T. (1998). Consequences for work, education and recreation. In M.A. McColl & J. Bickenbach (Eds.), *Introduction to disability.* London, UK: WB Saunders.

Lande, R.G. (1998). Disability law: Problems and proposals. *Southern Medical Journal, 91*(6) 518–521.

Law, M., Baptise, S., Carswell, A., McColl., M.A., Polatajko, H., & Pollock, N. (2014). *Canadian occupational performance measure* (5th ed.). Toronto, ON: CAOT Publications ACE.

LeClair, J. (2011). Global organizational change in sport and the shifting meaning of disability. *Sport in Society, 14*(9), 1072–1093.

Leete, E. (1989). How I perceive and manage my illness. *Schizophrenia Bulletin, 15,* 196–200.

Leipoldt, E. (2006). Disability experience: A contribution from the margins towards a sustainable future. *Journal of Futures Studies, 10*(3), 15–32.

Leiulfsrud, A., Ruoranen, K., Ostermann, A., & Reinhardt, J. (2016). The meaning of employment from the perspective of persons with spinal cord injuries in six European countries. *Work — A Journal of Prevention Assessment & Rehabilitation, 55*(1), 133–144. doi:10.3233/WOR-162381

Leo, J., & Goodwin, D. (2016). Simulating others' realities: Insiders reflect on disability simulations. *Adapted Physical Activity Quarterly, 33*(2), 156–175. doi:10.1123/APAQ.2015-0031

Leonardi, M., Bickenbach, J., Bedirhan Ustun, T., Kostanjsek, N., & Chatterj, S. (2006). The definition of disability: What is in a name? *The Lancet, 368*(9543), 1219–1221.

Lepofsky, D. (1998). *The Charter's guarantee of equality to people with disabilities: How well is it working?* Windsor Yearbook of Access to Justice. Windsor ON: University of Windsor.

Letizia, J.M. (2002). The Supreme Court helps employers by narrowing the definition of disability. *Home Health Care Management and Practice, 14*(6), 484–485.

Livermore, G., Goodman, N., & Wright, D. (2007). Social Security disability beneficiaries: Characteristics, work activity, and use of services.

Journal of Vocational Rehabilitation, 27, 85–93. doi:1052-2263/07/$17.00

Loi Assurant L'Exercisce des Droits des Personnes Handicapées en vue de leur Intégration Scolaire, Professionnelle et Sociale (1978). c. 31, a. 1.

Loreman, T. (2014). Special education today in Canada. In A. Rotatori, J. Bakken, S. Burkhardt, F. Obiakor, & U. Sharma (Eds.), *Special education international perspectives: Practices across the globe* (pp. 33–60). West Yorkshire, UK: Emerald Group Publishing Limited.

Lysaght, R., Ouellette-Kuntz, H., & Lin, C. (2012). Untapped potential: Perspectives on the employment of people with intellectual disability. *Work — A Journal of Prevention Assessment & Rehabilitation, 41*(4), 409–422. doi:10.3233/WOR-2012-1318

Macbeth, J. (2010). Reflecting on disability research in sport and leisure settings. *Leisure Studies, 29*(4), 477–485.

MacPherson, D. (2006). Damage quantification in tort and pre-existing conditions: Arguments for a reconceptualization. In D. Pothier & R. Devlin (Eds.), *Critical disability theory: Essays in philosophy, politics, policy, and law* (pp. 248–266). Vancouver, BC: UBC Press.

Martin, J. (2013). Benefits and barriers to physical activity for individuals with disabilities: A social-relational model of disability perspective. *Disability and Rehabilitation, 35*(24), 2030–2037.

Martin Ginis, K., Ma, J., Latimer-Cheung, A., & Rimmer, J. (2016). A systematic review of review articles addressing factors related to physical activity participation among children and adults with physical disabilities. *Health Psychology Review, 10*(4), 478–494.

Matsubayashi, T., & Ueda, M. (2014). Disability and voting. *Disability and Health Journal, 7*, 285–291.

Mays, J.B. (1995). *In the jaws of the black dogs: A memoir of depression.* Toronto, ON: Penguin.

McCabe, M.P., Cummins, R.A., & Deeks, A.A. (2000). Sexuality and quality of life among people with physical disability. *Sexuality and Disability, 18*(2), 115–123. doi:10.1023/A:1005562813603

McColl, M.A. (2005). Disability studies at the population level: Issues of health service utilization. *American Journal of Occupational Therapy Special Issue in Disability Studies, 59*(5), 516–526.

McColl, M.A. (2011). *Spirituality and occupational therapy* (2nd ed.). Ottawa, ON: Canadian Association of Occupational Therapists Publ.

McColl, M.A. (2017). *The disability policy lens* (2nd ed.). Kingston, ON. Canadian Disability Policy Alliance.

Mccoll, M.A., Adair, W., Davey, S., & Kates, N. (2013). The learning collaborative: An approach to emancipatory research in disability studies. *Canadian Journal of Disability Studies, 2*(1), 1–24.

McColl, M.A., Aiken, A., & Schaub, M. (2015). Do people with disabilities have trouble finding a family physician? *International Journal of Environmental Research and Public Health, 2015*(12), 4638–4651.

McColl, M.A., Arnold, R., Charlifue, S., Glass, C., Savic, G., & Frankel, H. (2003). Aging, spinal cord injury, and quality of life: Structural relationships. *Archives of Physical Medicine and Rehabilitation, 84*(8), 1137–1144.
doi: 10.1016/S0003-9993(03)00138-2

McColl, M.A., & Bickenbach, J. (1998). *Introduction to disability*. London, UK: WB Saunders.

McColl, M.A., Bickenbach, J., Johnston, J., Nishihama, M.A., Schumaker, M., Smith, K., Smith, M., & Yealland, B. (2000). Changes in spiritual beliefs after traumatic disability. *Archives of Physical Medicine and Rehabilitation, 81*(6), 817–823.

McColl, M.A., Bickenbach, J., Johnston, J., Schumaker, M., Smith, K., Smith, M., & Yelland, B. (2000). Spiritual issues associated with traumatic-onset disability. *Disability and Rehabilitations, 22*(12), 555–564.

McColl, M.A., & Dickenson, J. (2009). *Inter-professional primary health care: Assembling the pieces: A framework to build your practice in primary health care*. Ottawa, ON: Canadian Association of Occupational Therapists.

McColl, M.A., Forster, D., Shortt, S.E., Hunter, D., Dorland, J., Godwin, M., & Rosser, W. (2008). Physician experiences providing primary care to people with disabilities. [Experience des medecins offrant des soins de sante primaires aux personnes presentant une incapacite] *Healthcare Policy, 4*(1), e129–e147.

McColl, M.A., James, A., Boyce, W., & Shortt, S. (2003). Evidence based policy-making about disability: Evaluating the evidence. In D. Pothier & R. Devlin (Eds.), *Critical disability theory: Legal and policy dimensions* (pp. 25–46). Vancouver, BC: UBC Press.

McColl, M.A., Jarzynowska, A., & Shortt, S. (2010). Unmet health care needs of people with disabilities: Population level evidence. *Disability & Society, 25*(2), 205.
doi:10.1080/09687590903537406

McColl, M.A., Jaiswal., A., & Roberts, L. (2017). *A review of federal disability policy in Canada*. Kingston, ON: Canadian Disability Policy Alliance.

McColl, M.A., & Jongbloed, L. (2006). *Disability and social policy in Canada* (2nd ed.). Concord, ON: Captus Press.

McColl, M.A., Law, M., & Stewart, D. (2015). *Theoretical basis of occupational therapy* (3rd ed.). New Jersey: Slack.

McColl, M.A., & Shortt, S. (2006). Another way to look at high service utilization: The contribution of disability. *Journal of Health Services Research and Policy, 11*(2), 74–80.
doi:10.1258/135581906776318848

McColl, M.A., Shortt, S., Gignac, M., & Lam, M. (2011). Disentangling the effects of age and disability on health service utilization. *Disability*

344 | GLOSSARY, REFERENCES, AND INDEX

and *Rehabilitation, 33*, 13–14.
doi:10:3109/09638288.2010.526166.
McColl, M.A., Shortt, S., Godwin, M., Smith, K., Rowe, K., O'Brien, P., & Donnelly, C. (2009). Models for integrating rehabilitation and primary care: A scoping study. *Archives of Physical Medicine and Rehabilitation, 90*(9), 1523–1531.
doi: 10.1016/j.apmr.2009.03.017
McColl, M.A., Shortt, S., Hunter, D., Dorland, J., Goodwin, M., Rosser, W., & Shaw, R. (2010). Access and quality of primary care for people with disabilities: A comparison of practice factors. *Journal of Disability Policy Studies, 21*(3), 131–140.
McColl, M.A., & Schaub, M. (2013). *The lifetime costs associated with living with a disability.* Kingston, ON: Canadian Disability Policy Alliance.
McDermott, S., & Turk, M. (2011). The myth and reality of disability prevalence: Measuring disability for research and service. *Disability and Health Journal, 4*, 1–5.
McDonald, K., & Kidney, C. (2012). What is right? Ethics in intellectual disabilities research. *Journal of Policy and Practice in Intellectual Disabilities, 9*(1), 27–39.
McGinn, F., Gahagan, J., & Gibson, E. (2005). Back to work: Vocational issues and strategies for Canadians living with HIV/AIDS. *Work (Reading, Mass.), 25*(2), 163.
McKenna, I.B. (1997). Legal rights for persons with disabilities: Can the impasse be resolved? *Ottawa Law Review, 29*(1), 153.
Meaney-Tavares, R., & Gavidia-Payne, S. (2012). Staff characteristics and attitudes towards the sexuality of people with intellectual disability. *Journal of Intellectual and Developmental Disability, 37*(3), 269–273.
doi:10.3109/13668250.2012.701005
Meredith, T., & Chia, C. (2015). *Leaving some behind: What happens when workers get sick?* Institute for Research on Public Policy. Retrieved from http://irpp.org/research-studies/leaving-some-behind-what-happens-when-workers-get-sick/
Merriam-Webster dictionary. (1828). Retrieved from https://www.merriam-webster.com/dictionary/disability
Mezirow, J. (2000). Learning to think like an adult: Core concepts of transformation theory. In J. Mezirow (Ed.), *Learning as transformation: Critical perspectives on a theory in progress* (pp. 1–33). San Fransisco, CA: Jossey-Bass.
Miller, P., & Powell, S. (2016). Overcoming voting obstacles: The use of convenience voting by voters with disabilities. *American Politics Research, 44*(1), 28–55.
doi:10.1177/1532673X15586618
Minnes, P., Buell, K., Feldman, M., McColl, M.A., & McCreary, B. (2002). Community integration as acculturation: Preliminary validation of the AIMS interview. *Journal of Applied Research in Intellectual Disability, 15*, 377–387.

Mitra, S., & Sambamoorthi, U. (2014). Disability prevalence among adults: Estimates for 54 countries and progress toward a global estimate. *Disability and Rehabilitation, 36*(11), 940–947.

Mmatli, T. (2009). Translating disability-related research into evidence-based advocacy: The role of people with disabilities. *Disability and Rehabilitation, 31*(1), 14–22.

Monteith, M.J., & Mark, A.Y. (2005). Changing one's prejudiced ways: Awareness, affect, and self-regulation. *European Review of Social Psychology, 16*(1), 113–154.
doi:10.1080/10463280500229882

Moore v. British Columbia, 2012 SCC 61 (March 22; November 9, 2012).

Murphy, R. (1987). *The body silent.* New York, NY: W.W. Norton & Co.

Nierobisz, A,. & Theroux, C. (2008). *Disability complaints submitted to the Canadian Human Rights Commission: An analysis of systemic barriers reported by complainants.* Ottawa, ON: Canadian Human Rights Commission.

Nierse, C.J., & Abma, T.A. (2011). Developing voice and empowerment: The first step towards a broad consultation in research agenda setting. *Journal of Intellectual Disability Research, 55*(4), 411–421.

Nixon, S. (2017). *Presentation: Privilege 101: Power, privilege and oppression in the context of health equity.* Toronto, ON: Rehabilitation Sciences Centre, University of Toronto.

Notten, G., & Mendelson, M. (2016). Using low income and material deprivation to monitor poverty reduction. Caledon Institute of Social Policy.

Nova Scotia (Workers' Compensation Board) v. Martin; Nova Scotia (Workers' Compensation Board) v. Laseur, 2003 SCC 54, [2003] 2 S.C.R. 504.

Nussbaum, M.C. (2000). *Women and human development: The capabilities approach.* Cambridge, NY: Cambridge University Press.

O'Dea, S.M., Shuttleworth, R.P., & Wedgwood, N. (2012). Disability, doctors and sexuality: Do healthcare providers influence the sexual wellbeing of people living with a neuromuscular disorder? *Sexuality and Disability, 30*(2), 171–185.
doi:10.1007/s11195-011-9235-3

Office for Disability Issues. (2006). A way with words and images: Suggestions for the portrayal of people with disabilities. Retrieved from https://www.canada.ca/content/dam/esdc-edsc/migration/documents/eng/disability/arc/way_with_words.pdf

Oliver, M. (1990). *The politics of disablement.* Warminster, UK: MacMillan Education.

Oliver, M. (1992). Changing the social relations of research production? *Disability, Handicap and Society, 7*(2), 101–114.

Oliver, M. (1997). Emancipatory research: Realistic goal or impossible dream? In C. Barnes & G. Mercer (Eds.), *Doing disability research* (pp. 15–31). Leeds, UK: Disability Press.

Oliver, M., & Barnes, C. (2012). *The new politics of disablement*. New York, NY; Houndmills, Basingstoke, Hampshire: Palgrave Macmillan.

Ontario Human Rights Commission. (2016). *Policy on ableism and discrimination based on disability*. Human Rights Commission.

Ontario Human Rights Commission. (2017). *A bold voice: Annual report, 2016–2017*. Human Rights Commission.

Organisation for Economic Co-Operation and Development. (1999). *Inclusive education at work*. Stockholm, Sweden: OECD.

Organisation for Economic Co-operation and Development. (2003). *Transforming disability into ability: Policies to promote work and income security for disabled people*. Paris, France: OECD.

Organisation for Economic Co-operation and Development. (2010a). *Sickness, disability, and work: Breaking the barriers: A synthesis of findings across OECD countries*. Paris, France: OECD

Organisation for Economic Co-operation and Development. (2010b). *Sickness, disability and work: Breaking the barriers — Canada: Opportunities for collaboration*. Retrieved from www.oecd.org/els/disability

Organisation for Economic Co-operation and Development. (2010c). *Sickness, disability and work: Keeping on track in the economic downturn — Background paper*. Stockholm, Sweden: OECD.

Organisation for Economic Co-operation and Development. (2017). *Social protection: Public spending on incapacity*. Paris, France: OECD.

Oshima, S., Kirschner, K.L., Heinemann, A., & Semik, P. (1998). Assessing the knowledge of future internists and gynecologists in caring for a woman with tetraplegia. *Archives of Physical Medicine and Rehabilitation, 79*(10), 1270–1276.

Paetzold, R. (2005). Mental illness and reasonable accommodations at work: Definition of a mental disability under the ADA. *Psychiatric Services, 56*(10), 1188–1190.

Pal, L. (1992). *Public policy analysis: An introduction*. Scarborough, ON: Nelson Canada.

Palad, Y.Y., Barquia, R.B., Domingo, H.C., Flores, C.K., Padilla, L.I., & Ramel, J.M.D. (2016). Scoping review of instruments measuring attitudes toward disability. *Disability and Health Journal, 9*(3), 354–374. doi: 10.1016/j.dhjo.2016.01.008

Paradis, K., Misener, L., McPherson, G., McGillivray, D., & Legg, D. (2017). Examining the impact of integrated and non-integrated parasport events on volunteer attitudes towards disability. *Sport in Society, 20*(11), 1724–1744.

Parchomiuk, M. (2012). Specialists and sexuality of individuals with disability. *Sexuality and Disability, 30*(4), 407–419. doi:10.1007/s11195-011-9249-x

Paris, M.J. (1993). Attitudes of medical students and health-care professionals toward people with disabilities. *Archives of Physical Medicine and Rehabilitation, 74*(8), 818–825.

Parish, S.L., Grinstein-Weiss, M., Yeo, Y.H., Rose, R.A., & Rimmerman, A. (2010). Assets and income: Disability-based disparities in the United States. *Social Work Research, 34*(2), 71–82.

Parish, S.L., Rose, R., & Swaine, J. (2010). Financial well-being of US parents caring for coresident children and adults with developmental disabilities: An age cohort analysis. *Journal of Intellectual & Developmental Disability, 35*(4), 235–243.

Parsons, T. (1961). *Theories of society: Foundations of modern sociological theory*. New York, NY: Free Press of Glencoe.

Patrick, H., & Williams, G. (2012). Self-determination theory: Its application to health behavior and complementarity with motivational interviewing. *International Journal of Behavioural Nutrition and Physical Activity, 9*(18), 1–12.
doi:0.1186/1479-5868-9-18

Peloquin, S.M. (1997). The spiritual depth of occupation: Making worlds and making lives. *The American Journal of Occupational Therapy, 51*(3), 167–168.
doi:10.5014/1jot.51.3.167

Pension Benefits Act, S.O. 1965, c. 96.

Pentland, W., & McColl, M.A. (2008).Occupational integrity: Another perspective on "life balance". *Canadian Journal of Occupational Therapy, 75*(3), 135–138.

Pentland, W., & McColl, M.A. (2009). Another perspective on life balance: living in integrity with values. In K. Matuska & C. Christiansen (Eds.), *Life balance: Multidisciplinary theories and models* (pp. 165–179). Thorofare, NJ: Slack, Inc. and AOTA Press.

Peters, Y. (2004). *Twenty years of litigating for disability equality rights: Has it made a difference?* Winnipeg, MB: Council of Canadians with Disabilities.

Phelan, S.K. (2011). Constructions of disability: A call for critical reflexivity in occupational therapy. *Canadian Journal of Occupational Therapy, 78*(3), 164–172.
doi:10.2182/cjot.2011.78.3.4

Pooran, B., & Wilkie, C. (2005). Failing to achieve equality: Disability rights in Australia, Canada, and the United States. *Journal of Law and Social Policy, 1*, 1–34.

Porter, B. (2005). *Twenty years of equality rights: Reclaiming expectations*. Windsor Yearbook of Access to Justice. Windsor, ON: University of Windsor.

Porter, G. (2014). A recipe for successful inclusive education: Three key ingredients revealed. *Revista Journal Interacções, 10*(33), 10–17.

Potts, B. (2005). Disability and employment: Considering the importance of social capital. *Journal of Rehabilitation, 71*(3), 20–25.

Priestley, M. (2007). In search of European disability policy: Between national and global. *ScienceDirect, 1*, 61–74.
doi:10.1016/j.alter.2007.08.006

Priestley, M., Waddington, L., & Bessozi, C. (2010). Towards an agenda for disability research in Europe: Learning from disabled people's organisations. *Disability & Society, 25*(6), 731–746.

Primeau, L.A. (2003). Play and leisure. In E.B. Crepeau, E.S. Cohn, & B.A.B Schell (Eds.), *Willard & Spackman's occupational therapy* (10th ed., pp. 567–569). Philidelphia, PA: Lippincott Williams & Wilkins.

Prince, M.J. (2004). Canadian disability policy: Still a hit-and-miss affair. *Canadian Journal of Sociology, 29*(1), 59–82.

Prince, M.J. (2006a). A national strategy for disability supports: Where is the government of Canada in this social project? In M.A. McColl & L. Jongbloed (Eds.), *Disability and social policy in Canada* (2nd ed., pp. 97–111). Concord, ON: Captus Press.

Prince, M.J. (2006b). Who are we? The disability community in Canada. In M.A. McColl & L. Jongbloed (Eds.), *Disability and social policy in Canada* (2nd ed., pp. 160–175). Concord, ON: Captus Press.

Prince, M.J. (2007). *Working paper series on electoral participation and outreach practices: The electoral participation of persons with special needs.* Ottawa, ON: Elections Canada.

Prince, M.J. (2009a). *Absent citizens: Disability politics and policy in Canada.* Toronto, ON: University of Toronto Press.

Prince, M.J. (2009b). *Pride and prejudice: The ambivalence of Canadian attitudes toward disability and inclusion.* Toronto, ON: Institute for Research and Development on Inclusion and Society (IRIS).

Prince, M. (2010). What about a disability rights act for Canada? Practices and lessons from America, Australia, and the United Kingdom. *Canadian Public Policy, 36*(2), 199–214.

Prince, M.J. (2012). *Electoral participation of electors with disabilities: Canadian practices in a comparative context.* Elections Canada. Retrieved from http://www.elections.ca/res/rec/part/spe/dis_e.pdf

Prince, M.J. (2016a). Disability policy in Canada: Fragments of inclusion and exclusion. In J. Robertson & G. Larson (Eds.), *Disability and social change: A progressive Canadian approach* (pp. 99–114). Halifax, NS: Fernwood Publishers.

Prince, M.J. (2016b). *Struggling for social citizenship: Disabled Canadian, income security, and Prime ministerial eras.* Montreal & Kingston: McGill-Queen's University Press

Pryor, J., Reeder, G., Yeadon, C., & Hesson-McInnis, M. (2004). A dual-process model of reactions to perceived stigma. *Journal of Personality and Social Psychology, 87*(4), 436–452.

Putnam, M., Sherraden, M., Edwards, K., Porterfield, S., Wittenburg, D., Holden, K., & Saleeby, P.W. (2005). Building financial bridges to economic development and community integration: Recommendations for a research agenda on asset development for people with disabilities. *Journal of Social Work in Disability & Rehabilitation, 4*(3), 61–85.

Quinlan, E., Thomas-MacLean, R., Hack, T., Kwan, W., Miedema, B., Tatemichi, S., ... Tilley, A. (2009). The impact of breast cancer among Canadian women: Disability and productivity. *Work — A Journal of Prevention Assessment & Rehabilitation, 34*(3), 285–296. doi:10.3233/WOR-2009-0926

Rabiee, P., & Glendenning, C. (2010). Choice: What, when and why? Exploring the importance of choice to disabled people. *Disability & Society, 25*(7), 827–839. doi:10.1080/09687599.2010.520896

Rank, M., & Hirschl, T. (2010). *Estimating the life course dynamics of asset poverty. Centre for Social Development Working Papers No. 10-25.* Centre for Social Development: Washington University in St. Louis. Retrieved from http://csd.wustl.edu/Publications/Documents/WP10-25.pdf

Ravaud, J., & Stiker, H. (2001). Inclusion/exclusion: An analysis of historical and cultural meanings. In G. Albrecht, K. Seelman, & M. Bury (Eds.), *Handbook of disability studies* (pp. 490–514). London, UK: Sage.

Reaume, G. (2007). *Lyndhurst: Canada's first rehabilitation centre for people with spinal cord injuries, 1945–1998.* Montreal, Quebec: McGill-Queen's Press.

Reaume, G. (2012). Disability history in Canada: Present work in the field and future prospects. *Canadian Journal of Disability Studies, 1*(1), 35–81.

Reeve, D. (2014). Psycho-emotional disablism and internalised oppression. In J. Swain, S. French, C. Barnes, & C. Thomas (Eds.), *Disabling barriers — enabling environments* (3rd ed., pp. 92–98). London, UK: Sage.

Reuben, E., Gerold, S., Cieza, A., Davis, K., Strumbo, T., & Riddle, D. (2010). Creating an interface between the International Classification of Functioning, Disability and Health and physical therapist practice. *Physical Therapy, 90*(7), 1053–1063.

Riddle, C.A. (2010). Indexing, capabilities, and disability. *Journal of Social Philosophy, 41*(4), 527–537. doi: 10.1111/j.1467-9833.2010.01514.x

Riesen, T., Morgan, R.L., & Griffin, C. (2015). Customized employment: A review of the literature. *Journal of Vocational Rehabilitation, 43*(3), 183–193. doi:10.3233/JVR-150768

Rioux, M., & Sampson, R. (2006). Trends impacting disability: National and international perspectives. In M.A. McColl & L. Jongbloed (Eds.), *Disability and social policy in Canada,* (2nd ed., pp. 357–369). Concord, ON: Captus Press.

Robson, J., & Nares, P. (2006). *Wealth and wellbeing, ownership and opportunity: New directions in social policy for Canada.* Social and Enterprise Development Innovations (SEDI) Canada. Retrieved from http://www.sedi.org/html/resources/publications.asp

Rock, P. (1988) Independence: What it means to six disabled people living in the community. *Disability, Handicap & Society, 3*(1), 27–35. doi:10.1080/02674648866780021

Rohmer, O., & Louvert, E. (2012). Implicit measures of stereotype content associated with disability. *British Journal of Social Psychology, 51,* 732–740. doi:10.1111/j.2044-8309.2011.02087x

Rosen, R. (2007). Developing chronic disease policy in England. In J. Dorland, & M.A. McColl (Eds.), *Emerging approaches to chronic disease management in primary health care* (pp. 39–50). Montreal and Kingston: McGill-Queen's University Press.

Rothwell, D., & Goren, A. (2011). *Exploring the relationship between asset holding and family economic strain.* New America Foundation. Retrieved from https://newamerica.org/documents/114/exploring-the-relationship-between-asset-holding-and-family-economic-strain

Rotter, J.B. (1966). Generalized expectancies for internal versus external control of reinforcement. *Psychological Monographs: General and Applied, 80*(1), 1–28.

Ruddock, W., McColl, M.A., Benecki, L., & Wilson, R. (2007). *Family physician practice patterns and office accessibility.* Unpublished Manuscript.

Rudman, L.A., Ashmore, R.D., & Gary, M.L. (2001). "Unlearning" automatic biases: The malleability of implicit prejudice and stereotypes. *Journal of Personality and Social Psychology, 81*(5), 856–868. doi:10.1037/0022-3514.81.5.856

Ryan, R.M., & Deci, E.L. (2000). Self-determination theory and the facilitation of intrinsic motivation, social development, and well-being. *American Psychologist, 55*(1), 68–78. doi:10.1037/0003-066x.55.1.68

Sacks, O. (1984). *A leg to stand on.* Toronto, ON: Alfred A. Knopf.

Sakellariou, D. (2012). Sexuality and disability: A discussion on care of the self. *Sexuality and Disability, 30*(2), 187–197. doi:10.1007/s11195-011-9219-3

Sanchez, J., Byfield, G., Brown, T.T., LaFavor, K., Murphy, D., & Laud, P. (2000). Perceived accessibility versus actual physical accessibility of healthcare facilities. *Rehabilitation Nursing, 25*(1), 6–9.

Saunders, P. (2007). The costs of disability and the incidence of poverty. *Australian Journal of Social Issues, 42*(4), 461–480.

Scanlon, D. (2013). Specific learning disability and its newest definition: Which is comprehensive? And which is insufficient? *Journal of Learning Disabilities, 46*(1), 26–33.

Scheiber, N. (2015, November 30). Study using fake job letters exposes bias against disabled. *The New York Times,* p. B1.

Schneider, C. (2015). Social participation of children and youth with disabilities in Canada, France and Germany. *International Journal of Inclusive Education, 19*(10), 1068–1079.

Schur, L., Ameri, M., & Adya, M. (2017). Disability, voter turnout, and polling place accessibility. *Social Science Quarterly, 98*(5). doi:10.1111/ssqu.12373

Schur, L., Kruse, D., & Blanck, P. (2005). Corporate culture and the employment of persons with disabilities. *Behavioral Science and the Law, 23*, 3–20.

Schur, L., Shields, T., Kruse, D., & Schriner, K. (2002). Enabling democracy: Disability and voter turnout. *Political Research Quarterly, 55*(1), 167–190.

Schwartz, D., Blue, E., McDonald, M., Giuliani, G., Weber, G., Seirup, H., ... Perkins, A. (2010). Dispelling stereotypes: Promotions disability equality through film. *Disability & Society, 25*(7), 841–848. doi:10.1080/09687599.2010.520898

Seltzer, M., & Krauss, M. (1994). Aging parents with coresident adult children: The impact of lifelong caregiving. In M. Seltzer, M. Krauss, & M. Janicki (Eds.). *Life course perspectives on adulthood and old age* (pp. 3–18). Washington, DC: American Association on Mental Retardation.

Seltzer, M., & Krauss, M. (2001). Quality of life of adults with mental retardation/developmental disabilities who live with family. *Mental Retardation and Developmental Disabilities Research Reviews, 7*, 105–114.

Sen, A. (1980). *An approach to Naxalbari* (1st ed.). Calcutta, India: Institute of Scientific Thoughts.

Shakespeare, T. (1996). Rules of engagement: Doing disability research. *Disability & Society, 11*(1), 115–119.

Shakespeare, T. (2015). *Disability research today: International perspectives.* Amazon.ca: Kindle Store.

Shankardass, K. (2003). *Access to primary care for people with spinal cord injuries in Ontario.* Unpublished manuscript.

Shannon, D., Giancarlo, A., & McColl, M.A. (2015). More than voting booths: Accessibility of electoral campaigns for people with disabilities in Ontario. *Canadian Journal of Disability Studies, 4*(1), 89–110.

Shannon, P.D. (1970). The work-play theory and the occupational therapy process. *American Journal of Occupational Therapy, 26*, 169–172.

Sherraden, M. (1991). *Assets and the poor.* New York, NY: M.E. Sharp.

Shields, N., & Taylor, N. (2014). Contact with young adults with disability led to a positive change in attitudes toward disability among physiotherapy students. *Physiotherapy Canada, 66*(3), 298–305. doi:10.3138/ptc.2013-61.

Shier, M., Graham, J.R., & Jones, M.E. (2009). Barriers to employment as experienced by disabled people: A qualitative analysis in Calgary and Regina, Canada. *Disability & Society, 24*(1), 63–75. doi:10.1080/09687590802535485

Shikako-Thomas, K., & Law, M. (2015). Policies supporting participation in leisure activities for children and youth with disabilities in Canada: From policy to play. *Disability & Society, 30*(3), 381–400. doi:10.1080/09687599.2015.1009001

Silverman, A., Gwinn, J., & Van Boven, L. (2014). Stumbling in their shoes: Disability simulations reduce judged capabilities of disabled people. *Social Psychological and Personality Science, 6*(4), 464–471.
doi: 10.1177/1948550614559650

Sinclair, S., Pereira, J., & Raffin, S. (2006). A thematic review of the spirituality literature within palliative care. *Journal of Palliative Medicine, 9*(2), 464–479.
doi:10.1089/jpm.2006.9.464

Sinha, M. (2013). *Portrait of caregivers, 2012.* Ottawa, ON: Statistics Canada.

Sinha, M., & Bleakney, A. (2014). *Receiving care at home.* Ottawa, ON: Statistics Canada.

Sintas, J., de Francisco, L., & Alvarez, E. (2015). The nature of leisure revisited: An interpretations of digital leisure. *Journal of Leisure Research, 47*(1), 79–99.

Smith, E.M., Roberts, L., McColl M.A., Martin Ginis, K., & Miller, W.C. (2017) A national evaluation of the policies governing funding for wheelchairs and scooters in Canada. *Canadian Journal of Occupational Therapy, 85*(1), 46–57.
doi: 10.1177/0008417417719723

Smith, D. (2013). Disability, employment and stress regarding ability to pay for housing and healthy food. *Work, 45,* 449–463.
doi: 10.3233/WOR-121552

Smith, J. (2017). *How media can instill positive attitudes toward people with disabilities.* Ottawa, ON: CAIP Innovation Think Tank.

Smith, K., McColl, M.A., Aiken, A., & McColl, A. (2014). Primary care for people with SCI. In J.J. Eng, R.W. Teasell, W.C. Miller, D.L. Wolfe, A.F. Townson, J.T.C. Hrieh, S.J. Connnolly, V.K. Noonan, E. Loh, & A. McIntylre (Eds.), *Spinal cord injury rehabilitation evidence* (Vol. 5, pp. 1–28).

Snir, R., & Harpaz, I. (2002). Work–leisure relations: Leisure orientation and the meaning of work. *Journal of Leisure Research, 34*(2), 178–203.

Sobsey, D., & Calder, P. (2006). *Supports to families of children with disabilities: Systematic review: State of the evidence.* J.P. Das Developmental Disabilities Centre. University of Alberta with Alberta Centre for Child, Family, and Community Research.

Soffer, M., MacDonald, K.E., & Blanck, P. (2010). Poverty among adults with disabilities: Barriers to promoting asset accumulation in individual development accounts. *American Journal of Community Psychology, 46,* 376–385.

Soloman, A. (2012). *Far from the tree: Parents, children, and the search for identity.* New York, NY: Simon & Schuster.

Solstad Vedeler, J., & Schreuer, N. (2011). Policy in action: Stories on the workplace accommodation process. *Journal of Disability Policy Studies, 22*(2), 95–105.
doi:10.1177/1044207310395942

Stamou, A., Alevriadou, A., & Soufla, F. (2016). Representations of disability from the perspective of people with disabilities and their families: A critical discourse analysis of disability groups on Facebook. *Scandinavian Journal of Disability Research, 18*(1), 1–16.

Stapleton, D., Protik, A., & Stone, C. (2008). *Review of international evidence on the cost of disability*. Department for Work and Pensions. Research report No 52. Norwich.

Starfield, B. (1997). The future of primary care in a managed care era. *International Journal of Health Services, 27*(4), 687–696.

Statistics Canada. (1991). *Health and Activity Limitation Survey 1991*. Retrieved from http://publications.gc.ca/site/eng/9.509134/publication.html

Statistics Canada. (1992). *General Social Survey 1992: Overview of the Time Use of Canadians*. Ottawa, ON: Social and Aboriginal Statistics Division.

Statistics Canada. (2000). *National Population Health Survey: 1998–1999*. Retrieved from http://www23.statcan.gc.ca/imdb/p2SV.pl?Function=getSurvey&Id=4060

Statistics Canada. (2001). *Participation and Activity Limitation Survey*. Retrieved from http://www12.statcan.gc.ca/census-recensement/2011/ref/92-135/surveys-enquetes/participation-activ-eng.cfm

Statistics Canada. (2001). Children with disabilities and their families. Retrieved from https://www150.statcan.gc.ca/n1/pub/89-586-x/index-eng.htm

Statistics Canada. (2006). *2006 Census of Population*. Retrieved from http://www12.statcan.gc.ca/census-recensement/2006/index-eng.cfm

Statistics Canada. (2007). *2006 Participation and Activity Limitation Survey: Disability in Canada*. Retrieved from http://www5.statcan.gc.ca/olc-cel/olc.action?objId=89-628-X&objType=2&lang=en&limit=1

Statistics Canada. (2008). *Participation and Activity Limitation Survey 2006: A Profile of Education for Children with Disabilities in Canada*. Ottawa, ON: Social and Aboriginal Statistics Division.

Statistics Canada. (2010). *General Social Survey 2010: Overview of the Time Use of Canadians*. Retrieved from https://www150.statcan.gc.ca/n1/en/pub/89-647-x/89-647-x2011001-eng.pdf?st=fd9tOKKA

Statistics Canada. (2012). *Canadian Survey on Disability 2012*. Ottawa ON.

Statistics Canada. (2015). *A profile of persons with disabilities among Canadians aged 15 years or older, 2012*. Retrieved from http://www.statcan.gc.ca/pub/89-654-x/89-654-x2015001-eng.htm

Statistics Canada. (2016). *2014 General Social Survey, Cycle 28*. Retrieved from http://www5.statcan.gc.ca/olc-cel/olc.action?ObjId=12M0026X&ObjType=2&lang=en&limit=0

Stienstra, D. (2012). *Disability rights*. Winnipeg, MB: Fernwood.

Stienstra, D., & Ashcroft, T. (2010). Voyaging on the seas of spirit: An ongoing journey towards understanding disability and humanity. *Disability & Society, 25*(2), 191–203. doi:10.1080/09687590903534411

Stienstra, D., & D'Aubin, A. (2006). People with disabilities and political participation. In M.A. McColl & L. Jongbloed (Eds.), *Disability and social policy* (2nd ed., pp. 213–232). Concord, ON: Captus Press.

Stiker, H. (1999). *A history of disability.* Ann Arbor, MI: University of Michigan Press.

Stone, E., & Priestley, M. (1996). Parasites, pawns and partners: Disability research and the role of non-disabled researchers. *British Journal of Sociology, 47*(4), 699–716.

Strombolopolous, G. (2013). *12 facts and figures about having a disability in Canada.* CBC Canada. Retrieved from http://www.cbc.ca/strombo/news/by-the-numbers-international-day-of-persons-with-disabilities

Styan, J. (2012). *Good news for people with disabilities in the federal budget.* Caledon Institute for Social Policy.

Substitute Decisions Act, 1992, S.O. 1992, c. 30.

Sullivan, W.F., Berg, J.M., Bradley, E., Cheetham, T., Denton, R., Heng, J., ... McMillan, S. (2011). Primary care of adults with developmental disabilities: Canadian consensus guidelines. *Canadian Family Physician, 57*(5), 541–553.

Swain, J., & French, S. (2000). Towards an affirmation model of disability. *Disability & Society, 15*(4), 569–582. doi: 10.1080/09687590050058189

Sweet, S.N., Martin Ginis, K.A., Tomasone, J.R., & SHAPE-SCI Research Group. (2013). Investigating intermediary variables in the physical activity and quality of life relationship in persons with spinal cord injury. *Health Psychology, 32*(8), 877–885.

Taleporos, G., & McCabe, M.P. (2003). Relationships, sexuality and adjustment among people with physical disability. *Sexual and Relationship Therapy, 18*(1), 25–43. doi:10.1080/1468199031000061245

Tamaru, A., McColl, M.A., & Yamasaki, S. (2007). Understanding "independence": Perspectives of occupational therapists. *Disability and Rehabilitation, 29*(13), 1021–1033.

Tervo, R.C., Azuma, S., Palmer, G., & Redinius, P. (2002). Medical students' attitudes toward persons with disability: A comparative study. *Archives of Physical Medicine and Rehabilitation, 83*(11), 1537–1542.

Thomas, C. (2007). *Sociologies of disability and illness: Contested ideas in disability studies and medical sociology.* Basingstoke, UK: Palgrave Macmillan.

Thompson, A., Roberts, P., & Bittles, A. (2014). Navigating the maze: Ethics approval pathways for intellectual disability research. *Journal of Medical Ethics, 40,* 782–786.

Thompson, S., Lyons, W., & Timmons, V. (2014). Inclusive education policy: What the leadership of Canadian teacher associations has to say about it. *International Journal of Inclusive Education, 19*(2), 121–140.
doi: 10.1080/13603116.2014.908964

Till, M., Leonard, T., Yeung, S., & Nicholls, G. (2015). *Canadian survey on disability, 2012: A profile of the labour market experiences of adults with disabilities among Canadians aged 15 year and older, 2012.* Ottawa, ON: Statistics Canada.

Torjman, S. (2005). *What is policy?* Ottawa, ON: Caledon Institute of Social Policy.

Torjman, S. (2014). *Disability policy highlights.* Ottawa, ON: Caledon Institute of Social Policy.

Torjman, S. (2017). *Dismantling the welfare wall for persons with disabilities.* Caledon Institute of Social Policy.

Torjman, S., & Makhoul, A. (2016). *Disability supports and employment policy.* Caledon Institute of Social Policy.

Turcotte, M., (2013). *Family caregiving: What are the consequences?* Ottawa, ON: Statistics Canada.

Tweddle, A., Battle, K., & Torjman, S. (2017). *Welfare in Canada, 2016: Canada social report.* Caledon Institute of Social Policy.

Uniform Data Set for Medical Rehabilitation. (2012). *The FIM Instrument: It's background, structure and usefulness.* Retrieved from https://www.udsmr.org/Documents/The_FIM_Instrument_Background_Structure_and_Usefulness.pdf

United Nations. (1981). *General Assembly: International Year of Disabled Persons.* Retrieved from http://www.un.org/documents/ga/res/36/a36r077.htm

United Nations. (1982). *General Assembly: World programme of action concerning disabled persons.* Retrieved from http://www.un.org/documents/ga/res/37/a37r052.htm

United Nations. (2006). *Convention on the rights of persons with disabilities.* Retrieved from http://www.un.org/disabilities/convention

United Nations. (1948). *Universal declaration of human rights.* Retrieved from http://www.un.org/en/universal-declaration-human-rights/

United Nations Development Programme. (2016). *Sustainable development goals.* Retrieved from http://www.unpd.org/content/undp/en/home/sustainable-development-goals.html

United Nations Educational, Scientific and Cultural Organization (UNESCO). (1994). *The Salamanca statement and framework for action on special needs education.*

United States Department of Justice. (1990). *Americans with Disabilities Act of 1990,* 42 U.S.C. ch. 126 ss. 12101 et seq. Retrieved from https://www.ada.gov/pubs/adastatute08.htm

United States Department of Justice. (2008). *ADA Amendments Act of 2008,* Pub. L 110-325. Retrieved from https://www.eeoc.gov/laws/statutes/adaaa.cfm.

Unruh, A.M., Versnal, J., & Kerr, N. (2002). Spiritually and evidence-based practice. In M.A. McColl (Ed.), *Spiritually and occupational therapy* (pp. 145–160). Ottawa, ON: CAOT Publications ACE.

Valvano, A.K., West, L.M., Wilson, C.K., Macapagal, K.R., Penwell-Waines, L.M., Waller, J.L., & Stepleman, L.M. (2014). Health professions students' perceptions of sexuality in patients with physical disability. *Sexuality and Disability, 32*(3), 413–427. doi:10.1007/s11195-014-9347-7

van Kraayenoord, C. (2010). Agendas and disability research. *International Journal of Disability, Development and Education, 57*(4), 347–349.

Vanhala, L. (2011). *Making rights a reality: Disability rights activists and legal mobilization.* Cambridge, UK: Cambridge University Press.

Vanier, J. (1995). *The Heart of L'Arche: A spirituality for every day.* Toronto, ON: Novalis Publishing.

Vanier, J. (1997). *Our journey home: Rediscovering a common humanity beyond our differences.* Toronto, ON: Novalis Publishing.

Vanier, J. (1998). *Becoming human.* Toronto: Anansi.

Vaughn, M., Silver, K., Murphy, S., Ashbaugh, R., & Hoffman, A. (2015). Women with disabilities discuss sexuality in San Francisco focus groups. *Sexuality and Disability, 33,* 19–46. Retrieved from https://link.springer.com/article/10.1007/s11195-014-9389-x#citeas

Veltman, A., Stewart, D.E., Tardif, G.S., & Branigan, M. (2001). Perceptions of primary healthcare services among people with physical disabilities. Part 1: Access issues. *Medscape General Medicine, 3*(2), 18.

Ville, I., Crost, M., & Ravaud, J. (2003). Disability and a sense of community belonging: A study among tetraplegic spinal-cord-injured persons in France. *Social Science & Medicine, 56,* 321–332.

Wallace, P., & Seidman, J. (2006). Improving population health and chronic disease management. In J. Dorland & M.A. McColl (Eds.), *Emerging approaches to chronic disease management in primary health care* (pp. 15–20). Toronto, ON: McGill-Queen's University Press.

Watermeyer, B. (2009). Claiming loss in disability. *Disability & Society, 24*(1), 91–102. doi:10.1080/09687590802535717

Wenthold, N., & Savage, T. (2007). Ethical issues with service animals. *Topics in Stroke Rehabilitation, 14*(2), 68–74. doi:10.1310/tsr1402-68

Whalley Hammell, K. (2006). *Perspectives on disability and rehabilitation: Contesting assumptions, challenging practice.* London, UK: Churchill Livingstone.

Williams, C. (2006). *Asset-building approaches and the search for a new social policy architecture in Canada.* Wealth and Well-Being/Ownership and Opportunity: New Directions in Social Policy for Canada. Toronto, ON: SEDI.

Wilson, C., & McColl, M.A. (2017). *Attaining wider opportunities for disabled persons by constitution and statue: Evidence from time use data for Canada and the United States.* Manuscript submitted for publication.

Wilson, C., McColl, M.A., & Parsons, J. (2015). *Effects of post-secondary education on daily activity patterns of disabled persons: A measure of social inclusion.* Kingston, ON: Queen's University.

Wilson, C., McColl, M., Zhang, F., & McKinnon, P. (2017). Measuring integration of disabled persons: Evidence from Canada's time use database. *Canadian Journal of Disability Studies, 6*(1), 104–127.

Wing, L. (1995). Play is not the work of the child: Young children's perceptions of work and play. *Early Childhood Research Quarterly, 10*, 223–247.

Withers, A.J. (2012). *Disability politics & theory.* Blackpoint, NS: Fernwood Publishing.

Witt, W., Litzelman, K., Mandic, C., Wisk, L., Hampton, J., Creswell P., ... Gangnon, R. (2011). Healthcare-related financial burden among families in the U.S.: The role of childhood activity limitations and income. *Journal of Family and Economic Issues, 32*(2), 308–326.

World Bank, & World Health Organization. (2011). *World report on disability.* Geneva, Switzerland: World Health Organization.

World Health Organization. (1948) *Constitution of WHO.* Geneva, Switzerland: World Health Organization.

World Health Organization. (1986). *The Ottawa charter for health promotion.* Geneva, Switzerland: World Health Organization.

World Health Organization. (1991). *International classification of impairment, disability and handicap.* Geneva, Switzerland: World Health Organization.

World Health Organization. (2001). *The international classification of functioning, disability and health.* Geneva, Switzerland: World Health Organization.

Wright, B. (1960). *Physical disability: A psychosocial perspective.* New York, NY: Harper & Row.

Wullink, M., Veldhuijzen, W., Lantman-de Valk, H., Metsemakers, J., & Dinant, G. (2009). Doctor–patient communication with people with intellectual disability: A qualitative study. *BMC Family Practice, 10*(1), 82. doi:10.1186/1471-2296-10-82

Wunsch, S. (2014). To understand the origins of human sexuality. Neurosciences, ethology, anthropology. Comprende les origins de la sexualité humaine. Nuroosciences, éthologies, anthropologie. *L'Espirt du Temps.* Retrieved from http://humanbehaviors.free.fr/origine_sexualitie_humaine-extraits-2014_wunsch.pdf

Yoshida, K., Willi, V., Parker, I., & Locker, D. (2004). *The emergence of self-managed attendant services in Ontario: Direct funding pilot project*

— *an independent living model for Canadians requiring attendant services*, 177–204. West Yorkshire, UK: Emerald Group Publishing. doi:10.1016/S0275-4959(04)22010-5

Index

Note: T indicates Table and F indicates Figure.